Thank you fa[r] ... Greater Dubuque

a mod... !

Best wishes,

Tom

7/13/2017

D0698976

Praise for *Growing Jobs*

"Thomas Tuttle has captured how local elected officials are combining strategic and innovative decision making with professional local government management and dynamic not-for-profit partners for policy implementation. This implementation is disrupting and improving the status quo, leading to a more hopeful, resilient, and equitable future for communities and the businesses and individuals that call them home. Robust community engagement ensures that the personal values of citizens are aligned with the economic development strategies, accelerating the rate of growth and creating an environment that fosters investment in financial and human capital."

—Michael Van Milligen, City Manager, Dubuque, Iowa

"Creating quality jobs and filling them with a qualified workforce has become the challenge of our time because traditional strategies to promote economic growth have proven to be a zero-sum game at best. In this enlightening book, Tom Tuttle offers an engaging primer on the newest and best thinking for job creation at both local and state levels. It is a 'must read' for policy makers, economic development professionals, and all who care about America's economic future."

—William E. Kirwan, Chancellor Emeritus, University of Maryland System

"It is refreshing to see someone work so hard to create a holistic view of what community and economic development is all about. Never has it been more important to realize that successful economic development is nonpartisan and requires a powerful public–private partnership. Above all, what Dr. Tuttle has done is to prove once again that this work is complicated and that it is a 'team sport.' "

—J. Mac Holladay, CCE, PCED, LM, HLM, CEO, Market Street Services

"*Growing Jobs* is a 'must read' for local leaders across the country seeking to create good jobs and sustainable communities. Dr. Tuttle, a widely acclaimed expert on quality and productivity, draws upon decades of experience working with business, education, and government leaders and case studies of Austin, Texas, and Dubuque, Iowa, in this how-to guide, demonstrating that community values and engagement, along with education and business retention, are key strategies for successful, long-term, and sustainable economic development."

—Charles A. Stek, President and CEO, Environmental Stewardship Strategies

"In *Growing Jobs: Transforming the Way We Approach Economic Development,* Thomas Tuttle accurately assesses how traditional economic development approaches are no longer working. Tuttle's work will help economic development practitioners in developing plans and practices that leverage the significance of 'place' and 'talent' in driving local and regional economies."

—Jim Damicis, Senior Vice President, Camoin Associates

"Tom Tuttle approaches the topic of job creation and economic development from the experience that comes from many decades as a professor, consultant, student, and 'Guru' of productivity and quality improvement. His optimal mix of intellectual and practical real-world observations brings together, in this book, a very realistic account of the transformation of economic development and job creation approaches to succeed in today's global competition. The recommendations are understandable, implementable, and sustainable and should yield positive results for both the economic and social progress of municipalities, states, regions, and nations."

—Aris Melissaratos, Dean, School of Business and Leadership,
Stevenson University

"Tom Tuttle has opened the door to the next evolution of local economic development based on 'comprehensive community transformation.' His ability to identify the 'secret sauce' of building alliances, deep collaboration, and a shift to entrepreneurial ecosystems reflects his creative insight into a different kind of future that is emerging."

—Rick Smyre, President, Center for Communities of the Future

"Thomas Tuttle makes compelling arguments for why a transformation is required world-wide concerning existing economic development practices. There are not enough jobs of any kind for those seeking employment, and there is a growing mismatch between new job skill requirements and the qualifications of those seeking employment. In *Growing Jobs*, Tuttle provides compelling and useful examples of ways to consider and implement creative and innovative economic development frameworks."

—Dr. David V. Gibson, Associate Director, IC^2 Institute,
University of Texas at Austin

"Growing good jobs that satisfy community aspirations is the fundamental challenge facing local and state government leadership. *Growing Jobs* provides a national perspective on eco-nomic development practices with an in-depth look at two success stories—Austin, Texas, and Dubuque, Iowa. *Growing Jobs* provides transformational context and a values-driven pathway to individual and community innovation and productivity."

—Robert L. Hannon, President, Anne Arundel County
Economic Development Corporation

"Tom Tuttle's new book is a thought-provoking series of examples and findings on some of the most successful community and economic development initiatives from different regions of the country. It highlights the key ingredients of success by showcasing these 'best in class' examples. The keys include leadership, vision, best management practices, and a set of core community values that tend to drive the transformation to a highly effective system for com-munity building and job growth."

—Wayne A. Mills, Past Chairman of the Governor's
Workforce Investment Board for Maryland and Past Chair
of the Maryland Chamber of Commerce and Leadership Maryland

Growing Jobs

Growing Jobs

Transforming the Way We Approach Economic Development

Thomas C. Tuttle

Foreword by Jean-Claude Lauzon

 PRAEGER™

An Imprint of ABC-CLIO, LLC

Santa Barbara, California • Denver, Colorado

Library of Congress Cataloging-in-Publication Data

Names: Tuttle, Thomas C., author.
Title: Growing jobs : transforming the way we approach economic development / Thomas Clayton Tuttle; foreword by Jean-Claude Lauzon.
Description: Santa Barbara : Praeger, 2016. | Includes bibliographical references and index.
Identifiers: LCCN 2016005696 (print) | LCCN 2016021673 (ebook) | ISBN 9781440837227 (hardback) | ISBN 9781440837234 (ebook)
Subjects: LCSH: Manpower policy, Rural—United States. | Job creation—United States. | Rural industries—Government policy—United States.
Classification: LCC HD5724 .T88 2016 (print) | LCC HD5724 (ebook) | DDC 338.9—dc23
LC record available at https://lccn.loc.gov/2016005696

ISBN: 978–1–4408–3722–7
EISBN: 978–1–4408–3723–4

20 19 18 17 16   1 2 3 4 5

This book is also available on the World Wide Web as an eBook.
Visit www.abc-clio.com for details.

Praeger
An Imprint of ABC-CLIO, LLC

ABC-CLIO, LLC
130 Cremona Drive, P.O. Box 1911
Santa Barbara, California 93116-1911

This book is printed on acid-free paper ∞

Manufactured in the United States of America

To Judy, for her love, tolerance, and support
To Adrian, Cami, Cole, Drew, and Julia for giving me the strongest
reasons to care about these ideas

Contents

Foreword

I have worked with Dr. Tom Tuttle for the last 28 years in different locations around the world, and it is a distinct honor to introduce this book, which is dedicated to the future and well-being of America.

Tom and I have long been associated with the World Confederation of Productivity Science, a global think tank focused on "Peace and Prosperity through Productivity." For many years, I have acted as chairman of the organization, and Tom is still today the president of the World Academy of Productivity Science, which has some 500 distinguished members in more than 60 countries.

In his remarkable book, Dr. Tuttle explores new simple, doable, and practical avenues for creating favorable job opportunities. He challenges the status quo and proposes a clear action plan and great examples of cities that have already embraced new ways of defining and implementing economic strategies that fit with community needs. What is important is not only the number of jobs created but also the quality of said jobs, and this follows as the essence of his presentation. Dr. Tuttle points out that talent access and economic development go hand in hand. In this respect, rather than have a long debate on whether one is the chicken and the other the egg, he focuses on the output and predictable results to be obtained.

Good talent has always been and will continue to be the key ingredient of strong economic development in any part of the world, and this is very true for the United States of America. Executives and competent professionals are in high demand today in developed and developing economies, and now more than ever, these individuals weigh a wide variety of criteria when considering employment opportunities.

In my professional career as a global headhunter with Korn Ferry, candidates for top executive positions often asked me about local conditions—high-quality educational options for their children from kindergarten to university, a good and reliable health system, ease of local transportation and accessibility to air transport, security and ethics, and finally a city with varied and world-class cultural vitality. As one spouse once told me: "I don't care which city my spouse lives in as long as my family and I find comfort in the services that the city has."

I particularly enjoyed three major statements Dr. Tuttle provides: (1) resources must focus first on business retention and growth; (2) workforce development is a key ingredient for sustainable and long-term success; and (3) communities and citizens must help to create the kind of economy they want and need. His chapter on lessons from the past is an anthology of best practices and what everyone should be doing despite the many challenges.

In the examples of Austin and Dubuque, Dr. Tuttle helps us understand how his approach works and how collaboration and partnerships with leaders in the communities are vital to ensuring strong and solid economic growth. Hope, an aligned and engaged community, business growth and retention, and partnerships are discussed in great practical detail that should stimulate other constituents in the country to replicate these successes.

What I like most is the way Dr. Tuttle challenges how state and national initiatives in economic development are far removed from individuals' real everyday needs at the local level. He argues that the best way to ensure strong endorsement from communities and business leaders is to shift the decision-making process and policy philosophy back to the local community, city, or county. He writes:

> When citizens can see that their personal values are aligned with the community's economic development strategy, the result will be greater citizen ownership and support for the economic development process. Values alignment acts as an economic and employment development accelerator. (p. 10)

A job creation process that is values based and that stimulates innovation and productivity will act to accelerate the creation of good and valuable jobs.

One will find this approach echoed among local community leaders across the country, but it is all too often deterred by existing bureaucracies at state and national levels. The virtue of this book, therefore, is to initiate the discussion—as everything else in life, nothing is pure black or white, but rather light gray or lighter gray.

Enjoy this unique reading that showcases America's continuous process to improve itself and its desire and energy to constantly reinvent itself.

Jean-Claude Lauzon
Delegate General
Quebec Government Office in New York
January 6, 2016

Preface

There were two primary catalysts for this book. The first was the painful 2008 recession and the slow response of the economy in terms of employment levels, labor force participation rates, and the extent of underemployment. The second was that members of the economic development community were questioning whether traditional approaches to job creation and economic growth were working in light of new national and global forces that were impacting their states, cities, and regions. These two sets of facts suggested that the timing was right for an effort to define a new framework for transforming economic and community development approaches and strategies. However, for me, the preparation for this book began long before the second decade of the twenty-first century.

Very early in my life I learned to put a human face on unemployment statistics. This happened when my dad lost his job after working for over 20 years for a company that abruptly closed its doors and laid him off without notice or benefits. Since he was a union official, this was a traumatic situation not only for him but also for other members of the plant population whom he represented. Fortunately, he adjusted and managed to make a career change through additional training, several job changes, and the ability to maintain a positive perspective. However, a number of his colleagues never fully recovered from this job and career tragedy.

Like most kids growing up, my contact with the world of work was through stories told by my family, friends, and neighbors, and my own part-time and summer jobs. These included working in a gas station and being a bin loader in a warehouse. I also had many conversations with my friends and summer baseball teammates who had jobs ranging from hanging drywall to measuring the acreage of tobacco fields. From these conversations, I managed to form some early conclusions about the work world: there are many different things that people do, and jobs differ in terms of many attributes that have a lot to do with whether people are productive and happy or not. For example, in one of my jobs, I realized very soon that the way I was managed impacted my ability and motivation to perform the job well. On my first day I was told to do a certain task, I was given 15 minutes of instruction on that task and then I was expected to repeat that task over and over. After a few days of this, I realized that if I had been told what the purpose of this task was, how it related to the purpose of the department, and how it impacted the work of other people in the department, not only the job would have had more meaning for me but also I would have been in a better position to add value for the company through my job performance. I vowed that if I ever had the chance to manage other people, I would never put my employees in this position.

I was fortunate to have had positive role models who not only helped shape my work ethic but who also pointed me toward higher education as the way to create a better future. After college, I was commissioned as an army officer and attended the U.S. Army armor school followed by flight school. I was then assigned to the Korea Military Advisory Group as an aviator where my job was to fly U.S. and Korean military advisers around Korea on their training and advisory missions. Living in Korea opened my eyes to the world and served as my first real encounter with people from a different culture. It was enlightening not only to learn from my own interactions with Koreans but also to judge differences in the ways other Americans interacted with people in this culture. In some ways it was similar to the differences in the ways my dad and his colleagues reacted to the loss of their job. Some cherished the change and the opportunity to explore the richness of this cultural experience. Others could never escape the boundaries and limitations of their own culture and were constantly asking why the Koreans did not do things the "American way." Until I came to Korea, I was largely blind to the fact that my culture determined much of my behavior. One cannot see his or her own culture for the same reason that fish cannot see water. When you are immersed in it, you need a contrasting culture to enable you to see yourself and your own culture. Once that insight occurs, it is impossible to view the world in the same limited, culture-centric manner as before.

My deeper understanding of jobs was significantly expanded during my graduate school experience. As an industrial psychologist, I chose a dissertation topic that involved the study of jobs and a discipline known as job analysis. Guided by my adviser Dr. Bill Cunningham, I and my colleagues in the group developed methods and tools for analyzing jobs in terms of their interest, need, ability and cognitive attribute requirements. Our work was based on the assumption that performance and satisfaction of job incumbents resulted from a match between the job requirements and the incumbent's personal attributes. Improving incumbents' job satisfaction and performance involved helping them choose jobs which had requirements that matched their interests, needs, and skills. In order to do that, one requirement was to be able to analyze jobs in terms of the skills and abilities necessary to perform the tasks as well as the interests and needs that would promote motivation and satisfaction in doing so. Job analysis is a fundamental methodology that is an essential element of professional practice with respect to vocational counseling, employee selection and placement, employee training, job evaluation, and assessment of employees for promotion.

Even more relevant preparation for this book was developed during my 26 years as director of the University of Maryland Center for Quality and Productivity. This center was created by an advisory committee of the State Department of Economic and Community Development, which was led by Jay Jacobs, a visionary executive from the former Black and Decker Corporation. Jacobs and his colleagues, including the dean of the University of Maryland Business School Rudy Lamone, realized that productivity improvement was the key to improving the standard of living in a state and country. They developed the charter for an organization that would focus on improving productivity in the state of Maryland at a time (late 1970s), when U.S. productivity growth had declined from its traditional level of around 3 percent per year to less than 1 percent per year. The significance of this decline was that at a growth rate of 0.5 percent per year, the time required for the standard of living to double had increased from 22 years (at a 3 percent growth rate) to over 100 years. This meant that it was no longer possible for each generation to leave a world that was twice as affluent as that which it inherited from its parents' generation.

When I became director of this center in 1978, my learning accelerated. First, I learned about the importance of a group of influential people in building an organization and driving change. In my case this was the board of advisers for the center. According to the charter created by Jay Jacobs and his team, the center would be guided by a board comprising representatives from business, organized labor, government, education, and professional associations. The state's assistant secretary of economic development was a board member representing state government. This was my first experience with the power of collective action. The lesson learned was that whenever leaders from these various groups could come together and speak with one voice, change can happen—often very quickly.

A second key learning came from the fact that even though I was based in the university, I interacted regularly with state and local economic development representatives. Starting with the fact that the center was created by the Maryland Department of Economic and Community Development, the Center staff always stated that we existed to "retain and grow jobs in Maryland." In economic development jargon, that meant we were part of the job growth and retention function in economic development. Located in the university, we were able to view the state economic development department with some detachment. From that viewpoint it was possible to determine that the priorities of the department placed job retention below job attraction. In the 1970s and 1980s, there was virtually no focus on entrepreneurship at the state department level. There were some exceptions to this generalization. When the state feared that it would lose a high-profile employer, it spared no effort to retain this company. But in terms of the day-to-day focus, job attraction was the number one priority. I was biased of course, but I always felt that these priorities were wrong.

A third contributor to the motivation for this book came from my experiences as a participant in the U.S. Conference Board's Quality Council. The Quality Council was one of a number of learning councils operated by the U.S. Conference Board to promote cross-organizational learning among the largely Fortune 500 companies that were members of the Conference Board. Each council consisted of approximately 20 executives from organizations that are not direct competitors. The members of the Quality Council were individuals who were the "chief quality officer" of their corporations even though their job titles varied. I was invited to be one of two university representatives on this council. The group met for two days three times per year, with each meeting hosted by a member typically at one of the corporation's facilities. Meeting topics varied but fell under the broad topics of corporate quality and productivity improvement and organizational change.

It was through this group that I was introduced to the values framework described in Chapter 2. Tom Carter, an executive from Alcoa, brought one of their consultants, Dr. Brian Hall, to a meeting to discuss the topic of values-based management. I did not have any idea at the time how this experience would shape my worldview and thoughts about leadership, management, human development, and economic development. However, this council demonstrated to me the power of group learning and peer learning. Both types of learning require building trust between individuals and among group members because learning involves open and honest information sharing. As a colleague remarked, "the degree of trust in a group determines the size of the pipe that information flows through."

A fourth key influence on my thinking that is reflected in this book came from an encounter which led to a relationship with a retired executive from the Corning Glass Company named Forrest Behm. "Forry," the name he was known by, had held 14 different jobs within Corning from first-level supervisor in a plant to president of international operations for Corning. One of the stories that Forry shared with me dealt with the issue of executive leadership and the role of the CEO in leading change. James Houghton, then chairman of Corning, brought Forry back following his retirement and asked him to lead the total quality management initiative that Houghton was about to launch across the corporation. Forry stated that he deliberated for a day or so over this offer and then went back to meet with Chairman Houghton. Forry told the chairman, "I can't lead this effort. However, if you choose to lead it, I will help you." This story illustrates that the role of the CEO is to do the things that "only he or she can do." Because the total quality initiative was about changing the behavior of every manager and employee in the company in some fundamental ways, leadership of this function could not be delegated. Only the CEO could be seen as providing CEO leadership of this initiative.

This story provided one of the most significant lessons I have learned in terms of managing organizational change. There are some things that cannot be delegated in an organization. If the goal is to change the culture and operational practices which was the goal of the total quality initiative, only the CEO can lead the effort. That means serving as a personal role model, learning how to ask the right questions of subordinates, learning what to reward and what not to reward, and so on. This lesson is amplified in the book in the section on Dr. Deming in Chapter 3 and in Chapters 7 and 8 where I have focused on the frameworks for transformation of state and local economic development systems. If the goal is to change the economic development culture of a community, the key leaders of the community must lead this effort.

The lessons following the 2008 recession suggest that the timing is right for a transformation of economic development. My "past" has provided many lessons that underlie my perspective on the type of transformation that is needed. This brings me to the issue of what my hopes are for this book. The noted economist Joseph Stiglitz in his recent book with coauthor Bruce Greenwald frames the issue well. The book title is *Creating a Learning Society: A New Approach to Growth, Development and Social Progress.*[1] In this volume, the authors make the point that most of the increases in standard of living come from increased productivity and that productivity improvement is the result of learning. They further define the policy objective as follows:

a focal point of policy ought to be increasing learning within the economy; that is increasing the ability and the incentives to learn, and learning how to learn, and then closing the knowledge gaps that separate the most productive firms in the economy from the rest. Therefore, *creating a learning society should be one of the major objectives of economic policy.*[2]

My hope for this book is that it will contribute to moving economic development organizations to become learning organizations and that a major focus of economic and community development will be to create the conditions that will stimulate learning within the communities that they serve. We see considerable evidence of this in the three case examples in this book—Austin, Dubuque, and Maryland. Certainly much of the focus on job retention involves closing the knowledge gaps between the most productive firms and the least productive firms. In entrepreneurship and new job creation, there has been a key focus on developing "ecosystems." We should expand that focus to be "learning ecosystems" to imply not only that the ecosystem is about spreading existing knowledge among new and emerging firms but also that the ecosystem itself is dynamic and is evolving in terms of its knowledge assets. In order to develop and deploy effective policy, it is essential that policy makers focus on increasing learning among their citizens so that citizen engagement will become an even stronger force.

Like every book, this book has limitations. In the choice of case examples, there are many others that could have been included. The emphasis on state and local strategies does not address national policies and approaches that can enable and assist state and local development. We also do not address the significant global forces for change that state and local strategies must monitor and deal with as they develop and deploy their strategies. Originally a discussion of these forces that are driving change was presented as a chapter. However, it was omitted in order to allow a more complete presentation of the Austin and Dubuque stories. This decision was made in part due to the fact that many other volumes have addressed these global megatrends.

Chapter 1 of this book serves as the introduction as it defines the problem and provides an overview of the organization of this book. I invite you to read the book and then join the dialogue and learning process that will transform the economic and community development policies and organizations that you are able to influence.

Acknowledgments

A large number of people provided support, wisdom, and assistance during the process of deciding to write this book as well as critiquing the proposal and providing input during the writing phase. I would like to convey my sincere appreciation for their encouragement and involvement. For their assistance I especially want to thank R. V. Bartlett, George Creel, Karl Fooks, Dr. Charles Heller, Dr. Michael Hickey, John Kelly, William Liggett, Wayne Mills, Andrew Sonn, Erin Sonn, and Daniel Walton.

Throughout the proposal and book preparation, Robert L Hannon, president and CEO of the Anne Arundel County Economic Development Corporation, served as a valuable sounding board and friendly critic. An experienced and respected professional and an exceptionally clear thinker, he was an effective catalyst throughout in helping me clarify my thinking. We did not always agree but his viewpoints were always valuable.

At various stages of the book development I conducted a number of informational interviews with key economic development and workforce development professionals. Unfortunately, much of the valuable information they shared does not appear directly in the book. However, these interviews significantly aided me in the research done in Austin and Dubuque and with respect to the state-level examples. These interviewees were Dyan Brasington, Jim Damicis, John Dealy, Jim Dinegar, Don Frye, Stewart Gold, Kirkland Murray, Katherine Oliver, Rob Rosenbaum, J. Thomas Sadowski, Elliot Schwartz, Steven Silverman, Martin Simon, Sue Smith, Rick Smyre, Lawrence Twele, and John Wasilisin. I am very appreciative for your willingness to share your time and wisdom, and your ideas significantly broadened my perspective on state and local community and economic development issues and challenges.

For their assistance in the development of the Austin, Texas, case example, I want to thank John Baker, Scott Sherwood, Lauren Sherwood, and all of the interviewees who were extremely generous in sharing their time and knowledge. The interviewees were Jose Beceiro, Mike Berman, Charisse Bodisch, Paul DiGiuseppe, David V. Gibson, Julie Huls, Mitch Jacobson, and Joel Trammell.

Dr. David Dubois was extremely helpful in leading me to discover Dubuque, Iowa. Teri Hawks Goodmann, Michael Van Milligen, Rick Dickinson, and Nancy Van Milligen graciously welcomed me and opened the doors of their organizations. They also participated in interviews and generously enhanced the Dubuque story as did Mayor Roy Buol, Cori Burbach, Chad Chandlee, Brian Cooper, Kelley Deutmeyer, Eric Dregne, Sarah Harris, Douglas Horstmann, Maurice Jones, Russell Knight, Christine Kohlmann, Dave Lyons, Dan McDonald, Stan Rheingans, John Schmidt, Byron Taylor, and Tom Woodward. Rick Dickinson and Karen Kluesner of the Greater Dubuque Development Corporation deserve special thanks for arranging interviews with a number of their board members.

For the Maryland state-level case example, I especially appreciate the participation of the following interviewees: Richard Bendis, Brian Darmody, and Dr. William E. Kirwan. Robert Hannon also contributed significantly to this case example.

Three other interviewees made significant contributions to the book content. They are Elva Castaneda de Hall, Aris Melissaratos, and J. Mac Holladay. Thank you very much for your support.

Two people were invaluable in the actual production of the manuscript. My long-time friend and valuable colleague Jerry Elprin was a constant supporter and adviser as the editor for the project. For graphics assistance, Danielle Peterson of Briodesign provided timely and accurate support. Thank you, Danielle.

A book without a publisher is a book without value. I would like to provide my final thank-you to Hilary Claggett, Senior Editor, Business, Economics and Finance for Praeger/ABC-CLIO. Hilary has been extremely instrumental in guiding me through the proposal, writing, and production processes and in the publisher's decision to support this project. She has always been available promptly when I needed advice and her advice has always been spot-on.

None of these individuals are responsible for any errors or omissions in the document as that is the responsibility of the author. I accept that responsibility. Ultimately it will be up to the readers to decide the value of this work. I welcome your reactions and especially welcome feedback about how you are engaged in transforming community and economic development in your place.

Thomas C. Tuttle
Annapolis, Maryland
tctuttle1@verizon.net

CHAPTER ONE

The Jobs and Employment Challenge

We are defined by our work. Much more than a source of money, a job is a means of expression and a major source of self-esteem, dignity, and meaning in our lives. It is not surprising to learn, therefore, that the most significant finding of Gallup's World Poll, sampling opinion from 150 nations, was that what people all over the world want is a good job.[1]

The Gallup survey also found that not any job will do. What people want is not just a job, but a "good" job. While the definition of a "good job" varies from person to person as a result of individual differences, most would agree that a "good job" is at a minimum one that provides at least a living wage. Other factors desired from work include a chance for advancement, opportunity to have input to decisions that impact an employee on the job, the chance to learn new skills, safe and healthy working conditions, support from coworkers, challenging work, and so on.

From a policy maker's perspective, the difference between "creating good jobs" and "creating jobs" has not always been a primary focus. Too often policy makers have focused narrowly on metrics such as the unemployment rate and the number of jobs created without including metrics that address the quality of the jobs created.

We will argue in this book that, from a policy perspective, the difference between creating jobs and creating good jobs is the difference between a focus on traditional economic development and a focus on the new paradigm of values-based, innovation-driven economic development.

Current Economic Development Model

Traditional economic development has been defined by two principal activities. One is job attraction—the attempt to lure businesses or business investment from outside of the jurisdiction (e.g., state, region, county, city) into the target jurisdiction served by the economic developer. The second is business retention—efforts placed on working with businesses within the jurisdiction to assure they will remain in the jurisdiction and help them grow and add jobs.

In recent years the job development focus has also included a third emphasis on establishing and growing start-up businesses. This effort has focused on establishing and managing business incubators and accelerators and building an "ecosystem" to support entrepreneurship and innovation. If one examines the relative commitment of resources to these three primary strategies for job creation, the traditional economic development model has devoted a disproportionate allocation of resources to business attraction and much less to business retention and growth and new business creation. This is followed despite evidence that most new job creation comes from the expansion of existing firms. Professor John Haltiwanger and his colleagues of the University of Maryland argue that most new job creation comes from a subset of existing firms—those that can be identified as rapidly growing businesses and they tend to be start-ups and young firms.[2]

There are several reasons for this. First, luring a new corporation to the state or county generates a lot of favorable publicity as well as jobs and tax revenue. Attracting a new plant of a Toyota, General Motors, Siemens, or Samsung brings a defined number of new jobs and significant contribution to the tax base of a jurisdiction. It is also likely to have a multiplier effect in that a new plant will also help attract suppliers to the new plant and generate revenue for a range of service providers (e.g., restaurants, real estate agents, gas stations, dry cleaners). Second, and perhaps even more important, politicians like to attend "ribbon-cuttings" where they can claim credit for their efforts to land a number of new jobs for their constituents. Job attraction, when it is successful, produces visible and concrete victories that elected officials cherish.

Business retention—helping existing businesses remain in a jurisdiction and grow—is much less glamorous and produces few headlines. To use a baseball metaphor, job attraction is about hitting home runs. Business retention is what baseball players would call "small ball." It is hitting a single, stealing second, bunting the runner to third, and then relying on a sacrifice fly to produce the run.

Business retention efforts require a great deal of "hand-holding," dealing with interagency issues that impact businesses such as permits, regulations, inspections, tax issues, and so on. In general, it involves those activities that make the jurisdiction more "business-friendly." Business retention efforts can also impact business attraction efforts since companies that do their due diligence regarding a move or new investment will seek out existing businesses in the area to ask whether the jurisdiction is a place where it is easy to do business. If the existing companies in an area are not satisfied, they can share that dissatisfaction with potential new businesses and perhaps prevent a deal from getting done.

In the traditional paradigm, it is common for politicians at the state and county levels to run for office with promises to improve their local economy, create more jobs, and grow the local tax base. When they are elected they typically bring to their governing team a key supporter as the secretary of economic development or a comparable position. If the politician ran on a platform that the previous occupant—governor, mayor, or county executive—did not do a good job, there is little incentive to continue the policy initiatives of the past. Therefore, new policies are needed and usually new people are brought in to implement the new policies. If we assume four-year terms of office for elected officials, every four or eight years the economic development strategies are reinvented, and any continuity of policy from one administration to the next is lost. Often, knowledge capital is also lost with the replacement of staff.

The elected official typically brings her vision for economic development. Since elections in a democracy create winners and losers, the new administration comes into office with a substantial minority of citizens who do not share its vision. The professional economic development staff owe their allegiance to the elected official and therefore spend most of their time and effort on implementing the short-term promises made by the elected official during the campaign and implementing the vision of the "boss."

This system is dysfunctional for two primary reasons. First, economic development is a marathon, not a sprint. It is necessary to systematically create the building blocks that underpin a strong economy. This involves strategic planning, strengthening workforce skills, encouraging entrepreneurship, building the ecosystem—physical, social, and institutional—and supporting growth of the existing business base. This long-term perspective does not fit the needs of elected politicians who operate with a four-year time horizon.

The second reason the current system is dysfunctional is that sustained dynamic economic development requires that the entire community including citizens, businesses, and the nonprofit and educational sectors as well as all government entities, not just the economic development office, must be engaged in the effort. Obtaining broad-based community engagement requires the leadership of individuals and institutions that are outside of the political process. Certainly the elected leaders can be helpful in this community engagement process, but the focus and ownership must reside in the community institutions, not in the individual who happens to hold elective office.

The existing business attraction paradigm, founded on a "win–lose" zero-sum view of job development, has produced a great deal of dysfunctional behavior by states and counties. The dysfunctionality of the present system can provoke strong reactions from those who are participants in the system. An example comes from an individual who has seen this system from a range of perspectives. He has been a corporate executive of a major corporation and a secretary of economic development at the state level and now is a business school dean. In my interview he was very candid when reflecting on the current system:

> The norm in this country of trying to steal the next guy's company is completely a zero-sum game. There was talk a few years ago about legislating it out of existence, at the federal level, but it never happened. There is this whole industry that I will call "parasitic"—the so-called site development consultants—who have as their whole reason for being to squeeze the last penny out of any government body, whether it is state, county or municipality, as an incentive to bring that company there. Now if I am on the company side, and I was for many years, I felt that it was my civic duty to help the local economy. I hated it when corporations tried to get training dollars out of local government and that sort of thing. . . .
>
> The only real strategic investment for any region to make is an investment in education. You have to produce a workforce and it is a workforce that produces economic gains.[3]

As the quote points out, the bitter competition among states for business relocation or new business investment has enabled the site selector to pit states against each other in a bidding war to win the deal. As a result, politicians eager for the "home run" have often committed very significant public resources in the form of subsidies, tax incentives, and regulatory exemptions in order to improve their odds of winning the battle. Often the true costs of these arrangements are hidden from the public in order to disguise their true cost per job gained. The gains achieved coupled with loss of tax revenue are often outweighed by the loss of services which detract from the community quality of life needed to attract and keep the type of workforce required to support high-quality job growth.

Another type of dysfunctional behavior the traditional paradigm has produced is raids by one state on another in an effort to lure the other state's businesses without necessarily involving a site selection consultant. The negative impact of this behavior can be amplified by its partisan political overtones as Republican governors have openly targeted states with Democratic governors. As *Politico* has reported,[4] the GOP chief executives try to lure businesses by championing their states as "lower-tax, lower-regulation states." While this may be good politics for the Republican governors in their home states, it is hardly good for the overall U.S. economy. Not only is this behavior generating backlash from states that are being targeted, but it is also leading GOP governors to attempt to outdo each other as job raiders.

The dysfunctional mind-set the win–lose paradigm breeds can be seen even within states at the county level. When counties view economic development as a win–lose competition with other counties, we see behavior that is negative for the larger economic system, that is, the state and the nation. For example, there are anecdotes about an economic development professional in one county, who is showing a prospect sites in his county, driving to the county line and dropping the prospect off rather than delivering him to the office of the economic development person in the adjoining county. Competition of this sort destroys cooperation and alliance-building when the view is that if the other jurisdiction wins, I lose.

The current situation has driven organizations such as the International Economic Development Council (IEDC)[5] and National Governors Association (NGA)[6] to examine how the current approach should be changed. The pressure to change is driven by a number of forces. IEDC identifies the major drivers of the need for change as demographics, climate change, shifting global roles, and technology expansion. The NGA lists the major challenges facing states as the rise of global competition, structural inefficiencies in state economic development agencies, and the state fiscal crunch. There appears to be increasing agreement that the current paradigm and strategies for economic development are insufficient to meet the challenges that states and the nation face.

How should economic development strategies and processes change? The IEDC report points out some of the implications for current practice based on its analysis of the challenges. Some areas of needed change by economic development agencies and by individuals include changing practices, changing metrics, changing skills, and changing competition—the need to compete for talent by improving education and the quality of place. The NGA report identifies three areas in which state-level economic development strategy change is needed. These are: (1) the need to engage and sustain private sector involvement; (2) the need to create mechanisms to encourage collaboration among business, academic institutions, and government agencies; and (3) the need to institute a quantitative evaluation system—similar to the IEDC call for new metrics.

The Job Creation Challenge

The need for a more effective economic development system is also obvious when we consider the magnitude of the job creation challenges that we face. This challenge for the United States has been highlighted by the McKinsey Global Institute.[7] In order to reach full employment by 2020 the U.S. economy will need to create 21 million new jobs during the decade 2011–2020. The authors analyzed six sectors they regarded as the most promising for job growth in the economy for this decade. The sectors selected account for 65 percent of the forecasted job growth. They are health care, business services, leisure and hospitality, construction, manufacturing, and retail. Using the data from these sectors the authors created three scenarios for job growth across the sectors—high growth, moderate growth, and low growth. Only in the high-growth scenario could the economy create enough jobs to reach full employment by 2020.

Even if the economy creates a sufficient number of jobs, the authors point out that there will be considerable mismatches between the job requirements and the education and skills of the workforce. For example, their analysis forecasts a shortage of up to 1.5 million workers with bachelor's degrees or higher in 2020 and they estimate that nearly 6 million Americans who lack a high school diploma will not have a job. They also point out that students who attend college and vocational schools do not choose fields of study that are aligned with the likely needs of the future economy. They also forecast shortages in fields such as nutritionist, welding, and nurse's aides in addition to the fields of computer specialists and engineers that other analyses have identified.

Finally, the choices made by students regarding courses of study suggest that the labor-market information system is not providing information to students and other workers who may consider retraining that enables them to make wise and informed choices regarding future career opportunities. As the authors point out, business as usual will not help the U.S. economy reach full employment.

Need for a New Economic Development Model

The analysis by the McKinsey Global Institute calls for radical changes in current practice in order to increase the chance that the U.S. economy will reach full employment by 2020. The challenge is multifaceted. It will require significant increases in job creation. The challenge will also require significant changes and realignment in the education and skills of the workforce. Since the choice of an education or training program is a decision or a series of decisions made by individuals, there is a need for much better information to be available to people as they are making career choices.

There is some evidence that the old economic development model is changing. The NGA[8] has pointed out that, in January 2011, 29 new governors were inaugurated. The lingering impact of the 2008 recession and the high unemployment rate led them to launch a number of reforms and experiments to accelerate economic improvement. In analyzing these initiatives the report's authors identify six trends that have emerged across the states:

1. States are increasing their emphasis on the relationship between the state and its regions;
2. There is an increasing emphasis on job creation from within the state;
3. There is an increased emphasis on support for advanced manufacturing;
4. States are creating partnerships within the state to meet industry's demands for talent;
5. There is an increased emphasis by states to expect more from universities in terms of the commercialization of research into patents, new products, and new enterprises;
6. States are increasing their emphasis on assisting their businesses to develop new export markets and the capability to sell to those markets.[9]

Many of these ideas are not new. But the urgency of the situation seems to have ignited a search for identifying promising practices and deploying them more widely across the country.

Some of these initiatives do appear to represent new thinking in economic development and suggest that the new emphasis is evidence of an emerging new paradigm. The emphasis on job creation from within the state appears at least in part to have resulted from research results that show that most job creation is not the result of "job raids" from other states. A study in California, for example, examined the period from 1992 through 2006 and found that about 1 percent of the job gains in California resulted from the relocation of firms.[10] On the other hand, 40.6 percent of new job creation resulted from "expansions"—organic growth by existing businesses—and 58.4 percent came from "births"—the creation of new enterprises.

Data for the nation as a whole show that for all states 1.9 percent of job gains resulted from moves from one state to another, 41.6 percent came from expansions of existing firms, and 56.3 percent came from "births" or new firm creation. Data such as these seem to have influenced the new governors to put more emphasis on creating jobs from within the state. These in-state job creation strategies include helping existing firms grow, as well as starting new businesses through entrepreneurship initiatives promoting ecosystem growth and the support of incubators and accelerators.

The emerging economic development trend in states is to focus on economic development from within the state, rather than on the much publicized job raids to lure firms from other states. Such activities may generate headlines, but there is little data to support their effectiveness as job creation tools. The job and employment creation success of Texas is not the result of job raids, but of other policies and quality-of-life issues in progressive cities such as Austin that have stimulated the growth of firms in the state and entrepreneurship. Economic development job attraction officials will point out that there is a difference between "job raiding" (i.e., encouraging firms to move existing jobs out of a state) and encouraging firms considering new investments and new job creation to select another investment site. However, from the perspective of the state that loses the planned expansion, this may be a distinction without a difference.

Another trend that suggests new thinking in terms of economic development practice is an emphasis on identifying and supporting existing firms within a state with high growth potential. For example, Nebraska has developed a partnership with the Gallup organization to identify small to medium-sized firms with high growth potential. This process then focuses on the leaders of these firms and connects them with mentoring programs to improve their entrepreneurial ability in hopes of accelerating business growth and job creation.[11]

Such programs that appear to favor certain firms over others seem likely to encounter the political objections of government favoritism. However, the reality is that not all firms are equally likely to create above-average job growth. Whether states can design valid ways of predicting which will be the high-growth companies and whether they can make such targeting politically acceptable to citizens remain to be seen. But in an environment of limited resources, this approach appears to be one that merits attention.

Another illustration of new thinking is the increased emphasis on organizations and services that assist business to grow. For many years universities have partnered with their economic development agencies to support businesses through entities such as technology extension services, productivity centers, and centers of entrepreneurship. Typically, these have been relatively low-budget operations that were supported by a mix of funding from public and private sectors that existed to support job creation and business competitiveness.

Some of these initiatives also had as their mission to provide practical application experience to students and link businesses with faculty in order to create collaborative research opportunities for the faculty and business value for the companies. While these programs were generally well regarded by those businesses that became involved, the programs had limited impact on job creation because they lacked the resources to scale up to the level that would generate the impact. Cost–benefit analyses of these programs could demonstrate significant payback of the state's investment, but the old economic development paradigms did not appreciate their value.

This seems to be changing. In addition, there are new forms of assistance organizations that are more targeted to start-up and high-growth businesses. The two types of organizations that are evolving are incubators and business accelerators. Incubators tend to be a place where new businesses can develop. They typically provide space, support services, mentoring and networking opportunities, and access to investors. Some incubators charge a monthly fee and some trade the use of their services for equity in the new company. Some are hybrids that are supported by both fees and equity. Typically a firm would remain in an incubator for one to three years, and incubators are often most useful for first-time entrepreneurs. As of 2012, 1,300 incubators were operating in the United States.[12]

Business accelerators differ from incubators in that they typically offer less time in the program. They provide links to funding upon entry and typically take equity positions in the businesses they accept. They screen entrants to identify those that will attract venture funding in the near term so that the accelerators can get a quick return on their investment. As a result they tend to favor seasoned entrepreneurs—often in high-tech industries. Acceptance rates into accelerators are similar to acceptance rates into very selective universities. Seed-DB is an emerging database of accelerators and their companies.[13] As of April 2014, this database listed 213 programs worldwide with 3,712 companies accelerated and 16,129 jobs created. The total funding has been $4,835,682,545 or approximately $299,000 per job created.

Another aspect of the emerging new paradigm is that states appear to be increasingly viewing the business community as "their customer." One of the enduring lessons of the quality revolution that swept through U.S. businesses from the late 1970s into the 1990s was that it is customers that create jobs, not businesses. If customers buy the products and services of an enterprise, and if they market those products and services through word of mouth to their contacts, businesses grow. As employees gain this understanding that job security does not come from your employer, but ultimately comes from customers, they will be more willing to align their on-the-job behavior with the requirements of their ultimate customer.

It appears from the examples of new initiatives in state government that this lesson has made it to statehouses and to leaders of economic development and workforce development agencies. As a result, now that they realize existing businesses and new start-ups are the major job creators, it is important that state policy makers understand what these "job creators" need in order to be successful. This is also happening at a time when there are increasing pressures for businesses to act more responsibly in terms of environmental and social performance in addition to economic performance. Thus we may be in the very early stages of experiencing a "convergence" of goals between the public and private sectors to a greater degree than we have previously experienced.

We still hear much of the antitax, antiregulation rhetoric from the oldschool business community. And we still hear from some government officials and some "progressives" the distrust of business and the adversarial relationship between the sectors. However, we also see more businesses willing to be engaged in public–private partnerships, more businessesbuilding sustainability initiatives into their business strategies, and more governments taking a hard look at how to make their regulatory and tax structures less burdensome on the business community.

How This Book Is Organized

Chapter 2 will examine the role of values in economic development planning and implementation. As we examine different approaches to economic development not only in the United States but also across the world, we see that as cultures and communities have different values they reflect these values in the strategies they embrace in developing organizations, jobs and communities. In this chapter we frame the issue of values and economic development by posing the question, "What type of economy do we want to create?" What we find in talking with economic development professionals is that this question is not always asked.

A key premise of this book is that the answer to this question by citizens within the jurisdiction (state, region, county, or city) is the beginning point for a successful economic development strategy. When citizens can see that their personal values are aligned with the community's economic development strategy, the result will be greater citizen ownership and support for the economic development process. Values alignment acts as an economic and employment development accelerator. This chapter will describe a job creation process that is values based and that stimulates innovation and productivity in order to accelerate the creation of good jobs.

In Chapter 3 we will look at past job crises and identify themes, successful practices, and lessons learned that can have applicability today and in the future. Past jobs crises have included the Great Depression of the 1930s, a number of business cycle recessions, and competitive threats in the 1970s when Japan's manufacturing success peaked and we saw U.S. companies losing market share and jobs in industry after industry. The United States also assisted other nations to rebuild their economies following major wars. Chapter 3 will review these past efforts with a focus on the Marshall Plan to rebuild Europe after World War II and the response to the loss of jobs and market share to Japanese businesses in the late 1980s and 1990s.

Chapter 4 focuses on examples of changes in economic development practices that are being made at the state level in a number of states, including Arizona, Colorado, Tennessee, Massachusetts, Mississippi, Maine, Oregon, North Carolina, Michigan, Virginia, and New York. It will then focus in more detail on changes at the state level in Maryland as a way to look at state economic development not only at the executive branch level, but also from the legislative branch and higher education perspectives.

In Chapters 5 and 6 we will shift the focus from the state to the local level and examine two economic development success stories. Chapter 5 will focus on Austin, Texas, and Chapter 6 will focus on Dubuque, Iowa. We will examine these cases in some detail and extract principles that can help guide our development of a new economic development framework that is presented in Chapters 7 and 8.

Chapter 7 describes the proposed new framework for local community and economic development. Chapter 8 describes the proposed new framework for state-level community and economic development—focusing on how the state should support the local community and economic development systems.

In Chapter 9 the book will conclude with a discussion of the basic rationale for transforming community and economic development toward the new frameworks. We present this discussion in the form of a hypothetical dialogue between the author and an experienced and thoughtful economic development professional who is a bit skeptical of the new framework.

CHAPTER TWO

What Type of Economy Do We Want to Create?

In Chapter 1 we made the case for why new job creation is essential for regions, nations, and the world. How does job creation happen? How do we increase the number of good jobs? Job creation is the result of a sequence of actions and it can be viewed as a process. Figure 2.1 depicts an overview of that process. Like all models, this is a simplified view. It illustrates, however, that job creation is the result of innovation and improved productivity. When an organization creates a product or service that is valued by customers and when it can produce, market, and deliver that product or service with fewer resources than competitor organizations, that organization can grow and growth leads to new job creation. We will examine the logic for the process displayed in Figure 2.1.

In its report entitled "Growing State Economies: A Policy Framework," the National Governors Association (NGA) pointed out that:

> Productivity drives both prosperity and economic growth. Productivity growth (output per worker) is the basis for rising real wages for workers, increasing returns to shareholders and increasing per capita income for a state and the nation. . . . Innovation also is important to productivity growth. The value of goods and services increases not only as more workers are employed and as investors create more capital, but also because of new technologies and innovation in products, processes and management. Increasingly, it is innovation-driven productivity growth that is the basis for rising real wages for workers, increasing returns to shareholders, and increasing per capita income for a state and the nation.[1]

If we move upstream through the process in Figure 2.1, we see that productivity is driven by innovation. There are many forms of innovation. The

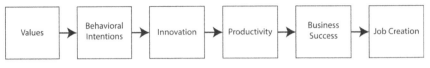

Figure 2.1   Values to Job Creation Process

NGA report mentioned three types of innovation: innovation in products, in processes, and in management practices.

Next we must ask, what is the source of innovation? The model points out that the behavioral intentions of people drive innovation. Whether this is an inventor in her garage, a scientist or engineer in the laboratory, or a frontline employee on the assembly line, new ideas, which are the source of innovation, come from people. The ideas may be from people acting as individuals or working in team settings, but innovations stem from the behaviors of people.

Architect, writer, consultant, and educator William McDonough has written and spoken widely about the way in which design thinking can benefit businesses and society. In an article published in the *Guardian*, McDonough discusses the way in which innovation occurs.

> The most successful companies embrace good design by loudly and clearly stating their positive intentions. When a CEO declares that his or her company will improve the water quality of an entire community or build a workplace that will generate more renewable energy than it requires, this statement alone can unleash enthusiasm, creativity and innovation. A statement of intention places values first. It stresses the good, such as "we will use and generate only renewable energy" rather than the more commonly stated less bad: "we will reduce our use of fossil fuels." . . . Putting values first produces far higher levels of innovation and performance than starting the design process with metrics, which tends to blur goals and aspirations with commonplace limits and benchmarks. When values and upcycling set the agenda, when—rather than inching forward bit by bit toward doing less harm—companies set purposeful goals and seek continuous improvement in everything they do, good design creates more value.[2]

Two authors from Babson College who have studied the factors that create an innovative organizational culture are Jay Rao and Joseph Weintraub.[3] They have defined the key elements that support innovation as falling into two categories which they call the "hard" and "soft" elements. The hard elements are resources, processes, and success. The soft elements are values, behaviors, and climate. They view these elements as "dynamically linked" and point out that values impact people's behaviors, the climate, and how success is defined and measured. Of the two sets of factors, they conclude that the hard elements are the most effectively managed, but in terms of stimulating innovation, the soft elements may offer the greatest potential for improving innovation.

From the evidence discussed, we can safely conclude that values are the foundation for understanding the behavior and behavioral intentions that ultimately produce innovation-driven productivity, business success, and job creation. Therefore we must begin our exploration of how to grow good jobs with an understanding of values and how values operate to shape behavior. More specifically, we will examine how values underpin the behaviors that are important to any effort to accelerate job creation.

Values do not completely account for behavior. Skills, knowledge, environment, and the like are also key factors. But values guide our decision making. They exert a significant influence over what skills and knowledge are acquired. Knowledge and skills are required for individuals to convert their values into action—that is, to live their values.

What are "values"? According to values theorist Brian Hall, "Values are the ideals that give significance to our lives, that are reflected through the priorities that we choose, and that we act on consistently and repeatedly."[4] Hall devoted his life's work to demonstrating that values can be identified and measured at both individual and organizational levels. His colleague Benjamin Tonna demonstrated that values can be assessed and tracked at the societal level using techniques of document analysis.[5]

Hall and Tonna cataloged and defined 125 human values which they formed into a taxonomy that will be discussed later in this chapter. This taxonomy of values can be considered to be to the science of behavior what the periodic table of elements is to chemistry. These elemental values are the building blocks for behavior analysis and for explaining human decision making.

The case for how values impact economic development practice can be made more concrete by considering a range of situations that present choices that are strongly influenced by value preferences. Consider the following situations:

1. An angel investor is presented with six business cases, all vying for his investment. Which business case(s) does he choose to fund?
2. A community foundation executive is charged with determining the community's needs that can be addressed through funding various charities. How are those community needs framed and which are chosen for funding?

3. A community that has been 98 percent white is faced with the need to make itself more welcoming to employees of businesses that are moving into the community with a diverse international workforce. What values need to be activated in order to build a more inclusive community?
4. To build a world-class workforce it is necessary to enable students in high school to develop higher levels of personal and vocational maturity to give them the ability and confidence to take charge of their learning and their life. What values must be activated in these students to enable this development to occur?
5. To address social problems in the community that have become business problems, for example, public safety, poverty, low educational attainment, and drugs, it is clear that no single organization is able to solve these problems. Business organizations must collaborate with other partners and be part of a larger systems initiative in order to address these complex societal and business problems. What values must be activated to enable this shift from a "go it alone" to a "collaborative" approach in which it does not matter who gets the credit?

All of these situations involve values-based choices and decisions for individuals, for organizations, and for jurisdictions and their leaders. Whether the values choices are implicit or explicit, values impact our decisions and behavior all the time. The more insight we can gain into the way values operate to shape our behavior, the more effective we will be in moving to a new paradigm of values-based economic development.

The Science of Values

One of the most significant contributors to the scientific study of human values was Milton Rokeach.[6] In his groundbreaking book he makes the distinction between beliefs, attitudes, and values. Rokeach points out that "an adult may have tens or hundreds of thousands of beliefs, thousands of attitudes, but only dozens of values."[7]

Rokeach also emphasized the distinction between "means" values and "ends" values. Means values, also called instrumental values, are preferences for specific ways of behaving. Ends values, also referred to as terminal values, address preferences for different end goals or states of existence. The question "What type of economy do we want to create?" that members of a community ask addresses their terminal values—their desired end-state.

A value system is a hierarchical arrangement of values that enables individuals to make choices between modes of behaving (instrumental) or desired end-states (terminal) when faced with situations that present values conflicts. For example, a person may have to make a choice between a course of action that is best for himself and one that is best for the group. Or a person may have to choose between acting truthfully and acting in a way that would be loyal to her organization. Or with respect to terminal values, a person may be confronted with a choice between self-fulfillment and prestige in the community. The way in which values are arranged in the hierarchy of terminal values and the hierarchy of instrumental values will guide the behavior choices in these conflict situations.

Brian Hall built on the work of Milton Rokeach and others, and with his colleague Benjamin Tonna, he built a theory of values that arrays 125 human values into a developmental values map.[8] The Hall–Tonna values framework defines eight developmental stages (Table 2.1). Within each stage there are both instrumental and terminal values. The authors point out that humans, as we develop, move through these eight stages. Hall and Tonna also introduce the concepts of foundation, focus, and vision values to describe the developmental process. Brian Hall provides the following definition for these three categories of values:

1.   *Foundation values* represent our basic needs and are the foundation for being able to act on and live out our focus values. Foundation values dominate during times of crisis or stress. People who are habitually very stressed can live out their whole lives in this development stage.
2.   *Focus values* are those value priorities in our day-to-day lives that describe our present worldview, our criteria for decision making, our attitude toward relationships, and the focus of most of our energy.
3.   *Future or Vision values* represent the motivational force in our lives. They are our future because they are not yet fully developed, although they are present, motivating us to move forward. They form the vision that pulls us into the future every moment of our lives.[9]

Development can stop at any one of the eight stages. However, people can choose to develop through all of these stages if they maintain the foundational values and develop the skills that allow them to proceed toward their vision values. Based on the value preferences within each stage, each individual's path through the development process can be quite variable. As a result the framework is not prescriptive and it recognizes that humans can develop in many different ways toward different visions.

As foundation values are addressed they lose their motivational power and the attention shifts to focus and vision values. Focus values are the values that are most active at any point in time, whereas vision values are values that one aspires to live but may not yet have the skills and competencies to live at the present stage of development. A key premise of the Hall–Tonna values framework is that people can choose to change their values through learning and experience. At any one time, only a subset of 20 or so of the 125 values will be activated. That subset however will change as

Table 2.1 Hall–Tonna Values Map*

Phases	Phase I SURVIVING		Phase II BELONGING		Phase III SELF-INITIATING		Phase IV INTERDEPENDENT	
World View	The world is a mystery over which I have no control.		The world is a problem with which I must cope.		The world is a project in which I want to participate.		The world is a mystery for which we care on a global scale.	
Stages	1. SAFETY	2. SECURITY	3. FAMILY	4. INSTITUTION	5. VOCATION	6. NEW ORDER	7. WISDOM	8. WORLD ORDER
Goals	Self-Interest/Control; Self-Preservation; Wonder/Awe/Fate	Physical Delight; Security	Family/Belonging; Fantasy/Play; Self-Worth	Belief/Philosophy; Competence/Confidence; Play/Recreation; Work/Labor	Equality/Liberation; Integration/Wholeness; Self-Actualization; Service/Vocation	Art/Beauty; Being Self; Construction/New Order; Contemplation; Faith/Risk/Vision; Human Dignity; Knowledge/Insight; Presence	Intimacy/Solitude; Truth/Wisdom	Ecority; Global Harmony; Word
Means	Food/Warmth/Shelter; Function/Physical; Safety/Survival	Affection/Physical; Economics/Profit; Property/Control; Sensory Pleasure; Territory/Security; Wonder/Curiosity	Being Liked; Care/Nurture; Control/Order/Discipline; Courtesy/Hospitality; Dexterity/Coordination; Endurance/Patience; Equilibrium; Friendship/Belonging; Obedience/Duty; Prestige/Image; Rights/	Achievement/Success; Administration/Control; Communication/Info Competition; Design/Pattern/Order; Duty/Obligation; Economics/Success; Education/Certification; Efficiency/Planning; Hierarchy/Order	Adaptability/Flexibility; Authority/Honesty; Congruence; Decision/Initiation; Empathy; Equity/Rights; Expressiveness/Joy; Generosity/Compassion; Health/Healing; Independence; Law/Guide; Limitation/Acceptance	Accountability/Ethics; Collaboration; Community/Supportive; Complementarity; Corporation/Stewardship; Creativity; Detachment/Solitude; Discernment; Education/Knowledge; Growth/Expansion	Community/Personalist; Interdependence; Minessence; Prophet/Vision; Synergy; Transcendence/Solitude	Convivial Technology; Global Justice; Human Rights; Macroeconomics

18

Leadership Style						
AUTHORITARIAN	**PATERNALIST**	**MANAGER**	**FACILITATOR**	**COLLABORATOR**	**SERVANT**	**VISIONARY**
Oppressive dictator with followers who are totally dependent.	Benevolent paternalist with followers who are dependent and obedient.	Efficient manager with followers who are loyally devoted to the organization.	Listener, clarifier, and supporter with followers who are also listeners, clarifiers, and supporters.	Facilitator, producer, and creator with active peer participation.	Interdependent administrator with collegial participation.	Liberator with a global network of peer visionaries.
		Respect Social Affirmation Support Peer Tradition	Honor Law/Rule Loyalty/Fidelity Management Membership/Institution Ownership Patriotism/Esteem Productivity Reason Responsibility Rule/Accountability Technology/Science Unity/Uniformity Workmanship/Art/Craft	Mutual Obedience Quality/Evaluation Relaxation Search/Meaning/Hope Self-Assertion Sharing/Listening/Trust	Intimacy Justice/Social Order Leisure Limitation/Celebration Mission/Objectives Mutual Accountability Pioneerism/Innovation Research Ritual/Communication Simplicity/Play Unity/Diversity	

*Reprinted with permission from Elva Castaneda de Hall, Principal Owner, Values Technology, Inc.

development proceeds. Progress toward one's vision values can be upset if foundation values are threatened. For example, if one experiences a medical crisis, a family crisis, or an employment crisis or if their safety and security is threatened in any other way (e.g., a 9/11 event), priority will shift from the focus and vision values to the foundation values.

Drawing on developmental theory, Hall points out that there is a very significant difference between the worldview of people who are operating (i.e., the central tendency of their focus values) in stages 1–4 and those operating in stages 5–8. They describe the developmental breakthrough as one moves from Phase 2 (i.e., stages 3–4) to Phase 3 (i.e., stages 5–6) as the "values shift"—hence the title of the book.[10]

In stages 3 and 4 the predominant worldview is that the world is a project and I need to find my place and fit into the environment around me. When people develop into stages 5 and 6, they shift their worldview. The new worldview is that I take charge of my life and I must create my own future. The differences between the values in these stages are displayed on Table 2.2.

Table 2.2   Comparison of Values from Stages 3–4 to 5–6

Stage 3	Stage 4	Stage 5	Stage 6
Goal Values	*Goal Values*	*Goal Values*	*Goal Values*
Family/ Belonging	Competence/ Confidence	Integration/ Wholeness	Being Self
Self-Worth	Work/Labor	Self-Actualization	Construction/New Order
	Belief/Philosophy	Service/Vocation	Human Dignity Knowledge/Insight
Means Values	*Means Values*	*Means Values*	*Means Values*
Being Liked	Achievement/ Success	Adaptability/ Flexibility	Collaboration
Control/Order/ Discipline	Duty/Obligation	Decision/ Initiation	Community/ Supportive
Friendship/ Belonging	Education/ Certification	Independence	Corporation/New Order
Obedience/Duty	Economics/ Success	Limitation/ Acceptance	Limitation/ Celebration
Rights/Respect	Responsibility	Sharing/Listening/ Trust	Pioneerism/ Innovation
	Law/Rule	Law/Guide	Mutual Accountability

When we examine the goal values in stages 5 and 6, we can see a shift from a focus on fitting into a world defined by others to becoming more of a participant in creating that world. This is most visible in stage 6 with values such as *Being Self*, which deals with one's capacity to know oneself and ability to act independently or cooperatively as one judges what is appropriate. *Construction/New Order* is a goal value that pertains to one's ability to transform an existing institution or create a new organization or institution that will benefit society. *Knowledge/Insight* refers to the pursuit of truth through structured or patterned investigation. The means values in stages 5 and 6 (*Independence, Decision Initiation, Adaptability/Flexibility, Corporation/New Order*, and *Pioneerism/Innovation*) support the "self-initiating" worldview that we see in these stages where individuals are not attempting to fit into the status quo but are active participants in trying to build a better world.

In Chapter 1 we made the case that the challenges facing states, counties, and cities demand a different approach to economic development. This new approach requires a different approach to economic development leadership. Transformational leaders who can enable a jurisdiction to move from the industrial age economy into the information economy or beyond are likely to be leaders whose focus is in stages 5 and 6, and who also have solid foundational values (stages 1–4). Peter Senge and his colleagues have addressed this issue in their call for what they call the system leader.

> The deep changes necessary to accelerate progress against society's most intractable problems require a unique type of leader—the system leader, a person who catalyzes collective leadership.[11]

Certainly the challenges faced by economic development leaders fall into the category of "intractable problems" that demand a system leader. The core capabilities required by system leaders are: (1) the ability to see the larger system, (2) the ability to reflect on how we think and see how our existing assumptions and mental models may limit us, and (3) the ability to shift the focus from reactive problem solving to co-creating the future. All three of these capabilities result from the values shift from stage 3–4 values to stage 5–6 values.

Up to this point we have focused on values of individuals. It is also possible and helpful for the economic development discussion to extrapolate the discussion of values to the organizational level. Following this we will shift the discussion to the "community level." At each of these larger units of analysis we can use the Hall–Tonna values framework to think of how organizations evolve and develop and how communities evolve and develop. This is particularly important since in our model in Figure 2.1 we pointed out that values drive the behavioral intentions of people who drive innovation and innovation drives productivity, which in turn drives job creation. When an organization achieves values alignment from top to bottom, that alignment acts as a productivity accelerator. People believe in the purpose of the organization, trust is strengthened, communication improves, and the organization becomes able to react more quickly to changes in the environment. All of these factors are characteristics of an innovative climate and they are productivity enablers and accelerators.

Values alignment does not mean that all people have the same set of values or become clones of each other. Values alignment means that there is sufficient overlap between the "values in practice" within an organization or a community and the personal values of each individual. This overlap creates an emotional bond between the individual and the organization that enhances trust, motivation, and communication and releases the personal energy of people to support the organization's purpose and mission.

Let me provide two examples of how this can work from my consulting experience in using values-driven organizational change. One was from a manufacturing organization and the other was from a county public school system. In both examples, the organizations were attempting to achieve breakthrough levels of performance improvement, and the values analysis was part of a larger organizational change initiative.

In both organizations the change process was led by a senior-level guidance team composed of the senior leaders of the organization. In the manufacturing case this was a team consisting of the top union and management officials in the plant. In the education example the team consisted of the top officials from the central office headquarters of a county school system as well as principals from individual schools. Each member of the guidance team was administered an individual values survey that produced a rank ordering of each of the 125 Hall–Tonna values. The scoring of the survey also produced additional statistics that were helpful in coaching individuals to understand their personal values priorities and to create an individual development plan. Individual values feedback sessions were held with each team member of both teams to prepare them to be able to discuss their values priorities in an open group session.

In the manufacturing case, one of the obstacles to productivity and performance improvement was the inability to create trust and collaborative decision making between the union leaders and management as they were facing the implementation of a new advanced manufacturing system that was being introduced by their new owner following an acquisition of the company. This new manufacturing system had the potential to increase the future competitiveness of the plant. However, to achieve this benefit it was necessary for the union and management to work together to implement the new technology effectively in order to obtain the performance benefits that were possible and therefore retain and grow good jobs. This required building a common vision, communicating this vision to employees, developing and implementing training for employees, and working together to do the day-to-day work of addressing the employee, technology, and maintenance issues that emerged. It was very important at the leadership level to have the union and management leaders speaking with one voice in support of the new manufacturing system implementation. This unity could only emerge through the development of a set of shared values between union and management leadership.

Once each member of the guidance team had completed the survey and participated in the individual feedback meeting, the next step was to bring the total group together for a group feedback and planning session. This session began with a presentation of the value rankings for the total group and separately for the union leadership and the management leadership. From this presentation, one observation was that the range of "diversity" of individual focus values was virtually identical for the management group and the union group. Both groups had individuals whose values profile focus ranged from stage 3 to stage 7. This means that with regard to their respective "teams"—management and union—each had to deal with people with widely different worldviews, which made intragroup consensus and communication challenging.

The data however also revealed a more profound insight. When the value priorities of the management group and union group were examined side by side, it became apparent that if one were attempting to create a consensus set of values to serve as the foundation for the management system for the plant, neither the values of the management group nor the values of the union group would be sufficient. What was needed was an integration of the values of both groups. The management team was stronger with respect to what is often called "left brain" values such as efficiency/planning, reason, productivity, and mission/objectives. The union team was stronger with respect to the more "right brain" human values such as rights/respect, peer support, empathy, sharing/listening/trust, and human dignity. In addition, there were a number of values that were shared by both groups.

What the discussion of the value analysis data made obvious was that the management system of the plant would be strengthened if the plant were operated on the basis of the combination of the management and union values rather than either set by itself. By having the value analysis data, a discussion that would have been contentious and emotional was able to be de-personalized and made more objective. By using the values "vocabulary," it was possible to talk in a common language about topics that are normally very private and difficult for people to discuss. The lesson learned was that the individual feedback sessions that preceded the group discussion were essential in order to build the common vocabulary and enable participants to gain insight into their own values. For most people who have never experienced such a development opportunity, values priorities are implicit and not easy to discuss. However, the Hall–Tonna values theory, its values list, and definitions of each of the 125 human values along with the values map and stages of development provide a system and vocabulary to enable conversations to occur that would otherwise be impossible.

Most importantly for this plant, gaining the insight and commitment to a set of consensus values between the union and management leadership built a foundation of trust that allowed the organizational transformation to proceed much more rapidly than it would have otherwise, if it could have happened at all.

A similar approach was used in the county school system. Here the split was not between union and management but between those who were located in central office departments and the principals located in schools. This school system, like many others, was dealing with a number of issues. However, the primary one was how to close the achievement gap between students from different ethnic subgroups.

The value analysis process followed the same steps as in the manufacturing example. Each member of the leadership team received individual feedback based on his or her personal values assessment. Then the total group was brought together for a session to begin to define a consensus set of values for the school district. After some preliminary discussion of the purpose of the session, I presented the ranking of the 125 values in priority order based on the compilation of all of the individual values analyses. As the group scanned the list moving down from the Number 1 ranked value to those ranked lower we came to the value "Human Dignity." This value was ranked at Number 40 out of 125. At that point there was a silence within the group. The silence was broken when a black elementary school principal turned to her colleagues and exclaimed "No wonder!" You could have cut the tension in the group with a knife. No one had to say it, but everyone in the group realized that it will not be possible to close the achievement gap when Human Dignity is ranked Number 40 out of 125 values.

This insight triggered a series of actions by the leadership team to acknowledge this as a problem and then focus on action plans that would begin to shift the importance of this value in the school system's operating principles, policies, staff development, and decision making. The values assessment alone will obviously not close the achievement gap. However, it enabled a conversation that launched actions that would make a difference. Before the school system can really make the commitment necessary to change, it was essential to look at itself objectively in the mirror that the values assessment provided. In a system that prides itself on making data-driven decisions, values assessment data are a very strong stimulus for change.

Values Shift and Community Behavior

In the Hall–Tonna values theory, when individuals develop from stages 3 and 4 to stages 5 and 6 there is a significant shift in their worldview. This same developmental challenge faces communities. Within cities, counties, and regions we face the challenge of people who do not believe that they can take charge of their life and the life of their community and create a better future. David Brooks, the *New York Times* editorial writer, addressed this issue in the context of an editorial following the Ferguson, Missouri, crisis.[12] In this editorial, Brooks makes the point that racial prejudice in the United States has shifted from a focus on genetics to a focus on social class. He states that:

> Today we once again have a sharp social divide between people who live in the "respectable" meritocracy and those who live beyond it. . . . In one world people assume they can control their destinies. In the other, some people embrace the now common motto: "It don't make no difference."[13]

The principal method that our society proclaims as the vehicle to enable people to move from one social class to another is through education. The American Dream has been that each generation will live better than their parents. Increasingly the evidence suggests that achieving this dream is no longer a given in the United States. In times of economic hardship such as the 2008 financial crisis and its aftermath, and for many trapped by poverty and extended unemployment, their values development fails to progress into the stage 5 and 6 levels where they believe they can create their own future.

Some people who may have been operating in stages 5 and 6 before the crisis reverted to stages 3 and 4 as their economic security deteriorated. It might be fair to argue that it is this "regression" in economic circumstances that has energized foundation values that are underpinning the rise of the Tea Party, the Freedom Caucus, and other political movements focused on people who have been left behind.

If we use values theory as a way to frame the challenges facing community and economic development, it becomes quite clear that successful economic development must build learning communities that encourage and enable most members of society and all of the key leaders to move from a stage 3 and 4 view of the world to a stage 5 and 6 view. As this shift occurs, the leadership style of economic development organizations must also shift toward that of the system leader as defined earlier by Senge and his associates. Society's primary tool for enabling these shifts is education and learning. This is the reason for comments such the one we heard earlier from Maryland's former Director of Economic Development Aris Melissaratos that "The only strategic investment that can be made to promote economic development is to invest in education."[14]

A Values Foundation for Rethinking Economic Development

For policy makers concerned with economic development, perhaps the most important question to address is "What type of economy do we want to create?" Equally important is a related question, "Who makes that decision?" If we go back to the values imbedded in the Declaration of Independence, we would have to conclude that the answer to the second question is "All of us." More pragmatically, the economic development vision for any political entity (i.e., town, city, county, state) must be developed through a process that ensures alignment to the greatest extent possible between the community vision and the values of all stakeholder groups. Increasing this alignment will serve as an economic development and job creation accelerator.

Building an effective economic development vision for a community cannot be decided by the results of an election. Elections create winners and losers. Developing an economic development vision must be done through a consensus process that engages people from all political, economic, social, and religious perspectives focused on creating their desired future. Winners of elections have the responsibility to be the stewards and enablers of the community's consensus vision. They cannot view an election as a license or mandate to impose the viewpoint of their constituency, even if it is a majority, on the total population. The development of an economic development vision, goals, and strategy must rise to a higher standard than electoral success.

The rationale for this view is straightforward. First, failing to engage the views of the total population violates the founding values of our nation. Second, and more pragmatically, it does not work. Economic development strategy requires continuity of purpose and sustained community support.

When elections determine economic development visions, both continuity of purpose and support of the entire community are impossible. Basing an economic development vision and strategy on the outcomes of elections every two or four years assures that there will be no continuity of purpose or sustained community support. To be successful, communities must shift to a values-based approach that engages the entire community in order to define the type of economy they want to create.

CHAPTER THREE

What Can We Learn from the Past?

Today's economic and job creation challenges are not the same as the ones we have faced in the past. However, that does not mean we cannot learn valuable lessons from our responses to past challenges. As we think about the job and economic challenges we have had since the beginning of the twentieth century, some of the most significant that come to our minds have been the Great Depression of 1929–1932; the rebuilding of Europe and Japan following World War II; the competitive threat to U.S. business and technology supremacy by so-called Japan, Inc. from 1978 to 1990; significant U.S. recessions in the 1980s; the dot-com crash in 2001; and the Great Recession of 2008.

Many of the lessons from these past challenges fall outside the scope of this book and deal with macroeconomic policy. However, two of these periods in particular have lessons that are quite relevant for our focus on economic development at the state, region, county, and city levels. We will focus on the rebuilding of Europe and the competitive threat posed by Japan, Inc. In particular, we will attempt to highlight the interaction of broad policy issues with more microeconomic development and management initiatives that are relevant to our focus.

Rebuilding of Europe Following World War II

A major "jobs crisis" resulted from the situation faced by the United States following the defeat of Germany and its Allies at the end of World War II. The jobs crisis in this case was in Europe. The United States had learned an important lesson following World War I when the country retreated into isolationism. Its failure to play a leadership role in rebuilding the economy of Europe allowed the development of the conditions that resulted in World War II.

Having learned that lesson, following World War II the Truman administration chose to pursue a very activist international agenda. A key element of this foreign policy was to focus on the rebuilding of the European economy. This decision was made for a number of strategic reasons; however, following the war, the U.S. economy was the only national economy with the resources to support this rebuilding effort.

The keystone of this rebuilding effort was the European Aid Program that has come to be known as the Marshall Plan, named for retired general George C. Marshall who became President Truman's secretary of state in 1947. The rationale for the aid program was announced by Secretary Marshall at a commencement address given at Harvard University on June 5, 1947.[1] In this speech, Secretary Marshall framed the problem in terms of the economic crisis confronted by European Allies as well as the defeated adversaries of the United States.

> Machinery has fallen into disrepair or is entirely obsolete. Under the arbitrary and destructive Nazi rule, virtually every possible enterprise was geared into the German war machine. Long-standing commercial ties, private institutions, banks, insurance companies, and shipping companies disappeared, through loss of capital, absorption through nationalization, or by simple destruction. In many countries, confidence in the local currency has been severely shaken. The breakdown of the business structure of Europe during the war was complete. Recovery has been seriously retarded by the fact that two years after the close of hostilities a peace settlement with Germany and Austria has not been agreed upon. But even given a more prompt solution of these difficult problems the rehabilitation of the economic structure of Europe quite evidently will require a much longer time and greater effort than had been foreseen.

Marshall provided an interesting analysis of the economic structure of modern civilizations as a way of explaining the rebuilding effort to the American people. He believed they needed to understand the complexity of the rebuilding effort in order to provide their support. Secretary Marshall was able to simplify this complex situation and explain it in terms that allowed the "person on the street" to realize how much pain and suffering Europeans were facing.

> The farmer has always produced the foodstuffs to exchange with the city dweller for the other necessities of life. This division of labor is the basis of modern civilization. At the present time, it is threatened with breakdown. The town and city industries are not producing adequate goods to exchange with the food-producing farmer. Raw materials and fuel are in short supply.

Machinery is lacking or worn out. The farmer or the peasant cannot find the goods for sale that he desires to purchase. So the sale of his farm produce for money which he cannot use seems to him an unprofitable transaction. He, therefore, has withdrawn many fields from crop cultivation and is using them for grazing. He feeds more grain to stock and finds for himself and his family an ample supply of food, however short he may be on clothing and the other ordinary gadgets of civilization. Meanwhile, people in the cities are short of food and fuel. So the governments are forced to use their foreign money and credits to procure these necessities abroad. This process exhausts funds which are urgently needed for reconstruction. This is a very serious situation that is developing which bodes no good for the world. The modern system of division of labor upon which the exchange of products is based is in danger of breaking down.[2]

Secretary Marshall went on to say that the situation faced by European leaders and their requirements for rebuilding will require resources that far exceed their ability to pay for them. Therefore Europe must have external assistance or face "economic, social and political deterioration of a very grave character." This is the basic argument for the multibillion-dollar aid package from the United States. By way of further justification for U.S. action, Marshall outlined the need for the size of the aid package.

It is logical that the United States should do whatever it is able to do to assist in the return of normal economic health in the world, without which there can be no political stability and no assured peace. Our policy is directed not against any country or doctrine but against hunger, poverty, desperation and chaos. Its purpose should be the revival of a working economy in the world so as to permit the emergence of political and social conditions in which free institutions can exist. Such assistance, I am convinced, must not be on a piecemeal basis as various crises develop. Any assistance that this Government may render in the future should provide a cure rather than a mere palliative.[3]

Two final parts of the speech relate to two key ideas that helped make this aid plan one of the most successful foreign aid programs in history. The first related to gaining acceptance of this program from the target nations.

It is already evident that, before the United States Government can proceed much further in its efforts to alleviate the situation and help start the European world on its way to recovery, there must be some agreement among the countries of Europe as to the requirements of the situation and the part those countries themselves will take in order to give proper effect to whatever action might be undertaken by this Government. It would be neither fitting nor efficacious for this Government to undertake to draw up unilaterally a program designed to place Europe on its feet economically. This is the business of the Europeans. The initiative, I think, must come from Europe. The role of this country should consist of friendly aid in the drafting of a European program and of later support of such a program so far as it may be practical for us to do so. The program should be a joint one, agreed to by a number, if not all European nations.[4]

The second related to gaining political support in the United States from a war-weary nation. He addressed the people of the United States by appealing to key U.S. values—sense of duty, responsibility, and patriotism, as well as empathy and the ability to rise above the passions that were engendered by the war effort.

An essential part of any successful action on the part of the United States is an understanding on the part of the people of America of the character of the problem and the remedies to be applied. Political passion and prejudice should have no part. With foresight, and a willingness on the part of our people to face up to the vast responsibility which history has clearly placed upon our country, the difficulties I have outlined can and will be overcome.[5]

This speech by Secretary Marshall is a powerful demonstration of how the launch of the Marshall Plan was anchored in the core values of the American people. Using the Hall–Tonna values map described in Chapter 2, we can see how the secretary appealed to foundation, focus, and vision values. The speech addresses values that stretch across the entire values map.

Lesson 1. The people who will be impacted by the plan must play a role in creating the plan

A key design element of the Marshall Plan was the involvement of the aid recipients in defining the requirements of the plan. The mechanism for this was the creation of the Organisation for European Economic Co-operation on April 16, 1948. The mandate of this group was not only to define the requirements, but also to supervise the distribution of aid. This organization has remained in existence and in 1961 became the Organisation for Economic Co-operation and Development.

Lesson 2. The commitment of the U.S. government to Europe through the aid program had the secondary benefit of reducing the perceived risk of investment in Europe by American firms

There was a "role-modeling" effect from the actions by President Truman and Secretary Marshall to assist European redevelopment. This helped create a safer climate for private investment, which brought additional investment in European production facilities and modernization of the plants which American firms previously had in Europe. Without the Marshall Plan these firms may have walked away from their prior facilities there which were in need of modernization. However, with the Marshall Plan, American firms could have more confidence that they would receive a return on their investments in a reasonable time period.

Lesson 3. The productivity councils established by the European Recovery Program acted as business accelerators to speed the transfer of technology and management practices and to help convince employees and labor leaders to accept these new practices

The productivity councils established in each country were a focal point for building awareness of world-class practices and for transferring and implementing advanced management practices, new marketing approaches, new forms of work organization, and technology-enabled business processes.[6] One of the key efforts of these councils was also to lead delegations of business, government, and labor representatives to the United States to tour major manufacturing facilities. They could experience steelmaking in Pittsburgh, auto production lines in Detroit, tire making in Ohio, and so on.

These visitors also experienced the benefits of a consumer society. They saw parking lots of factories filled with automobiles owned by employees. They visited department stores to see the merchandise choices that were available to consumers. The intent of these visits was not to have the visitors return to their home countries and replicate American practices. The hope was that they would be inspired to adapt what they saw to their own culture and create something new that would position their businesses and factories to be competitive in the global economy that was emerging. These productivity councils evolved into national productivity centers, and many still exist today and are members of the European Association of National Productivity Centres.

Lesson 4. A third party with resources can facilitate convergence and integration of participants who were formerly antagonists or adversaries

One of the additional benefits of the Marshall Plan was the extent to which it helped European countries develop more cooperative working relationships. Many of the historic differences remain. However, through the interactions with Americans and American institutions, and through the work which helped Europeans look beyond their national borders to see the benefits of greater European integration, some of the old walls that divided countries were removed. There seems to be little doubt that the Marshall Plan and its impact laid the foundation for building what has become the European Union. This process would have certainly taken longer if it had not been for the facilitation role that the United States played as a "third party" with resources to convene the countries, ask them to define their needs, and continue to work with them to support and assist in implementing the plan.

The Japanese Economic Threat: 1978–1990

Following the end of the Pacific campaign in World War II, the United States occupied Japan. Initially, the U.S. policy was to demilitarize Japan and punish its leaders who had led the country into war. However, the occupation began to shift its focus as events unfolded in Asia. The policy in Japan focused on helping Japan rebuild its economy without recreating an offensive military capability. As the United States became engaged in a war in Korea, Japan became the logical site to serve as a major logistics hub for U.S. forces. This had the dual advantage of supporting U.S. troops, and it accelerated the delivery of resources that Japan needed to rebuild its infrastructure and economy.

Part of the rebuilding effort of the Japanese economy involved bringing various advisers from the United States to provide technical expertise to Japanese managers. Two of those advisers were Dr. W. Edwards Deming and Dr. Joseph Juran. Deming and Juran were experts in the application of quality management practices to improve product and process quality. Deming and Juran were not well known in the United States outside the narrow quality field, although Deming was also known among statisticians for his work at the U.S. Department of Agriculture and the Census Bureau.

Deming's work in Japan began in 1947 when he was asked by General Douglas MacArthur's Supreme Command of Allied Powers (SCAP) to advise the command on a major census that would take place in Japan in 1951.[7] Deming, in his work at the U.S. Census Bureau, is credited with bringing the concept of statistical sampling to the bureau. It was at the Census Bureau that Deming first demonstrated the power of his statistical quality control methods to improve data accuracy. Census questionnaire data were keypunched onto punch cards which were fed into the computer for processing. Deming shifted the process from 100 percent inspection to 5 percent statistical sampling. This process improved accuracy because with 100% inspection the inspectors made many errors. Also they were reluctant to identify which keypunch operators made errors because they were friends and also because the inspectors were paid on a piecework basis based on the volume of cards inspected. Thus speed was the inspectors' concern rather than accuracy. Deming's statistical sampling method led to improved quality and reduced cost. It allowed identifying which operators needed additional training to bring their keypunching process into "statistical control." The key is that this method was not used to punish workers but was used to help them improve their process through additional instruction and training.

While in Japan, Deming developed a great respect for the Japanese people and created close relationships with a number of Japanese statisticians. He was made an honorary member of the Japanese Statistical Society. When his consulting on the Japanese census was completed in 1947, he returned to the United States.

One of the other initiatives of the SCAP was involved in improving the quality of Japanese products. The Civil Communications Section (CCS) of MacArthur's staff was given the responsibility to restart the communications equipment manufacturing industry from ground zero. In this process the CCS drew on the U.S. experts at Bell Labs. During the war, Bell Labs and Western Electric used the principles of statistical process control in manufacturing communications equipment for the U.S. war effort. These methods had been developed and taught by Walter Shewhart, a prominent Bell Labs statistician who had also been a mentor of Deming. Deming had met and became a colleague of Shewhart while Deming was at the Census Bureau. The lectures in Japan by Shewhart's associates from Bell Labs were beginning to be accepted by the Japanese statisticians and engineers. However, there was concern that the lectures were too technical and too difficult to understand for use by a broader audience.

Independent of this CCS work, statisticians who were members of the Japanese Union of Scientists and Engineers (JUSE) were developing an interest in these methods. They began reading the papers of Shewhart and Deming and some had known Deming when he had been in Japan in 1947. So in 1950 Deming was invited by JUSE, after receiving permission from CCS, to come to Japan and deliver a series of lectures. The first one was to a standing room only crowd of over 500 at Tokyo University.

The president of JUSE at the time was Ichiro Ishikawa, who was also chairman of one of Japan's most powerful business groups, the Keidanren (the Japanese Federation of Economic Organizations). With the assistance of Ishikawa, Deming was able to meet with 21 of the most senior executives of Japanese organizations on July 13, 1950. Deming knew that his methods and philosophy could only be effective if the shift in thinking it required was led from the top of an organization. After the first meeting, these executives were impressed enough to ask him to meet with them again.

His message to them was that "they could make good quality products if they would follow some of the common sense things he was advocating. . . . He said that if they followed his recommendations they would capture markets all over the world within five years."[8] In fact it began to happen in four years! He introduced the idea that the production process should be viewed as a system with inputs and outputs. He stressed that the process starts with the consumer and requires a close relationship with one's suppliers to make sure that the input quality will allow you to produce quality products.

Deming returned to Japan in 1951, 1952, 1955, and 1956 as a consultant to aid JUSE's efforts. In 1950 JUSE launched a national quality award called the Deming Prize. The recipients receive a medal with Deming's likeness imprinted on the front with the following inscription: "The right quality and uniformity are foundations of commerce, prosperity & peace."

By the late 1970s, U.S. companies who had enjoyed a seller's market following World War II were beginning to realize with some shock that the competition from Japan was a serious threat to their businesses. None articulated this more effectively than David Kearns, the CEO of Xerox. Xerox in the early 1970s enjoyed market share in the copier market of up to 70 percent or more. By the early 1980s, this had dwindled to 8 percent. As Kearns pointed out in many briefings, Xerox learned to its horror that Japanese competitors could sell copiers in the United States at prices that were less than Xerox's manufacturing cost. Not only that, the Japanese competitors were improving their performance at 18 percent per year compared to Xerox's rate of improvement of 7–8 percent.

This was a huge wake-up call. Xerox was not the only U.S. company to be suffering from this Japanese competition. U.S. companies in a range of industries from automobiles to copiers to electronics were experiencing competition unlike anything they had faced in the past.[9]

It was in this context that on June 24, 1980, NBC TV presented a landmark documentary: "If Japan Can . . . Why Can't We?" This program documented the rise of Japanese competition driven by a new breed of management. The program pointed out that much of what the Japanese were doing was taught to them by an American—W. Edwards Deming. It included interviews with Bill Conway, the CEO of Nashua Corporation, who had hired Deming in 1979 to work with them on their quality improvement initiative. Conway recounted that they had been buying copiers from a Japanese supplier and had begun to realize how much improvement the Japanese had made by using Deming's improvement methods.

Nashua, Conway said, was beginning to see major improvement as well. As you can imagine, the next day Dr. Deming's phone rang off the hook as desperate business executives said they needed to talk with him immediately. This TV program can be credited with helping launch the "Quality Revolution" in the United States.

What are the lessons that Dr. Deming taught the Japanese in the 1950s and then, after being discovered by executives in his home country, what did he teach to U.S. businesses?

Lesson 5. Work must be viewed as a system with inputs, processes, and outputs

The system begins with customer research, followed by system design, selection of suppliers of materials and equipment, receipt and test of incoming inputs, production, assembly, inspection, and distribution to consumers. Then it repeats itself. This systems view of an organization was a fundamental concept of this new management philosophy.

Lesson 6. The principle of continuous improvement using the Shewhart Cycle must be applied to all elements of the system repeatedly

The Shewhart Cycle, which many now call the Deming Cycle, involves four actions depicted as a continuous sequence of actions. The four actions are plan, do, study, and act, or PDSA.

P = plan a change or a test aimed at improving the system;
D = carry out (i.e., doing) the change or the test, preferably on a small scale;
S = study the results of the test or change and determine what we learned and what went wrong;
A = either adopt the change or abandon it based on the results of the change or test.

On a more macro level, the PDSA cycle can be used to think about how to incorporate the customer requirements into the system. In this context "P" involves doing the customer research to determine their requirements. "D" would involve making the product that you believe meets the customer requirements. "S" would involve determining how the customer liked the product, and "A" would be taking action to make the appropriate modifications based on customer feedback. Applying this cycle-guided thinking to all elements of the system is the essence of the concept of "continuous improvement."

Lesson 7. The level of quality produced by a system results more from the actions by management than from the actions of workers

This is the key lesson from Deming's famous "red bead" experiment. In this experiment, which is a manufacturing simulation, Deming would have a container that contains red and white beads. Most of the beads are white but there are a relatively large number of red beads—say 10 percent. Deming would ask for volunteers from the audience to be "willing workers," along with a quality inspector and a manager. Deming would be the customer and would tell the manager that he wanted to buy an order of beads but that he only wanted white beads. The manager would then instruct willing worker Number 1 of the task, which was to make white beads. The worker's task would be to use a small shovel, insert it into the container and withdraw a shovelful of beads. The quality inspector would examine the "product" and count the number of red beads which were considered to be "defects."

After each of three workers completed Round 1, the manager would then tell the workers to work harder because their first round production had too many defects. They would repeat the task in Round 2 with similar results. At that point the manager would pull them aside and this time offer an incentive—a financial bonus—if they can make error-free products. The workers then insert the shovel into the container and again they withdraw a number of beads which contains red as well as white beads.

The point this exercise makes very vividly is that when the worker is asked to work in a system that is designed to make defects, it does not matter how hard the worker tries or what management gimmick is used (e.g., financial incentives, warnings, training). The worker cannot produce error-free performance. The point is that "management builds the systems while workers work within the systems."

Lesson 8. A quality management system must be led by the most senior leader of the organization—the CEO. This leadership role cannot be delegated

Senior managers build the systems that determine quality levels. How do managers build the systems? They set the goals, strategy, and policies for the organization; they determine the compensation systems; they hire the leaders and employees; they decide what training will be provided; their behavior communicates what the organization values; they define roles and review performance; and they have responsibility for building the major business processes. If senior leaders do not understand their role, which is to focus the organization on meeting customer

Table 3.1 Deming's 14 Points—The Basis for Transforming American Industry*

1. Create constancy of purpose toward improvement of product and service, with the aim to become competitive and to stay in business, and to provide jobs.
2. Adopt the new philosophy. We are in a new economic age. Western management must awaken to the challenge, must learn its responsibilities, and take on leadership for change.
3. Cease dependence on inspection to achieve quality. Eliminate the need for inspection on a mass basis by building quality into the product in the first place.
4. End the practice of awarding business on the basis of price tag. Instead, minimize total cost Move toward a single supplier for any one item, on a long-term relationship of loyalty and trust.
5. Improve constantly and forever the system of production and service, to improve quality and productivity, and thus constantly decrease costs.
6. Institute training on the job.
7. Institute leadership (see point 12a and 12b). The aim of supervision should be to help people and machines and gadgets to do a better job. Supervision of management is in need of overhaul, as well as supervision of production workers.
8. Drive out fear, so that everyone may work effectively for the company.
9. Break down barriers between departments. People in research, design, sales, and production must work as a team to foresee problems of production and problems that may be encountered with a product or service in use
10. Eliminate slogans, exhortations, and targets for the workforce asking for zero defects and new levels of productivity. Such exhortations only create adversarial relationships, as the bulk of the causes of low quality and low productivity belong to the system and thus lie beyond the power of the workforce.
11a. Eliminate work standards (quotas) on the factory floor. Substitute leadership.
11b. Eliminate management by objective. Eliminate management by numbers, numerical goals, substitute leadership.
12a. Remove barriers that rob the hourly worker of his right to pride of workmanship. The responsibility of supervisors must be changed from sheer numbers to quality.
12b. Remove the barriers that rob people in management and in engineering of their right to pride of workmanship. This means, inter alia, abolishment of the annual or merit rating and of management by objectives.
13. Institute a vigorous program of education and self-improvement.
14. Put everybody in the company to work to accomplish the transformation. The transformation is everybody's job.

*Table created by the author based on W. Edwards Deming, *Out of the Crisis* (Cambridge, MA: Massachusetts Institute of Technology, Center for Advanced Engineering, 1986), 23–24.

| Improve Quality | Costs Decrease | Productivity Improves | Capture the Market with Lower Costs and Better Quality | Stay in Business | Provide Jobs and More Jobs |

Figure 3.1   The Deming Chain (Based on W. Edwards Deming, *Out of the Crisis*, Cambridge, Massachusetts: Massachusetts Institute of Technology, Center for Advanced Engineering, 1986, p. 3)

requirements and then fulfill it effectively, it is not possible for people lower in the organization to create defect-free products and services. Therefore, the launch of a quality management system must begin with the reeducation of the senior leaders of the organization. Until there is a change in the way leaders conceive of their role, little sustained progress can be made.

Lesson 9. To achieve sustained organizational performance improvement, leaders must understand the cause-and-effect relationships between management actions and performance results

Dr. Deming called this understanding of cause-and-effect relationships the development of "profound knowledge." Just as a scientist is able to develop understanding of complex physical systems, business leaders need to develop a deep understanding of organizational systems. The development of "profound knowledge" integrates the knowledge gained through the application of the methods discussed above—defining the organization as the interaction of multiple systems and processes, each of which can be understood and analyzed using the systems diagram. It includes understanding the principles of statistical process control and PDSA as a way of monitoring and improving business systems. Perhaps most importantly, "profound knowledge" involves understanding and applying the management and leadership philosophy outlined by Deming in his 14 points (Table 3.1).[10]

The overall impact of Deming's methodologies and their relevance to economic development can be summarized by a diagram that was on the blackboard of every meeting Deming had with top management in Japan from 1950 onward. This diagram, which has become known as the Deming chain, is shown in Figure 3.1.[11] That the success in Japan has been repeated in Deming's work with U.S. companies validates the logic of this management framework.

The implications of these "lessons from history" for economic development systems are in many cases obvious. In Chapters 7 and 8, where we present recommendations for transforming economic development systems, we will incorporate many of these lessons.

CHAPTER FOUR

Overview of Current State-Level Economic Development Strategies

Within the past two years, at least 12 states have created new entities focused on economic development or have consolidated existing agencies to streamline their approach to economic development.[1]

How States Are Responding to the Economic Development Challenges

The 2008 recession and its aftermath created a window of opportunity for many states to implement new economic development strategies and approaches, often under the banners of job creation, innovation, and competitiveness. The National Governors Association (NGA) report referenced above is a thoughtful attempt, from the executive branch perspective, to assess these changes, understand the forces that were driving them, and provide a framework for describing the types of changes that were under way.

The NGA report concludes that three broad strategies will help ensure success in state-level economic development efforts. The first is to engage and sustain involvement by the private sector. The second is to create mechanisms that encourage collaboration among businesses, government agencies, and other key stakeholders and between state government and regional initiatives. Third is the need for an evaluation system that promotes transparency and helps guide the investment of state funds where they can have the greatest impact.

Strategies to engage the private sector

Private sector involvement is being achieved through one of three organizational structures: public–private partnership, a semi-state agency, or an independent business organization or association. Public–private partnerships can take a variety of forms and have a variety of funding arrangements. An example is the Michigan Economic Development Corporation (MEDC). MEDC is a corporation directed by an executive committee of 20 individuals appointed by the governor. The executive committee appoints a chief executive officer who administers all programs, funds, personnel, and other administrative actions of the corporation. In addition, there is an oversight and performance board, which includes members of the executive committee along with approximately 90 additional private sector leaders, which meets once per year to review the performance of the organization.

The mission, vision, and customers of MEDC are described in the organization's concise and focused mission statement:[2]

> **Our Mission:** We market Michigan and provide the tools and environment to drive job creation and investment.
> **Vision:** We will transform the Michigan economy by growing and attracting business, keeping talented residents here and revitalizing our urban centers.
>
> **A top 10 State for:**
>
> - Low unemployment
> - Per capita income
> - GDP growth
> - Young adult population growth
>
> **Our Customers:** We engage with customers globally, including:
>
> - Businesses, entrepreneurs and communities
> - A talented workforce that adds value to Michigan businesses

The MEDC operates through two basic types of formal partnerships. These include agreements with public sector organizations called interlocal partnerships and agreements with "local agencies, utilities and non-profit economic development organizations."[3] This organizational structure allows the MEDC both to deal with statewide issues and to work regionally through the existing local and regional economic development organizational structure. MEDC is funded almost exclusively through public funds, including general funds, tobacco settlement funds, and casino revenue.[4] Alignment of local and regional initiatives with the overall state strategy is achieved through formal partnership agreements.

An example of a semi-state agency is the Arizona Commerce Authority (ACA). By executive order, Governor Jan Brewer transitioned the

Arizona Department of Commerce into the quasi-public agency. ACA is an independent agency created and funded by the government to perform a specific set of functions under private management. The ACA is governed by a board chaired by the governor but operated on a day-to-day basis by the vice chairman and the president, both of whom are elected by the board. Its main function is the retention and recruitment of high-quality jobs through the use of a $25-million deal-closing fund. The fund only provides incentives to businesses that are performance based with criteria such as whether or not the average employee wage of the new jobs exceed the county's average employee wage. The four functions of the ACA are business retention and recruitment, strategic planning, managing financial programs, and marketing. All other functions formerly performed by the old Department of Commerce have been transferred to other agencies.[5]

The third structure for involving the private sector is the independent organization. An example of this is the Oregon Business Council (OBC). OBC is a statewide focused organization run by a collective of supporting businesses with no organizational ties to state government agencies. OBC's directors are CEOs of Oregon-based companies and senior executives of Oregon-based divisions of national companies. Created in 1985, the organization exists to play a significant role in developing public policy for Oregon. The work of the council falls into four areas—economic development, education, health, and poverty reduction.

In 2002 the OBC, in conjunction with U.S. Senator Ron Wyden, created the Oregon Business Plan as a way to focus city and state initiatives as Oregon attempted to rebound from the 2001 recession. The focus of OBC is described on its website:

> The Oregon Business Plan initially set two goals: create 25,000 net new jobs per year through 2020 and bring Oregon's per capita income from 90% of the national average to above it by 2020. The Plan later added the goal of reducing poverty (currently at 16.7%) to below 10% by 2020. To achieve these goals, the Plan envisions Oregon building up a strong set of innovative and globally competitive industry clusters that sell products and services outside of Oregon, in turn producing payrolls that support families and communities while funding critical public services that improve life and attract even more businesses.
>
> As a strategy to enhance cluster success, the Plan recommends improvements in public policies that promote conditions essential for business success and growth in jobs that pay well. These conditions are grouped into what are called "4Ps for Prosperity." These are People (a talented workforce created by a good education system); Productivity (quality infrastructure,

resource utilization, and competitive regulations and business costs); Place (quality of life and communities); and Pioneering Innovation (a culture of research, commercialization and product and process innovation).[6]

The OBC revises the business plan annually through a process that engages public and private sector leaders. The priorities identified are vetted each year at a day-long leadership summit each December that draws over 1,000 business and government leaders, including the governor, two U.S. senators, and other elected and agency officials. Issues recommended are often taken up weeks later when the legislature convenes. The 2015 priorities are to (1) connect education with careers, (2) put natural resources to work, and (3) modernize its infrastructure.[7]

As an example of how the OBC priorities can shape state policy, consider the group's efforts to increase post–secondary education attainment. The OBC business plan goal for education attainment was that 40 percent of Oregonians would have at least a bachelor's degree, 40 percent would have at least an associate's or technical degree, and at least 20 percent would have a rigorous high school diploma by 2025. These goals were embraced by political and education leaders, and in 2007, the state legislature passed House Bill 3141 that established the 40–40–20 goals by statute. The governor organized his budget around these goals and many in higher education and K-12 school systems are working to achieve these goals.[8]

Strategies to promote collaboration within the state

The NGA report also highlighted strategies that are being implemented by states to encourage collaboration across sectors and between the state and regions. North Carolina has created a 37-member economic development board to: provide economic and community development planning; recommend economic development policy to the state secretary of commerce, the general assembly, and the governor; recommend annual appropriations for economic development programs; and coordinate agencies, foundations, and boards involved in economic development. The board membership is a "big tent" board consisting of government agencies, non-profit organizations, private businesses, and the state legislature. A major area of focus has been on better aligning the education system with the needs of high-growth industries and occupations.

Another trend highlighted in the NGA report is the increase in collaboration between states and regions. Colorado, Tennessee, and New York have initiated efforts to shift their economic development focus from a top–down to a bottom–up strategy.

New York is particularly interesting in that the state in 2011 established 10 regional public–private partnerships (regional councils) comprising local representatives from education, business, local government, and nongovernmental organizations. These councils then compete for funding from the state. The state has created a single application that allows the councils to apply for funding from multiple funding sources. The state committed $150 million for capital projects and $70 million for tax credits.

In terms of tracking performance of the regional councils, New York will track two sets of metrics for each region. One is a common set used to measure performance across all 10 regions, which will allow for benchmarking, identifying, and sharing successful practices. Included in this set are metrics associated with labor force indicators, educational measures, business starts, and minority and woman business certifications. The second set is a unique set of metrics for each region based on its specific regional goals.

Improved state economic development metrics

The NGA report[9] highlights the measurement initiatives of Virginia, Maine, Massachusetts, Mississippi, and Oregon. It provides some detail with respect to Virginia Performs and the Massachusetts Innovation Index. Virginia Performs is a measurement system that provides trend data on a range of performance indicators for each state agency. The indicators use data collected from a wide range of both public and private data sources and display that information as trend data on the state government website. Virginia also provides similar trend data for its economic development regions.

Massachusetts provides an annual detailed report comparing its performance on a range of innovation economy metrics compared to 10 states it characterizes as leading technology states. These benchmark data are compiled by the Massachusetts Technology Collaborative, which is a quasi-public agency that attempts to help advance the technology sector of Massachusetts.

For a state that is focusing on decentralizing its economic development strategy, the measurement approach outlined above in New York State is a thoughtful approach. By having a common set of metrics that apply across all regions, it enables the state to have an objective basis for allocating resources and permits regions to benchmark themselves against other regions and seek out promising improvement strategies. In addition, the measurement system includes region-specific metrics that are needed by each region to monitor those strategies and actions that are uniquely appropriate for its own area.

How the State of Maryland Is Redirecting Its Economic Development Strategy

To provide additional insight into the dynamics of economic development strategy at the state level, this section will examine the changes that have been occurring in the state of Maryland. When considering the leadership of state-level economic development, it is necessary to focus not just on the executive branch, as the NGA did, but also on the legislative branch and the higher education system in the state. Ideally, all three of these institutions will be active and aligned toward a shared vision for economic development in the state. We will examine this "ideal" with respect to the state of Maryland.

Overview

Maryland is a small state with a great deal of geographic and economic diversity and a number of significant economic development assets. Those assets include the natural environment—most notably the Chesapeake Bay, the Atlantic Ocean, and the mountains of Western Maryland. The state also has a large number of federal government assets. Its location adjacent to Washington, D.C. has led to the presence of more than 70 federal facilities in the state that account for $26 billion in capital assets and over 800,000 jobs. These facilities also provide much of the impetus for the state's innovation and entrepreneurship initiatives. The Baltimore–Washington region is also the home of major research universities, including Johns Hopkins, and three campuses of the University System of Maryland—the University of Maryland, College Park (UMCP); the University of Maryland, Baltimore County (UMBC); and the University of Maryland, Baltimore (UMB). Baltimore is home to two major medical schools and two major professional sports teams.

In terms of economic development statistics, Maryland's performance has been mixed. In 2013, Maryland was ranked first in the nation in terms of entrepreneurship and innovation by the U.S. Chamber of Commerce.[10] The same report ranked Maryland third overall in terms of its talent pipeline. However, in 2015, the Kauffman Foundation ranked Maryland 28th out of 50 states for start-up activity and Baltimore was ranked 17th with respect to major metro areas in start-up activity. In 2015, Business Insider ranked Maryland 's economy in a three-way tie with Virginia and Iowa for 27th place based on their index which considered six metrics: change in housing prices, nonfarm payroll job growth, unemployment rate, GDP per capita, average weekly wage, and state government surplus and deficit.

Maryland was ranked 27th despite having the 6th highest weekly wage and 10th highest GDP per capita.

As the last statement points out, national rankings must be viewed quite critically. Since the choice of the metrics is "value-laden," the rankings carry with them a set of values that may or may not align with the region being ranked. That does not mean that they do not matter in terms of how a state or region is perceived. It does matter in terms of how much the rankings should influence policy. For example, how should one interpret the finding that Maryland has the 6th highest weekly wage and 10th highest GDP per capita? If one believes that what is best for business climate is to have low-wage workers, this fact about Maryland would be seen negatively. On the other hand, if one believes that the purpose of economic development is to improve the standard of living and wealth of all citizens, this fact would be much more positive. This is only to say that "ratings chasing" can be bad economic development policy unless it is done in light of a clear understanding of the type of economy we want to create.

The executive branch in Maryland

Over the years, Maryland's economic development strategy has suffered from a lack of continuity as the policy direction has shifted as governors have changed. Compared to the nation, economic development in Maryland has not been excessively hampered by partisan politics. The shifts in direction have been due more to the focus of the governor rather than the influence of a political party. There is little evidence that in the past 30 years Maryland has had a statewide economic development strategic plan, created with broad citizen input, that was effectively communicated to stakeholders and that effectively enabled the key organizations and institutions to choose to align their efforts with the state's direction. As a result, economic development in Maryland has been characterized by frequent shifts in policy direction, and the establishment of a large number of promising and well-conceived initiatives that were underresourced and unaligned.

For many years, leaders in Maryland have pointed out what the U.S. Chamber of Commerce noted in ranking Maryland first in the nation in terms of entrepreneurship and innovation—that this strength is due in large part to the research universities that annually account for over a billion dollars in R&D, and the presence of a number of federal research laboratories. From an executive branch perspective what changed in Maryland in the second term of Governor Martin O'Malley was a series of decisions and accompanying legislation to significantly "ramp up" the emphasis on commercialization activities related to this concentration of R&D activity.

Former chancellor of the University System of Maryland, Dr. William E. "Brit" Kirwan, described this shift:

> Starting with the second term of the O'Malley administration (2011–2015) there has been a sea change with regard to the focus on commercialization of intellectual activity. It has remarkably changed the culture of our universities and our state government. Four key pieces of legislation were introduced and championed by the Governor. When he (Governor O'Malley) was called to testify in support of these key bills, the first witnesses he called were the President of Johns Hopkins and the Chancellor of the University System of Maryland, who locked arms in support of these bills.[11]

The four pieces of legislation Dr. Kirwan referred to were: Invest Maryland, Innovate Maryland, E-Nnovate, and RISE Maryland. Invest Maryland was passed by the legislature in 2011. This was a very creative initiative that auctioned tax credits to Maryland insurance firms through an online process to generate an $84-million-dollar fund that is being used to invest in new or rapidly growing Maryland technology companies. Two-thirds of the funds are being invested by a private venture fund manager and one-third is managed by the Maryland Venture Fund Authority. This state authority has a 17-year track record of having invested $25 million and returned $61 million, helping create 2,000 jobs and spurring $1 billion in additional private investment. Any return is reinvested in the fund.[12]

The second piece of legislation was Innovate Maryland. Innovate Maryland was launched in 2012. The state allocates $5 million, and each of the five qualifying research universities—UMCP, UMB, UMBC, Morgan State University, and Johns Hopkins University (JHU)—will match this contribution with between $100,000 and $200,000. The program is administered by the Maryland Technology Development Corporation (TEDCO) and will award start-up grants to university researchers best positioned to move their discoveries into the commercial marketplace.[13] Governor O'Malley, discussing the goal of this initiative stated:

> Our goal of moving 40 new discoveries and innovations out of the lab and into the marketplace each year will help create the next generation of jobs and fuel our Innovation Economy pipeline for decades to come.[14]

The third member of this legislative quartet was E-Nnovate. This legislation creates a $100-million matching fund to recruit the world's best scholars to endowed faculty chairs in Maryland in areas as diverse as cybersecurity, biotechnology, STEM education, autonomous systems, language science, and food safety. The fund will match campus private sector funds raised up to $100 million per year. The money must go to bring new talent to the state, and the endowed faculty member must agree to devote on average one day a week toward translational activities that will promote commercialization of his or her work.

The final legislative achievement in this quartet for Governor O'Malley was the Regional Institution Strategic Enterprise (RISE) Zone Program. This program designates a zone surrounding universities or federal laboratories as a location that provides credits toward local real property and income taxes to businesses that invest in these zones. In addition, these businesses receive priority consideration for other state business incentives. The intent of this legislation is to increase physical proximity between research institutions and businesses to encourage research commercialization and to enhance the amenities in these regions as a way to attract and retain talent.

Since 1970, the "Department of Economic Development" has undergone five name changes with the most recent being in 2015 when it was renamed the Department of Commerce by Governor Larry Hogan. Interestingly, this title did not originate with the governor, but resulted from the recommendations of a commission created by the legislative branch. To a greater degree than any recent governor, Hogan ran on a platform to reform economic development in Maryland. The next section describes how the legislature played a leadership role in this change.

Legislative branch

Governors are limited to two four-year terms. Therefore, if one is looking for continuity in Maryland state government leadership, it can be found in the legislative branch. Mike Miller has been president of the Senate since 1987. In the House of Delegates, the Speaker, Mike Busch, has been in office since 2003.

The legislative branch has led economic development in a number of cases. The most recent example is the formation of the Maryland Economic Development and Business Climate Commission (MEDBCC) which was convened in March 2014. This commission was asked to review the state's current economic development structure and incentive programs and make recommendations to keep Maryland competitive in economic and private sector growth and prosperity.

Several factors converged to cause the legislature to form this commission. One factor was the reduction in the federal budget. Nearly one-fourth of Maryland's economy depends directly or indirectly on federal spending. When the federal government reduced spending (6 percent in

2013 for contracts in the state and 2.6 percent for wages) Maryland suffered significantly. Second, a new governor was to be elected in 2014 and the state legislature leaders wanted to provide a set of recommendations for the new governor. Third, there was dissatisfaction by the legislative leadership with the performance of the Maryland economy and, by association, with the performance of the state's economic development establishment.

The commission chair, Norman R. Augustine, is the former chairman of Lockheed Martin, former secretary of the army, and a member of the Board of Regents of the University System of Maryland. Three members of the commission were state senators appointed by the president of the Senate and four were members of the House of Delegates appointed by the Speaker of the House. The remaining 18 members were appointed jointly by the Senate president and the Speaker and came from education and the private sector.

The commission's interim report[15] on February 2015 provided 32 recommendations grouped under the following headings: role and structure of state economic development; impact of the federal government; fostering a positive business climate; regulatory structure; tax structure (to be addressed in a second phase report); measuring progress; workforce development; and education and entrepreneurial support. Within these categories the report summarized 10 findings which led to the recommendations. As with any evaluation designed to improve the system, the findings were opportunities for improvement rather than celebrating the strengths, so they had a definite negative tone. The findings were:

1. Economic development entities need to be reorganized.
2. The state's economic development marketing strategy is ineffectual.
3. Federal activities in the state warrant increased attention and support.
4. The state is viewed as deficient in providing customer service.
5. Business in the state suffers from a lack of certainty and inconsistent time frames for agency decisions.
6. The state lacks sufficient data to assess the performance of business incentive programs.
7. Employment needs often do not match workforce skills.
8. Apprenticeships are seriously underutilized.
9. Education is a critical element in economic development.
10. Technology transfer at universities is crucial and is impeded by state laws.

The first of the 32 recommendations focused on reorganization and suggested that all economic development programs be consolidated under a newly created secretary of commerce. The stated intent of this change was to elevate the stature of economic development from simply one of

22 departments reporting to the governor to a Department of Commerce, located in the governor's office, that would increase its ability to work cross-functionally across state government to coordinate efforts of all agencies that impact businesses in the state. Legislation to implement the recommendation to create a Department of Commerce was passed by the House and Senate in 2015, and the new structure was announced on October 1, 2015.

The second recommendation addressed strengthening the Maryland Economic Development Commission (MEDC). One observer described this as the "uber-Commission" which would have the highest status of all the advisory bodies reporting to the governor's office. The new role of the MEDC should be expanded and empowered from just developing a strategic plan (which, in the past if it existed, was never effectively implemented) and making recommendations to the governor, to also having input over the budget of the department, and oversight responsibility for how the agency implements the plan. Basically the Augustine Commission concluded that there has been no effective accountability for state-level economic development. The recommendation was also made to create a subcabinet including all the cabinet secretaries whose policies impact business. One of the objectives for this subcabinet is to shift the culture of Maryland state government staff to view businesses as valued customers of state government agencies.

The Augustine Commission report points out what many would say is the obvious point that education is a critical element in economic development. It turns out that this is especially true in Maryland in both obvious and nonobvious ways. Education, particularly higher education, is another lens we can use to view the Maryland economic development scene.

Higher Education and Economic Development in Maryland

With two exceptions, all public higher education institutions (not including community colleges) in Maryland fall under the administration of the University System of Maryland headed by a chancellor. There are 12 academic institutions in this system, two regional higher education centers, and a system office. Maryland also has a number of private higher education institutions. However, the one that is most significant from an economic development perspective is the JHU and its medical school and its other affiliated research institutions such as the Johns Hopkins Applied Physics Laboratory.

The University System of Maryland and JHU can also be viewed as forces for continuity with respect to Maryland economic development efforts by providing a technology and knowledge infrastructure that has continued to grow and develop as leadership in the executive branch has come and gone. While this fact was recognized by the Augustine Commission, it pointed out that there were significant opportunities to improve the commercialization of technologies that have and are being developed in the state's higher education institutions. The commission made a number of suggestions in this regard, such as establishing an executive in residence within the new Department of Commerce to improve communication and coordination between government, business, and the research universities. Other recommendations emerged from finding Number 10 that technology transfer from universities is impeded by state laws.

The economic impact of higher education on the economy of the state is partially reflected by the income and sales tax receipts that result from Maryland graduates who remain in the state to work. With a $5.5-billion state investment in higher education institutions the tax receipts from graduates are estimated to be $1.1 billion annually. This estimate does not include other benefits that accrue to the state in terms of new business formation, technology transfer, and so on. Investment in the 16 community colleges of $300 million annually (not counting capital budgets) is estimated to produce an annual benefit of over $600 million per year.[16]

In a speech to a business group discussing the work of the MEDBCC, Norm Augustine, chair of the commission, stated:

> How do you increase GDP (Gross Domestic Product)? Eighty-five percent of the increases in GDP have come from advances in science and technology. Advances in science and technology are based on advances in education and research. These are two areas where our state (Maryland) is extremely strong. Where we fail is in terms of the transfer of that into jobs and better businesses. Only 5 percent of the workforce in the country are scientists and engineers. That 5 percent disproportionately creates jobs for the other 95 percent.[17]

The infrastructure for enhancing commercialization was given a strong boost by the legislation passed by Governor O'Malley and the legislature between 2012 and 2014. The recommendations of the Augustine Commission have also given increased new emphasis to these initiatives. One of the benefits of the programs that were created by the four legislative initiatives discussed previously was the fact that the funding streams they created provided incentives for the major research institutions in the state to increase their collaboration.

Also in 2011, the Maryland legislature challenged the University System of Maryland Board of Regents to find ways to increase its impact on the state. This led the Board of Regents to challenge two of the major research campuses—the UMB and UMCP, two campuses separated by about 40 miles—to find ways to increase innovation through collaboration between the two campuses. This led to a program that has been labeled MPower. We know that many new innovations come from the intersection of traditionally separate disciplines. For example, when clean energy research is combined with information technology, it can produce synergies that create innovation that would not come from the separate disciplines acting alone. To spur such synergies, MPower is a structured collaboration between the UMCP and the UMB. Since this program was launched in 2012, it has increased technology licensing by almost 50 percent and doubled the number of start-up businesses and joint research proposals.

Another example of how higher education is seeking collaboration to promote economic development is illustrated by a two-year-old public–private partnership that was initiated by several bio-health private sector companies in Maryland. One of the cluster strategies in Maryland has been the focus on biotechnology and bio-health. Two years ago an organization named BioHealth Innovation (BHI) was created as a unique public–private partnership in Maryland that is unique if for no other reason than the fact that it has access to 59 federal laboratories, centers, and institutes as well as the state's higher education research institutions. BHI is a partnership between private industry, academia, federal government, county government (Montgomery County, Maryland), foundations, and nongovernmental organizations. It does not receive direct state government support. The organization describes itself as a regional innovation intermediary that accelerates and facilitates technology transfer and commercialization of market relevant research from federal labs, research universities and bio-health companies. The outcomes that the organization seeks to create include new jobs, new start-ups and spinoffs, leveraged investment dollars, existing company growth, regional branding, additional risk capital, and technologies progressed. Richard Bendis, founder, president, and CEO of BHI, describes two aspects of the organization—its operating philosophy and its Entrepreneurs in Residence program:

> BHI's operating philosophy is to shift the Innovation Paradigm from proof of concept (where the focus is on technological feasibility) to proof of commercial feasibility (where the focus is on showing that it solves a problem and demonstrating that the market will buy it). The primary vehicle for this is

the Entrepreneurs in Residence (EIR) program and the Commercial Relevance Advisory Board (CRAB).

Our EIRs are experienced venture capitalists, business development people, and entrepreneurs who work for BHI full time. They are on our payroll and their primary mission is to identify commercially relevant science and technology that BHI can add value to. Unlike other EIR programs, when necessary, sometimes the EIR will even take an operating role in the start-up company until we can raise the money to bring in the professional manager. That is what differentiates our EIRs from a lot of others out there. A lot of them "don't get their hands dirty." They may give advice but they don't actually run companies.[18]

A less obvious contribution of higher education is the way it has and can influence policy making in the state. An example is the story of how one of Maryland's most successful economic development organizations was born. A Maryland organization singled out by the Augustine Commission for praise was TEDCO. TEDCO's mission is to facilitate the creation of businesses and foster their growth in all regions of the state through the commercialization of technology. TEDCO is also Maryland's leading source of funding for technology transfer and development programs and entrepreneurial business assistance.[19] The Augustine Commission report commended the work of TEDCO:

> Testimony before MEDBCC indicated that TEDCO is regarded as being a highly effective facilitator of early stage business development and entrepreneurship. One strength often cited is its ability to understand the unique needs of entrepreneurs and to respond quickly to changing business conditions.[20]

TEDCO publicly cites its origin as a bill in the state legislature that created the independent organization in 1998. This is true. However, it does not tell the story of how this bill came to be. The initiative to create TEDCO came from the UMCP. Brian Darmody, currently the associate vice president for Corporate and Foundation Relations, was in 1998 the lawyer for the flagship campus of the University of Maryland, and he describes the origin of the bill to create TEDCO:

> I drafted the bill, and gave it to Speaker Taylor. It was House Bill 7. When the Bill came out, DBED (the Department of Business and Economic Development as it was known at the time) was caught by surprise and did not know whether to support it or oppose it. There was no blue ribbon commission, the bill just appeared. I got into a little trouble with the executive branch

who asked "What in the hell are you doing?" My boss, Brit Kirwan, President of the University of Maryland-College Park at the time, gave me a long leash but said "Brian I'm not sure what you do, but keep doing it and don't go to jail." We needed an organization that was separated from politics and state regulations that could speed up the process of commercializing technology in the State.[21]

This is a very good example of how a university can take an economic development leadership role behind the scenes. To go through the usual process to create an organization such as TEDCO would have taken several years and still may not have been created as an independent agency with the freedom to act that has made it very successful.

Traditionally, public universities in the country, especially "land-grant" universities such as the UMCP, have had three missions: teaching, research, and outreach. The best known of the outreach organizations have been the Agricultural Extension Service. These extension organizations played a major role in the productivity revolution that has shaped U.S. agricultural production. They served as the "translators" of research results from the university laboratory to individual farmers. This "outreach" role has been expanded by universities to other disciplines as well. There are engineering extension programs, extension programs that serve local government, and productivity centers that have focused on assisting business organizations to improve quality and productivity through improvements in their management systems.

Another dimension of the university's role in economic development is its contribution to community building. The concept of the "college town" has always been a part of American lore. Today as universities are being forced to "break down the walls of the ivory tower," the "outreach" idea is being displaced by a broader sense of engagement with the community that becomes a part of the educational and research experience. Wallace Loh, president of the UMCP, described the redevelopment that the university is spearheading within the town of College Park, Maryland:

> We are building a community here. If we are to recruit and retain the world's best faculty and staff, we need housing options, stores and restaurants, green spaces. And we need to intrinsically tie together our academics and research with our surrounding communities.[22]

Dr. William E. "Brit" Kirwan, the recently retired chancellor of the University System of Maryland, noted that there are a number of forces at work that are leading to systemic change in higher education. A number of these changes are increasing the significance of this "outreach" mission and will increase the positive contributions to economic development by higher education.

> In the past, state universities could count on steady increases in their annual appropriation from the state and an ever-growing volume of federal dollars supporting research. Today, neither is happening. State funding is flat at best and research funding is stagnating. As state budgets come under ever increasing pressure, we know that it is unlikely that we will return to the funding levels of the past. States would have to increase taxes to fund the university at prior levels and in this political environment that isn't going to happen. Given the dysfunction in Congress, the same dim prospect holds for research funding as well and, as a result, research partnerships with industry are becoming more essential.
>
> But there is another reason university/private sector partnerships in research are critical. These partnerships are now in the national interest because most companies have significantly reduced or totally eliminated their R&D operations, especially in basic research. It used to be that a talented person could graduate with a Ph.D. and have choices of going to work at a major research university or to a corporate research lab such as Bell Labs or IBM Watson, etc. But no more. Our nation needs our universities engaged in translational research if we are going to have the technology and other innovations to keep the U.S. at the forefront of the global economy.
>
> In response to these changing dynamics, research universities are becoming enablers of translational activities, e.g. technology transfer, technical assistance to firms, technology commercialization, etc. Translational research activity is now part of the mission and goals of many research universities. Here within the University System of Maryland, we have gone so far as to change the promotion and tenure criteria for faculty in relevant disciplines to include translational research and the commercialization of intellectual property activities as an important option in the review process for merit pay and promotion. These changes are shifting the culture of the university in ways that promote economic development. I believe this is a good thing because these kinds of activities at our major research universities are becoming critical for our nation's future well-being. However, in these partnerships, it is vital that the university's ethical guidelines regarding the integrity of the research process are maintained to avoid conflict of interest and conflict of commitment issues on the part of the faculty.[23]

As we have seen in this chapter, a great deal is happening at the state level to enhance economic development outcomes in response to the significant challenges state economies are facing. Improved state strategies are important and necessary as we attempt to address the job challenges faced by the United States. However, state strategies alone are insufficient. Some would argue, as Jim Clifton, chairman of Gallup, has done in his book *The Coming Jobs War*, the real hope for the United States is based on what happens in cities. Clifton states "Fixing America's biggest problems and re-winning the world can only be accomplished one city at a time. Ultimately, all solutions are local."[24] Clifton goes on to say that cities will only succeed if they declare an all-out war on the problems.

> I don't use the term "war" lightly. This really has to be a war on job loss, on low workplace energy, on healthcare costs, on low graduation rates, on brain drain, and on community disengagement. Those things destroy cities, destroy job growth, and destroy city GDP. Every city requires its own master plan that is as serious as planning for war.[25]

Our next two chapters will look at how two cities, Austin, Texas, and Dubuque, Iowa, have and are waging that war. From these two case examples, we will seek to learn some key principles that have helped Austin and Dubuque claim key victories in the global war for jobs.

CHAPTER FIVE

Austin, Texas: The Human Capital

Why Austin?

It is rare today to pick up any ranking of economic development success stories in the United States without finding Austin at or near the top of the list in terms of business friendliness and job creation. For example, Austin has been named:

- Number one city for start-ups—Kauffman Index, June 2015
- Number one city for creating the most middle-class jobs—*Forbes*, October 24, 2013
- Number two city for future job growth—*Forbes*, July 23, 2014
- Number one city in economic performance from the recession to the recovery—Brookings Institution, April 2, 2014
- Fastest growing large metro economy through 2020—U.S. Conference of Mayors, June 20, 2014
- Number one "Aspirational City" offering both jobs and culture—NEWGEOGRAPHY.com, July 30, 2013
- One of the hottest start-up cities in the United States—RJMetrics, April 24, 2014
- Most business-friendly city—Kauffman Foundation, April 2, 2013
- The top city for net migration of adults with college degrees—NEWGEOGRAPHY.com, August 20, 2014
- Number two in best performing large cities for 2014—Milken Institute, January 8, 2015

If we can distill the factors that have made Austin's job creation story a success, we should be able to use these insights to help create a new framework for economic development. We should ask two key questions:

(1) Has Austin's success come from better execution of the traditional model of economic development? or (2) Has Austin's success resulted from a rethinking of the traditional economic development approach? These are the questions we will examine in depth in this chapter.

What Is the Job Creation Story?

The recognition and rankings above demonstrate that Austin has had great success in creating jobs. The Greater Austin Chamber of Commerce in its 2014 annual report provided detailed results of its economic development efforts that began in 2004 under the banner initiative "Opportunity Austin." The scorecard over the following 11 years is shown in Table 5.1.

It is not surprising that these results have garnered many accolades for the city and surrounding counties in the Austin region. In this chapter we will examine how Austin's history, leaders, institutions, strategies, approaches, and principles influenced and contributed to these accomplishments.

A Brief History

Before we examine the more recent Austin economic development story, it is helpful to consider some of key points of the history of this city from its founding in 1839 until 1982 where we begin the present story. First, it is important to point out that competing for economic development "wins" is not new for Austin. Its citizens chose to compete and win both the site selection to be the permanent Texas state capital in 1872 and in 1881 to be chosen as the site for the University of Texas—the flagship institution of the Texas higher education system. These two institutions continue to serve as key anchors of the Austin economy.

A second lesson from this history is that Austin has benefited substantially from visionary leadership in both the city and the private sector, and

Table 5.1   Opportunity Austin Scorecard

Performance indicators	2003–2014 results*
New jobs created	263,400
Payroll increase	$13.9 billion
Corporate relocation announcements	370
Out-of-region visits	2,483
Prospect visits to central Texas	1,468

*Based on the Greater Austin Chamber of Commerce, 2014 Opportunity Austin Annual Report (Austin, TX: Author, 2014).

from political leadership in Washington that could channel federal funds to the city to assist its growth and development.[1] A key public policy decision by the city involved the creation of Austin Energy, a municipal electric system that provided relatively low-cost electric power that was a boon in attracting and retaining businesses, and contributed a source of funds (currently approximately $100 million annually) to the city's general fund and to its economic development efforts and helped reduce tax rates.

A third lesson is that Austin has a strong history of paying attention to policies that promote improvements to the quality of life of its citizens—at least for most of its citizens. This focus on building the quality of place has served Austin well in its economic development success.

The fourth lesson is that from slavery to more modern times, a number of Austin's citizens have endured a history of discrimination based on race and ethnic identity. These scars still remain in terms of the difficulty of integrating the entire population into the workforce.

Finally, the city's history is a testament to the fact that the people of Austin have been resilient, innovative, competitive, and have demonstrated the courage and ability to set large goals and achieve them. These traits have continued to exemplify Austin's character in more recent times.

How Did They Do It?

Leadership

In 1982, Mark White, a former attorney general of Texas, was elected governor of Texas. The recession of 1981–1982, which some called the "Reagan Recession," created serious problems for the state as oil prices plummeted. This economic crisis led the new governor to conclude that Texas needed to diversify its economy from its dependence on oil and gas. As it turned out, this decision by the governor would have a seminal impact on Austin.

From a leadership perspective, it was also the governor's chief of staff who would play a key role in Austin's economic development successes over the next four decades. This was Pike Powers, who has been described as the "super-lawyer-turned-entrepreneur whose leadership helped turn Austin from a university town into a high-tech powerhouse."[2] Powers led the efforts to achieve two major economic development victories in the 1980s—the location in Austin of the Microelectronics Computer Technology Corporation (MCC) and Semiconductor Manufacturing Technology Initiative (SEMATECH). These two research collaborations formed the backbone of Austin's development as a major information technology and semiconductor research and manufacturing innovation hub.

As early as the mid-1950s, Austin gradually began to build a foundation for a technology industry as the third major anchor of its economy. One early "homegrown" success was Tracor, Inc., a defense-related R&D company founded by Frank McBee, a University of Texas faculty member, and several of his engineering collaborators.[3] At its peak in the late 1970s and early 1980s, Tracor had over 2,000 employees. In addition, more than 25 high-tech companies were spun out of Tracor as subsidiary businesses.[4] Pike Powers more recently put the number of spin-offs from Tracor at more than 435 businesses.[5]

The University of Texas produced a number of other individuals who served as leaders in Austin's success story. One was George Kozmetsky, an American technology innovator, businessman, mentor to business executives, educator, author, and philanthropist. Before coming to Austin, Kozmetsky cofounded Teledyne, Inc. in 1966 in California. He came to Austin that same year and served as dean of the University of Texas College and Graduate School of Business Administration for 16 years. In 1977, he founded the IC^2 Institute, a "think-do" tank focused on research on the intersection of business, government, and education. Created to test the belief that technology can catalyze regional economic development through the active collaboration of these three sectors, IC^2 stands for innovation, creativity, and capital.

At the University of Texas, Kozmetsky was a pioneer in developing and integrating technology knowledge into the business administration curriculum, as well as integrating technology into the teaching process. More than 20,000 students graduated under his deanship. Michael Dell, the founder, chairman, and CEO of the Dell Computer Corporation, had this to say on the value of his assistance:

> George Kozmetsky's guidance in management issues, workforce motivation, and strategies needed to remain technologically competitive has been invaluable in helping Dell Computer Corporation grow to be a more than $2 billion company—and he has done the same for many other entrepreneurs in technology. His wisdom and guidance have enabled many innovative ideas to reach fruition, directly benefiting not only their creators but also the American people at large.[6]

Kozmetsky was given the National Medal of Technology by President Bill Clinton in 1993.

It was Kozmetsky who, along with his colleagues at IC^2 D. V. Gibson and R. W. Smilor, developed the "Technopolis Framework," which has served as the conceptual basis for Austin's technology-driven economic development. Kozmetsky and his colleagues proposed four fundamental steps required for a region to develop as a technopolis:

1. Achieve scientific preeminence in technology-based research;
2. Develop new technologies for emerging industries;
3. Attract major technology companies;
4. Create homegrown technology companies.[7]

The third major leadership player in this story is an institution that had played leadership roles in Austin's economy since the late 1800s, known today as the Greater Austin Chamber of Commerce. In 1957, the chamber, led by Vic Mathias, engaged consultants from University of Texas–Austin's faculty to provide recommendations on ways the city could grow and diversify its economy. These consultants provided a report to the chamber that recommended that the city take steps to attract light manufacturing industries.

It took a while, but in 1966 the chamber's efforts succeeded in attracting IBM's Selectric typewriter manufacturing plant. Motorola located a facility in Austin in 1974. When asked what attracted them to Austin, a Motorola representative said it was three things:

1. University of Texas–Austin—the university was a source of well-trained engineers for Motorola's design centers and production lines;
2. Quality of life—Austin was known throughout the Southwest as a place of extraordinary natural beauty and a friendly atmosphere conducive to easy living; and
3. Cost of living—Austin boasted among the lowest rental, property and utility rates anywhere in the United States.[8]

The chamber's influence and effectiveness waxed and waned over the years as a function of its leadership. From 1984 to 1987 the chamber was led by C. Lee Cooke, a visionary, ex-corporate executive, and ex-member of Austin's City Council. Cooke felt that the chamber and Austin needed a new vision—beyond the efforts to attract branch plants of large manufacturing companies such as IBM and Motorola recommended by the 1957 study. He believed that Austin could capitalize on its assets—state capital, lifestyle, and great research university—through what he called "civic entrepreneurship"[9] and seek to become a world-class economy. Later to become mayor (1988–1991), Cooke successfully helped the city raise its sights in terms of its economic development aspirations.

Another group of key leaders instrumental in Austin's success were elected officials at the city, state, and national levels. As previously noted,

Lyndon Johnson's assistance following the Depression was beneficial to Austin. Another key public official in Washington was Congressman J. J. Pickle. He was involved in coordinating the legislation that exempted research consortia from antitrust liability and in assuring that legislation providing federal budget support for both the MCC and the SEMATECH successfully found their way through the committees of Congress and was passed.

Decision to diversify the Austin economy

As is the case in many areas of human endeavor, a crisis can drive change and innovation. In the case of Texas, the early 1980s' "bust" in the oil and gas industry—the largest economic engine in the state—provided the impetus to accelerate the development of the technology sector in Austin. The intent was to shift Austin from a place where innovation and design was conducted somewhere else and shipped to Austin to be manufactured to a place where homegrown innovation and development would take place.

Even though Austin lay outside the oil and gas production areas of Texas, it felt the effects both as the state capital and due to the fact that the crisis also impacted the real estate, banking, housing, and other sectors that depended on the oil and gas industry. So, when in 1983, the governor was presented with an opportunity to implement his economic diversification strategy, the university and business community leadership of Austin were ready to assume a key role.

Attraction of MCC

The opportunity resulted from a response by U.S. computer companies to the news that Japan had announced in April 1982 that the Ministry of International Trade and Industry (MITI) would fund a 10-year $850-million research effort to bring together computer companies in Japan to leapfrog existing computer technologies to produce a Fifth Generation Computer System. This new computer would be designed to support artificial intelligence applications and would give the Japanese a major competitive advantage in a critical global technology. The U.S. response led by William Norris, founder and visionary leader of Control Data Corporation, would be to form a private sector R&D corporation to collaborate to produce breakthrough basic technologies that each consortium member could then take back to his or her corporation to commercialize into his or her own proprietary product lines. While the MITI initiative was government driven, the U.S. consortium would be totally private sector funded.

This organization was called the Microelectronics and Computer Technology Corporation (MCC). MCC was first announced in 1982 and held its first board meeting in February 1983. Ten companies—DEC, Harris, Control Data, Sperry-Univac, RCA, NCR, Honeywell, National Semiconductor, Advanced Micro Devices, and Motorola—were the initial funders and members. Admiral Bobby Inman, former head of the National Security Agency, was chosen as the first head of MCC.

In order to select its headquarters location, MCC conducted a national search that involved 57 cities in 27 states. Governor White and his Chief of Staff Pike Powers learned of this site search from Mayor Henry Cisneros of San Antonio. Through the persuasion by Cisneros and other influential government and business leaders, Governor White came to realize that if he could bring this consortium to Texas it would lay the foundation for building a major information technology industry in the state. Led by Governor White and Powers, Texas mounted an unprecedented statewide effort to secure this prize. In the words of Pike Powers, the governor "believed that winning MCC was critical to charting the future for the state in terms of new and emerging technology rather than continuing to rely on an oil- and gas-based economy."

In describing Austin's winning bid for MCC, Pike Powers wrote:

> The key ingredient to Austin's victory was careful collaboration among government, business and the University of Texas. The MCC experience dramatically brought these forces together for the first time in Texas, to develop incentives and present a very aggressive bid. Among the key participants were the governor's office, The University of Texas at Austin and its College of Engineering and the Greater Austin Chamber of Commerce. . . . A statewide task force was created to focus on and ensure the commitment of financial resources and talent that MCC required. In a show of solidarity, Henry Cisneros, then mayor of San Antonio, threw his city's support behind Austin's bid when it was clear that San Antonio could not be a finalist in the competition. Unselfishly, Texas A&M University and its engineering school stepped up to support and collaborate with The University of Texas at Austin.
>
> Texas' bid for MCC, with more than $20 million in incentives, raised and altered forever the stakes for such economic development competitions in the United States. Major incentives in Austin's bid package, among others, included: (1) a facility and laboratory . . . leased for $10 a year and financed by university and private statewide contributions; (2) the creation of 32 $1-million endowed chairs in engineering and natural sciences; and (3) other benefits to MCC employees, including fellowships, teaching positions, and job-hunting assistance for spouses.[10]

The story of Austin's pursuit of MCC is wonderfully described in a compelling book by David V. Gibson and Everett M. Rogers.[11] The authors frame the case not only as an economic development story, but also as a treatise on the factors that impact the successful operation of a R&D collaborative effort among competing firms.

A key contribution of the ongoing research which led to this book is the development and description of the "technopolis" model (Figure 5.1).[12] The authors depict this model as a wheel that has seven major elements: government (1. federal; 2. state; and 3. local); business (4. large and 5. small); support groups (6); and education (7).

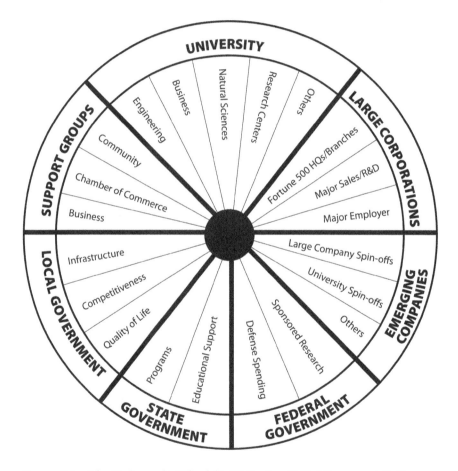

Figure 5.1 The Technopolis Wheel (R. W. Smilor, D. V. Gibson, and G. Kozmetsky, "Creating the technopolis: High-technology development in Austin, Texas," *Journal of Business Venturing* 4(1), 1989, p. 51. Used with permission of D. V. Gibson)

Within each of these major elements are "spokes" that capture the major contribution of each element to the economic development mix. The authors emphasize that success results not just from the elements themselves, which are important, but even more importantly from the linkages among the elements.

> New kinds of relationships/alliances between public and private sectors—especially government, business, and academia—are having far-reaching consequences for the way people think about and implement economic development. This emerging reality is captured in the term "technopolis."
>
> The modern technopolis interactively links technology commercialization with public and private sectors to promote regional economic development and technology diversification. Four factors are fundamental in the development of a region as a technopolis: (1) the achievement of scientific preeminence in technology-based research, (2) the development of new technologies for emerging industries, (3) the attraction of major technology companies, and (4) the creation of homegrown technology companies.[13]

Another significant contribution of this research is the identification and emphasis placed on the essential role provided by two types of people and institutions. These are first- and second-level "influencers" who promote collaboration among the players at the same time the players are also competing against each other.

First-level influencers have several characteristics in common:

- They provide leadership in at least one segment of the technopolis wheel because of their established success in that segment.
- They maintain extensive personal and professional communication linkages to their counterparts in the other segments of the wheel.
- They have high credibility and function effectively within all segments of the wheel.
- They are visionaries who inspire others to action.[14]

While first-level influencers set the vision, inspire, and get things started, it is the second-level influencers who carry through and enact these visions. Second-level influencers have the confidence and support of the first-level influencers in their own sector of operation, which facilitates their linkages with influencers in the other sectors of the technopolis wheel.[15]

In the MCC case, some key examples of first-level influencers are Henry Cisneros as mayor of San Antonio; Governor Mark White; Ross Perot, chairman of Electronic Data Systems; Jon Newton, chairman of the Board of

Regents, University of Texas System; Donald Walker, chancellor, University of Texas System; and Ben Head, CEO and chairman, Republic Bank of Austin, and president, Austin Chamber of Commerce.

Key second-level influencers included Pike Powers, executive assistant to Governor White; Narciso Cano, director of economic development, city of San Antonio; and Professor Ben Streetman, Department of Electrical Engineering at University of Texas–Austin. It was Streetman's presentation at the site selection meeting to choose finalist cities that helped "make the sale" for Austin.

According to Admiral Bobby Ray Inman, the CEO of MCC, it was Streetman's two-minute presentation on the "nature of the microelectronics research" at the University of Texas that truly excited the site selection team.[16]

The key factors that led to Austin's selection by MCC over the three other finalist cities—San Diego, Atlanta, and Raleigh-Durham—were not only what the Austin group did, but also what the other cities did not do or did not have. For example, from the beginning, the Austin (really the Texas) team made it obvious it wanted MCC more than the other sites. This was shown in a variety of ways. For instance, the Austin team had gathered a huge amount of intelligence on each of the site selection team members and developed an understanding of what the team wanted. This intelligence also included what the "negatives" were about Austin from the initial site selection team interviews with candidate cities.

One of these was a concern about "quality of life" in Austin. The Austin team was prepared to address this directly when the site selection team came to Austin for its final round of interviews. It had commissioned a public relations firm to conduct a scientifically valid survey of citizens in each finalist city with respect to their views of the quality of life in each city on 16 separate factors.

Austin fared well on these measures compared to the other cities. However, as is often the case when such data are presented, the manner in which they are presented may have as much or more impact than the data themselves. In this case the presenter was an employee of the public relations firm that conducted the survey. By coincidence he had lived in all of the four finalist cities. As he was presenting the survey results he came to the section on crime and he "spontaneously blurted out, 'You know, I've got a sister that lives in San Diego [one of the competitor cities], and I was talking to her just a couple of weeks ago. Some guy got killed out in her front yard.' Although this was not planned, the comment—quite irrationally—planted a negative impression in the site selection team's eyes with regard to crime in San Diego."[17]

In addition to the survey, the site selection team was given a helicopter tour of the Texas Hill Country surrounding Austin. The selection team saw lakes, rivers, and hills, all of which did not fit the stereotype that many selection team members had of Texas and Austin.

All the finalist cities except Raleigh-Durham offered a significant incentive package to attract MCC. However, Austin's approach to incentives was a bit different. "In the eyes of MCC's site visitors, the university component of the Texas incentive represented a brilliant strategy. It wasn't just 'what we can do for MCC' but 'what we can do together with MCC to improve university research in microelectronics.'"[18]

Not only did this approach make sense from the standpoint of the city, state, and university, but it also reflected what the Austin team had learned about the desires of the MCC site selectors. They wanted a collaboration that would bolster research and technology development over time, not simply a one-shot infusion of money to attract the MCC organization to Austin.

Another key element of the strategy was to make the appeal to MCC a Texas statewide appeal, not just an Austin appeal. None of the other three finalists were able to present as compelling a case on how their entire "state" wanted MCC, not just the particular city that had been named a finalist.

In Texas, this approach was essential not only to persuade MCC to choose Austin, but also to sell the idea of supporting the MCC recruitment process in other geographic areas in Texas that would be asked to contribute funds to the Texas Incentive for Austin. Having people like Ross Perot and Henry Cisneros involved in the entire effort reinforced this view that Texas, not just Austin, wanted MCC and that the state would ensure the ongoing relationship received the support required.

Other aspects of this were the fund-raising effort to fund 30 endowed professorships with 15 each in the departments of computer science and electrical engineering, the offer for two years' use of a Lear jet, and funding for graduate student support and equipment for research at the University of Texas.

Austin's success in recruiting MCC resulted in large part from the ability of its first-level influencers to create a compelling vision of why MCC was crucial to Texas's ability to diversify its economy and was critical to the nation in terms of regaining technology leadership that was being claimed by Japan.

Following its selection by MCC, expectations rose for an immediate economic bonanza for the region. This was accompanied by the fact that there was also an economic boom occurring in Texas's traditional oil and gas industry. Because of unrealistic expectations of how fast Austin would become a high-tech superstar, land and housing prices escalated rapidly. "The ride up the roller coaster of rising land prices was breathtaking, but this rapid increase was followed by a sickening jolt and a steep plunge," according to Gibson and Rogers.[19]

> From 1980 until 1984 total employment in Austin's metropolitan area increased by 41%. . . . From 1982 to 1985, Austin added 10,000 manufacturing jobs, two-thirds of which were in the high-technology research, manufacturing and service sectors. . . . Between 1983 and 1985 the average price of a house in Austin increased by 21%. . . . Twelve major office buildings were built, creating the highest office vacancy rate (41%) in the nation.[20]

Two quotes from John Gray from the Greater Austin Chamber of Commerce describe the situation well.

> A tremendous speculative boom happened. Everybody overhyped the fact that MCC was coming to Austin and would attract other business operations here. The uninitiated expected it to happen overnight. Speculators are always looking for something to fuel a boom like that. Any piece of land you could get your hands on, you could sell it even before you closed your contract. Contracts were "flipped" in some instances as much as 20 times before they closed. MCC was just the triggering device to set off this boom.[21]
>
> In the early 1980s, when Austin was undergoing significant growth, some people felt that the way to stop growth was to oppose funds for expanding the utility infrastructure. The tactic backfired. Inadequate wastewater treatment facilities polluted the river, and farmers downstream claimed that their cows would not drink the water. The city came under attack from the state, environmental organizations, and downstream communities. Fortunately, the city cleaned up its act and the river. That lesson must be told over and over again, so the same is not repeated.[22]

The rapid growth and escalating land and housing prices increased antigrowth sentiment. In 1985, Mayor Ron Mullen was running for reelection. Mullen was the pro-growth mayor and his opponent, Frank Cooksey, was an antigrowth candidate and defeated Mullen. One of the most strident no-growth advocates was Sally Shipman, who was elected to the city council. One of her first actions on the council was to coauthor a letter that was sent to Fortune 500 companies telling them *not* to come to Austin unless they checked with the council first. This tension between the pro- and antigrowth communities has been a fact of life in Austin throughout its history, as it has been for many cities. As we proceed with the Austin story we will periodically revisit this issue.

Stanford Research Institute strategic plan for Austin

Its success in attracting MCC put Austin "on the map" nationally as an emerging technology hub. Pike Powers pointed out that "In 1985 Austin began to realize the true magnitude of possibilities."[23] To pursue these possibilities, the Greater Austin Chamber of Commerce contracted with Stanford Research Institute International (SRI) to conduct the research that would lead to the development of a new long-range plan for Austin's economic development. As Powers recounts it, the "charge" given to SRI was to "tell us what we need to know, not what you think we want to hear."[24]

The authors of the SRI report authors framed their view of Austin this way:

> Austin has all of the elements needed to build an advanced information and knowledge economy that would provide opportunity for all residents within a uniquely livable environment. If Austinites together chart a sound course for the next 15 to 20 years, the city has a unique opportunity to create the diversity and richness that will ensure a bright and healthy future. What is required to build this future is a shared vision, strategies to achieve the vision, and—most of all—public and private action to make the vision real.[25]

This strategic plan charted a new direction for Austin. For the first time in the city's economic development planning, it stressed the need to develop an explicit linkage between quality of life and economic development. In addition,

SRI's recommendations included:

- Continuing collaborations among business government and educational institutions, especially the University of Texas—using the MCC experience;
- Creating a climate for science and technology innovation and start-ups by creating business incubators, encouraging spin-offs, and increasing venture capital availability;
- Developing programs to attract, recruit and grow technology information firms (e.g. software, electronic publishing); and
- Providing training through educational institutions that is more aligned with industry.[26]

By linking quality of life and economic development explicitly, the plan helped address the tension that Austin experienced. In addition, it provided a competitive differentiator for Austin as it worked to attract both businesses and talent. More recently, communities have come to understand the connection between attracting members of what has come to be called "the creative class."[27]

Attracting SEMATECH

While Austin and Texas were dealing with the boom–bust cycle that followed the MCC win, another opportunity for Austin was being formed. Gibson and Rogers describe the alarm that was building in the U.S. semiconductor industry:[28]

> In 1985, Sanford (Sandy) Kane, IBM vice president for industrial operations, produced an alarming IBM report about the U.S. semiconductor industry. Why was IBM concerned? The survival of the U.S. semiconductor industry was critical to us for several reasons. . . . We like to source locally, and we didn't want to be in a position where we had no choice but to be dependent on our competition. (Kane interview by Strain, March 7, 1989).[29]

In February 1987, the U.S. Department of Defense's (DoD) Defense Science Board sounded another call to arms. This group argued that the national security of the United States was dependent on its leadership in the semiconductor technology industry. Since that leadership had seriously eroded, it recommended that the DoD establish a semiconductor manufacturing institute to enable the United States to reclaim global leadership in semiconductor manufacturing technology.

Following several rounds of political negotiations involving the DoD and Congress, SEMATECH was created in 1988 by Public Law 100-180. As with MCC, the site selection process for SEMATECH sparked a national bidding war. The "prize" was the lure of "800 high paying research jobs, a $200 million annual budget, the expected relocation or expansion of semiconductor equipment suppliers, and the predictions of technology spin-offs from SEMATECH's research."[30]

In the competition for SEMATECH, Austin prevailed over 134 other proposals from 34 states. This competition was more expensive and more complex than the MCC competition. Not only did the Austin team have to convince a site selection team, but it also had to work the process in Congress to assure that SEMATECH's federal funding would be provided. This was a major accomplishment as some influential members of Congress threatened to use their political clout to eliminate its funding if their state was not selected. Such threats were only part of the political hurdles that had to be surmounted.

Gibson and Rogers, who provide a detailed account of the many facets of this selection process, conclude that Austin won the competition for three reasons: (1) political clout, (2) geography, and (3) "avoiding the 'fatal flaw' during the site-selection competition."[31] Much of the political clout was achieved through the efforts of Texas congressman Jake Pickle. He had been instrumental in the MCC decision as well by working to resolve the anti-trust concerns in Congress regarding competing companies collaborating on research efforts. In the SEMATECH competition, Congressman Pickle worked with others to unite the Texas congressional delegation, including Speaker of the House Jim Wright from Texas, to push the funding bill through the various congressional oversight committees—Armed Services, Energy, Commerce, and Appropriations. On the Senate side, Senators Lloyd Bentsen and Phil Gramm, along with Florida Senator Lawton Chiles, pushed the funding bill through the Senate. (Chiles had had a change of heart, as he was one of the senators who had earlier threatened to kill the bill if Tampa was not chosen as the site.)

The site selection team chair, IBM's Sandy Kane, provided this assessment of the impact of the Texas congressional delegation:

> Texas has a congressional delegation that . . . will get together and stand behind [an issue] as one. . . . The other two states . . . that have comparably sized congressional delegations, one in California and the other one in New York, do exactly the opposite. They couldn't get together on the same time of day.[32]

The second factor in Austin's favor was geography. Its location virtually halfway between each coast created cost advantages whenever the consortium wanted to convene its board for a meeting. At the beginning of the consortium's formation, 11 of the 14 companies had a presence in Austin already. Six of the original members already had manufacturing facilities in Austin—AMD, AT&T, IBM, LSI Logic, Motorola, and Texas Instruments.[33]

Another favorable aspect of Austin's geography is that, of the companies with a presence in the region, no single company had a dominant presence, which tended not to be true for some of the other leading competitors. This meant that no single firm would be able to dominate the consortium.

With regard to financial incentives, Austin's proposal was not the largest by far. The total value of Austin's incentive offering was $68 million. Other sites presented packages worth two, three, four, and as much as seven times as much. However, in many cases the "apparent value" of the competitor proposals would not stand close scrutiny. Sandy Kane addressed this point:

The biggest problem that the media had, and others had, as they analyzed our selection afterwards, was that they couldn't understand how we could have picked Austin, who offered a package worth $68 million, while other states offered us packages that were two and three and four and in one case seven times as much. They said that didn't make any sense. . . . For instance, the Massachusetts proposal was $441 million. . . . But a couple of things deflated it rather rapidly. First, about half of the amount, $200 million or so, was a low-interest loan. A consortium of companies with a very large partner called the U.S. government doesn't really need to borrow money. . . . Secondly, if I wanted to borrow $200 million at 1% better than prime, that's not worth $200 million. It's worth 1% of $200 million or a couple of million bucks annually.[34]

The Austin proposal on the other hand was smaller, but it was solid. It contained very little "soft money." The cash was on the table, not a promise to pass a bill to get the funding.[35]

The third reason Austin won was its ability to avoid the "fatal flaw" that could sink the effort at a crucial decision point. This point was addressed by Pike Powers, who, using lessons learned from the MCC competition, was a critical player in creating the alignment among all the participants in the Austin initiative. Powers said in an interview:

That's the value of the MCC experience. The overlap of being able to know what it takes to really run hard and compete in one of these national public economic development sweepstakes competitions permitted us to know that you had to address in a very straightforward fashion your weaknesses, and find a solution to them and admit them right up front, and address them before anybody can pull the rabbit out of the hat on you and say "Voila! What about this?" and lay you on the carpet.[36]

In Austin's case one of the "rabbits" Powers referred to was the existence of a "clean room," which was a requirement for the proposal. The Austin proposal contained the offer to build a clean room in the facility that was being offered to SEMATECH. In its feedback prior to the site visit, the site selection team raised a number of objections and concerns about Austin's plan. In addition, the Austin team realized that several of the competitor sites had an existing clean room that was ready for occupancy on day one. To deal with this potentially fatal flaw in the proposal:

[Pike] Powers and [Peter] Mills (of the Austin Chamber of Commerce) located Al Tasch, a University of Texas engineering professor who had constructed a dozen clean rooms, including facilities for TI and Motorola, two of SEMATECH's members. Tasch assembled a team of 20 specialists who met every morning at 7:30 at Austin's chamber of commerce to plan the clean room's construction. They began meeting in July 1987, and by September when SEMATECH's technical team visited the Data General plant, Professor Tasch and his people had formulated a detailed plan.

Led by Ray Tyx, an Austin resident who worked with Tasch, the Texans built a complete clean room mock-up inside the Data General building. Tyx convinced vendors from all over the United States to display their products for SEMATECH: model floors, walls, lights, fans, filters and other equipment. Otherwise said Tyx: "You could not expect the SEMATECH people to just come into the Data General site with rose-colored glasses on and imagine what a clean room would look like."[37]

As of 1993, when Gibson and Rogers completed the research for their comprehensive assessment of MCC and SEMATECH, there were a number of direct benefits to Austin in terms of job creation and other economic benefits from the SEMATECH win. Perhaps the most direct benefit was the construction of a new facility in Austin by Applied Materials Incorporated. Applied Materials is one of the world's largest semiconductor manufacturing equipment providers.

Applied Materials came to Austin to be near SEMATECH as well as two major and growing customers (Motorola and AMD), and because of the University of Texas and the availability of skilled workers. In summer 1990, Applied began construction of a $21 million facility that began operation in 1992 and employed about 250. By summer 1993, the company was beginning construction of a second Austin-based manufacturing plant at a cost of $20 million. By the year 2000, Applied plans to have an eight-building campus in Austin with roughly 1 million square feet and as many as 2,000 workers. . . .

During its relatively short residence in Austin (as of 1994) Applied Materials has attracted and spawned a network of about 30 businesses that supply crucial goods and services that have helped vertically integrate the city's semiconductor manufacturing infrastructure. . . .

In 1989, the University of Texas at Austin committed to a $22-million construction project that would double the school's computer chip research operations and provide students with 12,000 square-foot clean room laboratories as sophisticated as those found in private industry. . . . As Ben Streetman (Director of the Balcones Research Center where the new facility would be located) stated, "Our interest is in looking at processes that are beyond what is currently used in industry. We want to look at new ways of growing and processing materials."

In 1991, using the SEMATECH's prototype clean room as a model, Motorola began construction . . . of an $800 million, 76,000 square foot facility. . . .

In 1992, IBM, Apple and Motorola announced they would form an Austin-based alliance to create a new computing standard. The Power PC was to use reduced instruction set computing (RISC) and was a major challenge to Intel's popular Pentium chip. This . . . alliance, called Somerset, was staffed by 340 engineers and required a massive investment in hardware and software research and technology.

. . . In summer of 1993, Motorola announced it would build another new chip laboratory and factory in Austin. . . .

(the facility would) cost upward of $1 billion, occupy nearly 800,000 square feet, and add 700 jobs to Motorola's Austin employment base of 7,700. . . . Also in the summer of 1993, AMD began construction of its new chip factory. . . . The 700,000 square foot state-of-the-art facility will cost upward of $1 billion when fully equipped and by 1997 will add 1,000 workers to AMD's Austin-based workforce of 2,500.

. . . According to SEMATECH's records, more than 300 of the consortium's direct-hire employees were recruited from within Texas and nearly all of the 100 manufacturing technicians were recruited from Texas schools. Residents of East Austin (where many blacks and Hispanics live) represented 22% of SEMATECH's workforce, taking home about $4.8 million annually. SEMATECH's procurement of goods and services pumped more than $13 million into east and south Austin businesses between June 1990 and February 1992.[38]

It is impossible to know how much of this development would have occurred without the SEMATECH win. A very conservative assessment would have to conclude that the presence of this R&D consortium helped accelerate the development of the semiconductor equipment and semiconductor manufacturing industries in Austin. A more realistic assessment would likely conclude that the $68-million-dollar incentive provided by Austin to win the competition for SEMATECH has led to the development of a vertically integrated semiconductor industry in the region that has added several thousand jobs, several billion dollars of investment in facilities, and several billion dollars of "multiplier impact" with respect to procurement dollars and personal consumption expenditures for housing, food, clothing, entertainment, and more.

ICF Kaiser economic blueprint

Previously we noted that the Greater Austin Chamber of Commerce engaged SRI to develop an economic development plan for Austin in 1985, between the two consortium wins. This plan was significant in that, for the first time, it made explicit the connection between Austin's quality of life and its economic development performance. In addition, the plan helped define the path to create the innovation ecosystem that would later become one of the city's greatest strengths.

A second strategic economic development plan was developed in 1998 when the chamber commissioned the ICF Kaiser Consulting Group to conduct an analysis and provide an economic development "blueprint" for the region. This study emphasized the focus on "industry clusters" that would leverage Austin's economic strengths in terms of information technology and software.[39]

Emphasis on "industry clusters" as an economic development strategy gained prominence in academic circles in part as a result of Michael Porter's influential *Harvard Business Review* article "Clusters and the New Economics of Competition."[40] In this article Porter asks why, in a global economy, when executives can source most of the key inputs to their business with the click of a mouse, does location matter? His response was that compared to the past, where competitive advantage was driven heavily by input costs, today's source of competitive advantage is different.

> Companies can mitigate many input-cost disadvantages through global sourcing, rendering the old notion of comparative advantage less relevant. Instead, competitive advantage rests on making more productive use of inputs, which requires continual innovation. . . . What happens inside companies is important, but clusters reveal that the immediate business environment plays a vital role as well.[41]

In his 2013 book, Enrico Moretti elaborates on how this business environment impacts competitive advantage. He focuses particularly on cities and regions that have become innovation hubs and asks why these companies often chose these locations when they could be anywhere. Boston, Silicon Valley, and San Francisco are some of the most expensive places to do business and to live in the country. He asks why, for example, when Wal-Mart chose to move into e-commerce, did it locate its division in Brisbane, California, rather than Bentonville, Arkansas?

> Wal-Mart saw three important competitive advantages to a San Francisco location which economists refer to collectively as the forces of agglomeration: thick labor markets (that is, places where there is a good choice of skilled workers trained in a specific field), the presence of specialized service providers, and most important knowledge spillovers.[42]

What are knowledge spillovers? Moretti states: "The answer has to do with a simple fact: new ideas are rarely born in a vacuum. Research shows that social interactions among creative workers tend to generate learning opportunities that enhance innovation and productivity."[43]

The relevance of this line of reasoning to help explain the success of Austin is explicitly addressed in a very insightful article by David V. Gibson and John S. Butler of the University of Texas's IC^2 Institute, which has played a key role in Austin's development as a technology and innovation hub and has assisted in the development of knowledge-based economies in over 30 countries. In the article "Sustaining the Technopolis: The Case of Austin, Texas," Gibson and Butler conclude that:

> A main conclusion of the current research is that the "momentum" for successful regional cooperative activity in Austin, Texas, has continued to come from key influencers—visionaries and champions—within and working across sectors or sub-sectors to connect and leverage unconnected and perhaps competing actors for a common purpose through formal and informal collaboration, coordination and at times synergy during key targets of opportunity.[44]

From complacency to sustained action—The origins of a systematic economic development strategy

Despite having a new blueprint for economic development from the Kaiser strategic planning effort, it did not spur an aggressive implementation effort. However, the industry cluster concept continued to influence the thinking and strategy in Austin. In 1998, the successes of the past two decades may have led to a bit of complacency. It was not until the dot-com crisis hit that the leaders of the community realized the need to launch a more systematic and comprehensive economic development strategy.

The 2001–2002 dot-com bust hit Austin very hard. Since Austin's economy had been focused on the technology sector, the ripple effects of this national recession were felt disproportionally in Austin. Between 2000 and 2003, the Greater Austin area lost 25,000 jobs (3.7 percent) and unemployment began to increase. "For the first time since the 1980s," noted an article on Austin's economic vision, "the Austin region experienced no net in-migration and declining population growth."[45] Unemployment rose from 1.6 percent in December 2000 to 5.7 percent in March 2003. There was a drop in real per capita income of $1,800 for the first time since 1987.[46]

Professional service firms, lawyers, accountants, and real estate firms saw their revenues fall as revenue to the technology sector plummeted. This economic crisis created a desire on the part of the professional services and technology firms who were the main funders of the Greater Austin Chamber of Commerce to look for strategies that could deliver more consistent development. As stated by Jose Beceiro, a long-time participant in Austin's economic development efforts:

> These major players decided to invest in a long-term economic development program that ultimately helps their business by providing economic stability in the region.[47]
>
> Believe it or not, Austin is still somewhat new to economic development in terms of a sustained, focused program. Prior to 2001, the Chamber was not able to sustain economic development programs through multiple years. Sometimes they would have funding for projects, sometimes they would not. As a result, you would see Austin's economy bump along up and down as the national economic trends bounced up and down.[48]

In 2003, the leaders of Austin realized that the city that had experienced such great economic development wins in the past was no longer in the "game." Its annual economic development funding was only $500,000 and the chamber had only one full-time staff member focused on economic development.

The chamber brought in another consulting organization in 2003 to help it craft a systematic, multiyear economic development plan and strategy. This initiative, labeled "Opportunity Austin," was officially launched in 2004 and continues today. Austin is currently in its third five-year plan under the Opportunity Austin banner.

The firm hired to assist in this new effort, Market Street Services, described the evidence of complacency that had set in prior to its engagement. It pointed out that:

- The Chamber's economic development funds were diverted to operations.
- Their website for site selection and business relocation/expansion was "under construction" for over five years.
- A city employee skipped meeting with a Big Three auto manufacturer visiting Austin for site search.[49]

Opportunity Austin 1.0
Opportunity Austin 1.0 was launched in 2004. This initiative was preceded by a comprehensive analysis that had the following elements:

- Economic and demographic profile
- Business climate assessment

- Leadership input process
- Assessment of priority target industries
- Economic development strategy development

The comprehensive plan had five goals and several objectives under each of the goal areas.[50] The goals were:

1. Capitalize on existing strengths—local headquarters, computer software, digital media, wireless, semiconductors, and tourism—and focus on retaining and growing each strength.
2. Recruit and target new businesses—focus on automotive, medical products and pharmaceutical manufacturers, wireless regional offices and headquarters, and transportation and logistics.
3. Stimulate entrepreneurship and new enterprises—focus on emerging technology sectors such as biosciences, digital film and entertainment, clean energy, nanotechnology, and export assistance.
4. Market Austin effectively—identity building, getting the word out that Austin is "in the game," and positioning the chamber as the economic development focal point for the region.
5. Improve regional competitiveness—focus on improving workforce quality, transportation system, and infrastructure and the permitting and regulatory climate.

In order to carry out this plan, the Greater Austin Chamber of Commerce led a fund-raising effort to fund Opportunity Austin and raised over $14 million for the five-year plan. The chamber expanded its economic development staff from 1 to 12 people and Opportunity Austin became a new economic development division of the chamber. Led by the chamber, the process engaged the city of Austin, Travis County, and the five surrounding counties and towns, and the major school districts that came together to offer economic development incentives.

Opportunity Austin 1.0 was extremely successful. The five-year goal for job creation was 72,000 new jobs. Between 2004 and 2007 the region created 104,200 new jobs. The plan had a target of increasing the region's payroll by $2.9 billion and exceeded that goal with an increase of $4.5 billion. The business attraction target was to obtain 100 corporate relocation announcements and it actually obtained 123 between 2004 and 2007. The initiative also set five-year targets for key "process metrics." Process metrics are those activities that drive the desired results and include out-of-region visits, prospect visits to Central Texas, serious relocation inquiries, and regional business retention visits. On all of these metrics except serious relocation inquiries, the target was exceeded in four years. For the serious relocation inquiries, the target was 5,000 and the actual in four years was 4,492.[51]

In 2008, Austin was ranked first by *Forbes* magazine's Fastest Growing Metros. It was ranked third in terms of *Forbes*'s Best Cities for Jobs.[52] Throughout the twentieth century the Austin chamber had been an effective and credible institution that had led efforts to develop and improve Austin as a place to live and work. In an interview, Jose Beceiro, who has been a participant in the Austin economic development story from the perspective of the chamber as well as from his former role at the University of Texas, pointed out that, around 2004, the economic development functions for the region were handed to the Greater Austin Chamber of Commerce. The chamber proactively proposed that this be done.

> The reason for that was to create some separation between incoming and outgoing elected officials and city council members and create a sustained economic development program that would have a strategic plan and funding in place to execute on that plan over time regardless of who is mayor or who is on city council at any point in time.[53]

The reasoning that led Austin to separate its economic development from the control of elected politicians will be one of the fundamental principles that we draw from this case study.

Opportunity Austin 2.0

Based on the success of Opportunity Austin 1.0, the Greater Austin Chamber of Commerce engaged Market Street Services to develop a new five-year strategy to move Austin to the "next level." Opportunity Austin 2.0 was launched in 2009 at the onset of the Great Recession. Despite the economic slowdown, $21 million was raised by the Greater Austin Chamber to fund the five-year initiative.

Prior to the launch, the consultants performed a competitive analysis that benchmarked Austin against other metro areas selected as "peer" regions. These were Denver, Colorado; Raleigh-Durham, North Carolina; Nashville, Tennessee; and Phoenix, Arizona. In addition, Austin was compared with Texas overall and with the nation. The analysis looked at five areas of comparison—education and workforce development, infrastructure, business costs, innovation and entrepreneurship, and quality of life.

The analysis pointed out that Austin in 2008–2009 was a different place than it was in 2004. Growth had returned. Jobs had been created at a rate that exceeded the rate for Texas and the nation. Unemployment had declined and job and wage growth occurred in every business sector.

However, among challenges that were identified was the fact that there was a growing mismatch between the jobs that were being created and the talent pipeline that existed to fill them. If one examines the population in the public schools it appears this mismatch will continue to grow based on reasonable projections. In addition, Austin's success over the 2004–2008 period was creating challenges in terms of transportation infrastructure, affordable housing, and the availability of certain classes of job skills.

The target business review led to the conclusion that two of the sectors targeted in Opportunity Austin 1.0 were no longer viable sectors to target. Instead, the analysis recommended two new "base targets"—convergence technologies and creative media. In addition, to promote further diversification of the economy the analysis revealed opportunities for Austin to grow green industries, corporate and professional operations, and health care and life sciences.

Based on the strategic analysis, the goals and objectives established for Opportunity Austin 2.0 were:

1. Economic diversification—This goal area included objectives that related to (a) growing jobs in existing businesses and promoting the start-up and success of new enterprises, (b) continued external marketing to targeted sectors, (c) developing businesses in sectors targeted for diversification, and (d) developing awareness in the community of the Greater Austin Chamber's programs to assist business and job growth.
2. Talent development, recruitment, and retention—This goal area focused on developing career awareness and skill alignment in the pre-K–12 school systems, higher education, and workforce development programs.
3. Keeping Greater Austin "Great"—The objectives in this goal area focused on improving the infrastructure—for example, to reduce commuting time and traffic congestion—as well as more affordable housing, reducing energy costs to businesses, and improving air routes into and out of the Austin–Bergstrom airport.

The targets set for Opportunity Austin 2.0 were prerecession targets that turned out to be unrealistic as the nation experienced the most serious economic shock since the Great Depression. As a result, in 2011 the Market Street consultants were asked to do a "mid-course analysis" with recommendations for adjusting the plan.

Despite the recession, the Greater Austin Chamber's economic development program raised over $20 million and fell just short of the prerecession target. This funding enabled the program activities, with a few exceptions, to continue as originally planned.

The relevant evaluation question for the economic development effort was not whether it met its prerecession targets but whether the region outperformed other "peer" regions in terms of how they survived the recession. By this standard, the Austin region performed very well. The Milken Institute rated the Austin metro area number one in 2009 and number two in 2010 in its best performing cities index. In terms of employment change among Sunbelt cities, only Austin outperformed its peers (Table 5.2).

In addition, during the recession (2007–2009), the Austin metropolitan statistical area (MSA) experienced (0.7%) wage growth which exceeded that of any of the comparison MSAs. Following the recession (2009–2010), wages in Austin grew faster than any of the comparison cities as well at a rate of 4.6 percent.[54]

Table 5.3 provides an analysis of the job growth in Austin between 2009 and 2014 as a result of business relocations and as a result of expansions of existing businesses. During this period 46,199 new jobs were created with 60.6 percent of the growth resulting from relocations.

Opportunity Austin in its second five-year plan sharpened its focus on its economic development targets, became more strategic in its use of incentives, and began to broaden its focus to address infrastructure issues that are essential to supporting economic development and building community support for additional economic development. In examining Opportunity Austin 2.0, we also need to look at two other major streams of economic activity that were occurring in parallel.

The first of these is the focus on entrepreneurship and new business start-ups. A focal point for the start-up activity in Austin is the IC^2 Institute's Austin Technology Incubator (ATI). ATI was established in 1989 and its first occupant was the first "spin-off" company from MCC.

Table 5.2   Comparison of Employment Change for Austin Metro Area and PEER Metro Areas

Metro area	Employment change January 2009–July 2011
Austin	1.5%
Nashville, Tennessee	−0.3%
Raleigh, North Carolina	−0.5%
Denver, Colorado	−2.6%
Durham, North Carolina	−4.7%
Phoenix, Arizona	−5.0%

Source: Created from a presentation by Market Street Services.com, original data derived from the U.S. Bureau of Labor Statistics and Moody Analytics.

Table 5.3   Job Creation from Relocations and Expansions 2011–2014*

Year	Number of company relocations	Number of jobs from relocations	Number of jobs from expansions	Hi-tech employ- ment	Annual change in hi-tech employment
2009	17	547	2,115	N/A	N/A
2010	29	3,128	2,307	N/A	N/A
2011	34	3,779	3,955	103,520	7,375 (7.6%)
2012	31	7,047	2,568	109,080	5,560 (5.0%)
2013	50	5,131	3,520	114,428	5,348 (4.9%)
2014	64	8,380	3,722	N/A	N/A

*Created by author from data presented in Opportunity Austin annual reports 2011–2014. Data are approximate due to differences from year to year in reporting format.

ATI, while a unit within the University of Texas, is not funded by the university. It depends totally on external funding. Unlike some incubators, ATI does not take an equity position in its start-up companies. It is viewed as a partner of the Chamber of Commerce in the Opportunity Austin initiative and receives some annual funding from the chamber as well as from Austin Energy, the City of Austin, federal contracts and grants, and private contributions. The purpose of ATI is to work with "seed and pre-seed stage technology startups, helping to prepare these businesses for commercial success. The Incubator . . . (has) a dual mission: create jobs and wealth in Central Texas through technology entrepreneurship, and provide unparalleled teaching and research opportunities for the UT-Austin community."[55]

According to Mitch Jacobson, codirector of the ATI Clean Energy Incubator,

> ATI focuses on the hard sciences—energy, biotech, etc. There are a number of other incubators and accelerators in Austin. We all work very well together. One of the things Austin does really well is the collaboration between the city, chamber of commerce, the incubators and accelerators, the non-profits and the private business community. You will not find a friendlier city. . . . Austin grew up on high-tech—computers, software and semiconductors. It has grown into clean tech—ATI started the clean energy incubator in 2001, the oldest clean technology incubator in the country. Then in 2007 bio-tech was added. It is not a coincidence that these incubator focus areas align with the economic development focus areas. It is deliberate.[56]

ATI contracted with a third party, the Bureau of Business Research of the University of Texas, to conduct an economic impact study of ATI incubator alumni companies. Over its first 25 years, ATI has graduated 142 companies. Six of these companies were publicly traded or went public after ATI graduation, while over 40 have merged with or been acquired by larger firms. Fifty are still in operation as viable businesses.[57]

The economic impact evaluation focused on the period from 2003 to 2012, which corresponded roughly with the first nine years of Opportunity Austin.[58] During this period there were 39 alumni companies—that is, companies that graduated from ATI. Thirty of these responded to a survey used for the assessment. Based on these responses, it is found that the 30 companies created $772.1 million in total economic benefits. They created 5,558 direct or indirect jobs and $20.1 million in local tax revenue. A subsequent analysis incorporated a methodology to estimate the economic benefits that were created by the nine companies that did not respond to the original survey. When the estimated results from the 9 nonrespondent companies were added to the reported benefits from the 30 responding companies, the total benefits from the 39 incubator graduates were:

- $880 million in total economic benefits
- 6,524 direct and indirect jobs
- $20.1 million in tax revenue.

ATI helps its member companies gain access to external angel funding, venture funding, and public funding. Of the companies that graduated in 2012, 85 percent received funding while at the incubator. Between 2007 and 2013, ATI members and alumni companies received over $431 million in external funding.[59]

A second force for economic development that began during the Opportunity Austin 2.0 time period is the most recent Austin public–private collaborative partnership known as the "Pecan Street" initiative. ATI's Mitch Jacobson pointed out that the idea for Pecan Street emerged from the IC^2 Institute. "Isaac Barchas, Brewster McCracken and my predecessor Joel Serface were the ones who sat around at a 'whiteboard' and said what if we do this—what if we applied for this."[60] What they applied for is a grant for $10 million from the U.S. Department of Energy to conduct a smart grid demonstration project at Austin's Mueller community—a community built on the former site of Austin's municipal airport.

Jacobson continued:

In my world (the world of clean tech) Pecan Street has created this clean tech ecosystem. We are coming out with a report . . . that shows that the clean tech business community has created an economic impact of $2.5 billion last year in Central Texas—the five county area surrounding Austin. This group of 250 companies account for 18,000 jobs in this region. This is roughly one-tenth of the total tech community and twice as big as the biotech industry which is approximately $1 billion but that will grow rapidly due to the new hospital and academic medical center that is under development.[61]

In addition to his role as codirector of the Clean Tech Incubator, Jacobson was also for a number of years board chairman of an organization of clean tech companies called CLEANTX. He was replaced as chairman in 2015 by Jose Beceiro. Jacobson's description of how he operated to facilitate the networking of clean tech companies is a very good example of how to leverage what Moretti refers to as "knowledge spillover" and also illustrates what Gibson and Butler describe as the source of momentum for building regional cooperative economic activity. The key is creating connections between otherwise unconnected and possibly competing individuals and organizations toward a common purpose. Talking about his two "hats" with CLEANTX and the Clean Energy Incubator, Jacobson says:

> We have events to get people together. They find jobs through these events. They find customers, vendors and partners. These events allow the ecosystem to talk. I make it a point to get to know every one of these 250 companies in our ecosystem. We have people come in and make talks. We bring them in to be on panels. That is important since it is the existing companies that help attract additional companies. We work with the Greater Austin Chamber of Commerce to help attract companies outside of the city and outside of the country. We (the incubator) also have a program called "Landing Pad." If we attract a company from outside the area or outside the country, this Landing Pad gives them a great place to start. I am brought in by the Chamber to talk about our ecosystem as they try to sell other companies on the resources that exist here. I talk about the University, the incubator and about CLEANTX.[62]

The team spirit that permeates the culture in Austin is, as Charisse Bodisch CEcD, senior vice president of economic development for the Greater Austin Chamber, describes it, our "secret sauce." Bodisch explains:

> This is, hands down, one of the top regions I have ever seen in terms of collaboration and creativity. The Austin region is attractive to companies who have more of a holistic outlook. The creative environment generates the free exchange of ideas and people here genuinely desire to be part of a larger solution, making a difference in the world. I call it a "caring and sharing" culture. The caring part is that altruistic nature you find permeating our culture where people are passionate and want to feel part of something larger than themselves and their own organization. The sharing part is the

openness to collaboration across all platforms with an eye on a more global end result yielding a bigger impact. That translates into new innovative technologies making lives better and more efficient. Locally, it is the personal human impact of sharing with others for the betterment of the overall community. Austin Gives is an excellent example of how committed companies are giving back to the community. This caring and sharing attitude is what sets us apart and is our secret sauce to success![63]

Pecan Street

The Pecan Street initiative that grew from the whiteboard discussion described by Mitch Jacobson began in 2008. The founding members included the city of Austin, Austin Energy, the University of Texas, the Austin Technology Incubator, the Greater Austin Chamber of Commerce, and the Environmental Defense Fund. The 501(c)(3) nonprofit Pecan Street Project Inc. was incorporated in August 2009—the same year that the project received its smart grid demonstration project grant from the U.S. Department of Energy.

An article in *Time* magazine in 2014 entitled "Is This America's Smartest City" described the project centered in Mueller, a planned green community in Austin. The article recounted the experience of Dan McAtee and Laura Spoor, whose electric bill for 2013 was –$631. Yes, that is minus $631.

They actually produced more electricity than they consumed and returned the excess to the grid. The generation came from a very large array of solar panels on their rooftop. The article points out, however, that the most interesting part of the story is what cannot be seen. Within the home "smart circuits are tracking their electricity use on a minute-by-minute and appliance-by-appliance basis, providing a running record of how power flows through their home."[64]

> The capability to monitor customer energy usage at this level is the essence of the project carried out by Pecan Street, Inc. The project tracks the energy use of more than 500 homes in Austin (along with 400-plus in Houston and the Dallas area), including both green homes and conventional ones, along with dozens of electric vehicles. Their meters collect nearly 90 million unique electricity use and voltage reads per day.[65]
>
> That kind of data is unprecedented in the electricity industry, whose essentials have remained largely unchanged since 1882, when Thomas Edison opened America's first commercial power plant. The Pecan Street team is already using it to upend long-held theories about electricity use and test provocative new distribution methods, which could make our power cleaner and cheaper. . . . Mueller is the community of the near future, says Suzanne

Russo, chief operating officer at Pecan Street. "But everything we're learning is going to be applicable to every community in America."[66]

In addition to the Mueller demonstration project, which has now evolved to involve other cities around the country, Pecan Street has a second division called the Pike Powers Laboratory and Center for Commercialization. This group offers specialized expertise in developing and testing a wide range of hardware and software products used in smart grid development and residential and commercial energy management systems.

Recently, Pecan Street has expanded its focus from its original work on smart electric grids and consumer electricity management behavior to address water as a key resource. It is applying many of its same methods and technologies to develop knowledge about consumer water use. It has long been known in the Southwest that water may be the most important resource that can determine the course of economic development in the region. Therefore, it makes great strategic sense for Pecan Street to broaden its focus to include water as a topic for its research and commercialization activities in order to improve how that resource is used and conserved.

It is too early to fully evaluate the impact of Pecan Street. However, Jose Beceiro, who served on the board of Pecan Street at the beginning, says, "Pecan Street is enhancing the ecosystem, it is working with start-ups, and increasing the community knowledge of energy usage issues. We are seeing large employers (e.g., Sun Power) move to the area. . . . Clearly Pecan Street has accelerated the growth of the clean tech industry."[67]

With Pecan Street, Austin has again demonstrated what Beceiro calls the Austin Model for growing new industry sectors. This model begins with a vision by key influencers, followed by collaboration on the part of key community leaders to implement the action plan that emerges from the vision, foundational R&D to build a knowledge base, business attraction to augment and leverage the knowledge base, and nurturing the growth of an ecosystem through data-driven business support to help create start-ups and growth of existing businesses. Once a certain level of momentum is reached, the "pull" of the ecosystem builds momentum and the snowball starts rolling.

What is clear regarding the Austin Model is that it receives and requires political support, but is not driven by politicians. It requires a time horizon that exceeds the time horizon of people seeking elective office. Pecan Street, for example, has been evolving for six years and only recently began having a significant job creation impact that is not yet fully realized.

Another aspect of Pecan Street compared to the two previous public–private initiatives—MCC and SEMATECH—is the high degree of transparency that characterized Pecan Street from the beginning. The board made a conscious decision to launch this initiative in a very transparent fashion. As Beceiro points out, part of the motivation for this decision was that Pecan Street had the benefit of learning from the difficulties faced by a number of other smart grid projects around the country led by investor-owned electric utilities that were not transparent and experienced significant consumer backlash.

With Pecan Street we see many of the characteristics of a more evolved economic development system. These include, in addition to greater transparency, limited use of financial incentives, strategic alignment between the job creation focus and the needs of the jurisdiction, and engagement with the broader community—the state, nationally, and internationally.

Similarly, there is a comparable move toward increased transparency in the Greater Austin Chamber's Opportunity Austin 3.0, along with much more strategic targeting of financial incentives for business attraction and growth, and greater alignment with the more holistic needs of the jurisdiction. This is visible in the plan's increased attention to the K–12 school systems, focus on infrastructure that limits growth, and emphasis on a new sector that is promoting business development and job creation in the medical, biotech, and health areas.

The technopolis model builds off a solid technical foundation, which will be the new University of Texas–Austin medical school and the associated academic research community. The school and its associated research form a solid knowledge base that will propel the development of knowledge businesses to support, leverage, and extend the impact of this research. The entire process of developing the medical school required great transparency since the community was required to vote on a tax increase to fund the development of the new campus. Much more than any previous Austin economic development initiative, the development of this "next" industry sector required transparency and broad scale community understanding and engagement.

Future Challenges

The Austin region faces a number of challenges as it strives to sustain its economic development momentum. Some of its challenges are unique to Austin, while others are challenges that many if not most cities and regions face. Austin has faced challenges before, and is responding to the current challenges with its characteristic "problem solving" strategy characterized by systematic analysis, action, evaluation, and more action. Let's look at some of the challenges.

Talent attraction and development

Julie Huls, president and CEO of the Austin Technology Council (ATC), pointed out that the rapid growth of the technology industry in Austin has created a "skills gap." As a result, the ATC commissioned a study to assess the dimensions of that skills gap, and the results were reported to the members of ATC at an event in May 2015. Austin has 108,310 tech jobs, which represents 11.1 percent of the total workforce. In 2013–2014, the tech job market grew by 5.3 percent.

Five industries in the tech sector contribute at least $1 billion per year to the regional gross domestic product. They are computer and peripheral equipment, IT services and applications, Internet and telecommunications, semiconductors, and software. It is expected that Austin will have 2,500 to 3,500 tech job openings per year between 2014 and 2024.

The regional education institutions are currently providing approximately 1,500 degrees per year in the core tech fields. Approximately 70 percent of the tech employers surveyed report moderate to significant difficulty in filling their tech job vacancies. Another conclusion from the analysis was that while a substantial number of the tech jobs do not require a bachelor's degree, the career and technology education programs offered in the K–12 education system do not produce graduates with skills that are aligned with the needs of employers. This study, supported by the ATC, has helped focus policy makers on a problem that can, if not addressed, limit the future growth of the technology sector in Austin.

Michael Berman, senior vice president of communications/strategy for the Greater Austin Chamber of Commerce, provided a broader perspective of the skills gap that the chamber is working to reduce:

> In the broader job market including technology, the Greater Austin Chamber of Commerce tracks monthly open job positions throughout the five county region. We know that at any one point in time there could be as many as 40,000 jobs open in Austin. Approximately 8,400 of those are in high technology jobs. Approximately 62% of those jobs require an associate's degree or higher to be considered for those roles. Even with our unemployment rate at just over 3% this means that approximately 35,000 of our neighbors are unemployed. Of those 35,000 over 80% do not have an associate's degree or higher. So most of the unemployed lack the degree or certificate that is needed to fulfill the requirements for the open jobs. This data points out that

the skills mismatch in the workforce is a challenge not only in the tech sector but in the broader job market as well.[68]

Affordability

The ATC study asked employers to share the reasons that candidates living outside Austin typically turn down job offers. The most significant reason cited was salary. There are significant salary differences between Austin salaries and those of other major technology hubs. Since the cost of living in Austin has historically been considerably lower than places like Silicon Valley, Boston, Seattle, and Washington, D.C., the salary gap has been less of a problem in the past. However, as Austinites view the future, the "affordability" gap is growing as housing costs in Austin have increased significantly. For the period between 1998 and 2008 the median single-family house price increased by almost 90 percent while median family incomes increased by only 36 percent. A similar increase is occurring in rental housing prices.[69]

In an interview, Joel Trammell, former chair of the ATC and a local investor and entrepreneur, pointed to one of the factors that is driving the accelerating housing prices. Trammell told a story about his friend who ran the largest residential appraisal firm and declared in 1996–1997 that the Austin economy could not support the increase in home prices. Several years later as housing prices continued to rise, Trammell said:

> I called my friend and asked him what did he miss in his prediction? He said "I missed the fact that Austin would become a national destination for a whole group of people who could live anywhere." Once a month I meet someone who is worth tens of millions of dollars and could live anywhere in the world that he wants to. But he has chosen to live here in Austin. His business may be somewhere else—California, New York—but they want to raise their kids here, retire here or whatever.[70]

Affordability as a growing concern has been recognized by leaders in the region as a challenge. ATC's Julie Huls pointed out that traffic and affordable housing are just beginning to become business issues in Austin.[71] The city of Austin's comprehensive plan, adopted by the city council in 2012 and called "ImagineAustin," states the concern as: "Median household and family incomes may be higher than those of the rest of the state, but Austin's high housing and transportation costs may consume greater proportions of household budgets, relative to other Texas cities."[72]

Paul DiGiuseppe, who was one of the key staff involved in developing the ImagineAustin comprehensive city plan, participated in a number of individual interviews and community engagement activities associated with obtaining over 18,000 community inputs to the plan development over two years. He stated:

> The majority of people who participated in this plan approached the issue as "we know that growth will happen, let's do the best we can do with it." . . . The focus of the plan on sustainability gives you the opportunity to bridge your gaps—environmental issues, social issues, etc. . . . Affordability is a big issue in this town now. We have become a very expensive city. We are now starting to see the loss of our lowest income groups from the city. We saw this anecdotally in some recent data where the number of people in the lowest income groups fell. Coincidentally, Bastrop County's low-income groups went up by the same amount.[73]

Thus we see that affordability is likely to increase as a concern in Austin. It is a business issue as it is beginning to impact the ability to attract needed talent to the area. It is also apparently beginning to have the effect of causing some potential members of the workforce to leave the city. As the affordability issue disrupts traditional neighborhoods, it also becomes a political issue, which energizes the antigrowth forces. As this sentiment resurfaces it becomes more difficult to address other issues such as traffic congestion.

Traffic and transportation

Another infrastructure challenge to Austin is the issue of traffic congestion and overall transportation planning. Speaking from the standpoint of an employer regarding how the traffic situation in Austin has changed, Joel Trammel remarked, "When I first moved to Austin you did not think much about where you worked in relation to where you lived. Now there are four quadrants, and if you are going to work in the west you will probably want to live in the west. Otherwise you can have one of these hour-long transitions."[74]

The traffic and transportation challenge has become an issue that both public and private sector policy makers are working to address. The "traffic light" metaphor can be used to describe different infrastructure issues where green means all is well, yellow means caution, and red means we are in trouble. Using this frame of reference ATC CEO Julie Huls points out that:

> As far as a culture for innovation, Austin is still very much in the green zone. However, as it relates to life styles we are approaching the "yellow" range.

In November 2014, we had a billion-dollar transportation bond issue that was shot down by 65–70%. It was a miserable failure. No one knew what we could be getting for a billion dollars and it would have meant a property tax increase. There was a lack of education and awareness. So because of that we have started to have these conversations in the boardroom about infrastructure. We have partnered with Mobility ATX, a brand new non-profit funded by Daimler-Chrysler, which will go back to citizens and solicit ideas about solving our transportation problems.[75]

Transportation is also a key challenge identified in the city of Austin's comprehensive plan. The challenge is identified as:

Expanding Transportation Choices
  Austin is a big city, so it's time to build a "big-city" transportation system. We need good roads, and we need to move people around the city and the region conveniently and safely, with or without a car. How can we offer more transportation choices? How can we encourage Austinites to walk, bike and take transit? How can we build the kind of transportation network we'll need for sustainable development?[76]

Capital availability

Another challenge identified by the ATC and one of its strategic imperatives is capital availability.[77] Chris Pacitti, general partner of Austin Ventures, observes that the issue of capital availability in Austin is not unlike the issue in most of the rest of the country other than Silicon Valley.

The data indicate that the Austin market isn't starved for venture capital. Mr. Pacitti says the region now has a raft of angel investors, three or four credible incubators and several Series A investors. In his view, the real capital gap, not only in Austin but across the U.S. save for Silicon Valley, is in what he calls midstage venture, a point at which a company has traction in its market and needs capital for growth but hasn't yet hit a breakout that would draw big-time investors.[78]

A similar point was made by Joel Trammell, former chair of the ATC, when he described the situation he faced in attempting to grow his company to a stage that would have made a public offering feasible. He chose to sell the company but would have preferred to be able to attract the funding needed to make a strategic acquisition as a way of growing the company.

We were not trying to sell the company. We decided to sell the company because it became our best option. I had talked to 46 Venture Capitalists, literally, and after 31 consecutive quarters of double-digit growth—as good of a success story as you could possibly have—we could not raise money at anywhere near a rational valuation of the company. We had a deal that would have doubled the size of the company and then we could have taken it public. But we could not fund the deal to acquire the company we needed to acquire. If we could have, we might be operating a billion dollar, home-grown company today.[79]

This situation appears to represent the key capital challenge for start-up companies in Austin, and perhaps much of the nation. Austin is rich in innovation and start-up businesses. It has a significant supply of "angel" investment, which, along with the rich ecosystem for entrepreneurs described earlier by Mitch Jacobsen, contributes to the area being one of the very top places in the country to start a business. However, as the businesses grow and begin to gain traction in their market they encounter the situation described by Trammell. As a result there are very few, if any, homegrown, multibillion dollar tech businesses in Austin. The only exception is Dell and some point out that Dell is now more of a logistics business than a tech business. Instead, the active start-up culture in Austin becomes a rich hunting ground for larger enterprises, based elsewhere, who are doing technology scouting for new ideas and new products to energize their business growth. With the appropriate capital availability, these Austin companies could become major job creators in Austin. Instead they often end up creating jobs elsewhere after they are acquired.

Poverty and the digital divide

The Austin comprehensive plan, ImagineAustin,[80] has identified the "Ethnic Divide" as one of the key six challenges for the next 30 years. Earlier in this chapter we addressed the racial history of Austin, which included the fact that the city had legally enforced racial segregation. While this ended long ago, there are remnants of this history in terms of land use and housing patterns.

In the 2010 Census, non-Hispanic whites represented 48.7 percent of the population compared to 52.9 percent in 2000. The Hispanic population in 2010 was just over 35 percent, Asians represented 6.3 percent, and African Americans represented 7.7 percent. In 2011, 21 percent of the residents lived below the poverty line, which was $22,350 in 2011 for a family of four. Almost one-third of all children live in poverty. Eighty-three percent of these children are Hispanic.

The ethnic divide is evident when we look at educational patterns. In 2010, 44 percent of the residents aged 25 and above had a bachelor's degree and almost 16 percent had advanced degrees. This compares very favorably to the state of Texas, where only 27 percent had a bachelor's degree and 9 percent had advanced degrees. However, on the other end of the education attainment spectrum 14 percent of Austinites aged 25 and older lack a high school degree.

The economic challenge of this demographic picture is made obvious by this projection in the comprehensive plan:

> If no intervening actions are taken, the percentage of Austinites with post-secondary education levels is expected to decline from 65% to 55% by 2040. The cost to Austin will be a loss of $2.4 billion in annual income due to reduced career opportunities and earning capacities.[81]

To their credit, these problems are on the radar of economic development policy makers in the city as well as in the private sector organizations that recognize these as emerging, critical business issues. For example, the city has developed an economic development "decision matrix" that scores potential investment opportunities in terms of the extent to which they address key city economic development priorities such as location in targeted economic development zones and the extent to which they will offer employment prospects to "hard to employ" populations. Both the Greater Austin Chamber of Commerce and ATC have developed programs to better align the K–12 and community college education curricula with the needs of employers and to generate increased student interest in the science, technology, engineering, and math disciplines.

Community engagement

In many aspects, there is extensive involvement of targeted groups of stakeholders in Austin. One of the best examples was the process used by the city of Austin to develop its comprehensive plan. This systematic two-year effort to engage citizens has been recognized as a best practice by the International City Management Association.

However, in the economic development sphere, especially in many of the examples we have highlighted in this chapter, such as the competition for MCC and SEMATECH and the development of Opportunity Austin, broad involvement of the community has not occurred. The decision to pursue the technopolis model and the actions to implement that approach to economic development were made by a group of community leaders who were visionary, competent, and extremely successful. But one would have to conclude that this approach to economic development was "done to the community" rather than "done with the community." Could it have been done differently and still have been so successful in bringing business and jobs to the community? Given the history of Austin, the political climate, and periodic waves of antigrowth sentiment, to say it should have been done differently would be "Monday morning quarterbacking."

There are signs, however, that the situation Austin faces today is different than the one community leaders faced from 1980 to 2010. There already is considerable evidence that the approaches have also changed to address that new reality. The comprehensive plan, for example, was a very ambitious effort to ask the community to define what type of city they would like to create over the next 30 years.

The establishment of the most recent major public–private initiative— the Pecan Street Project—was developed and deployed in a much different manner, with more transparency and, owing to the nature of the project, with significant target community involvement. It also appears that one of the lessons learned from the failure of the transportation bond issue in 2014 was that there is a need for more citizen involvement, awareness-building, and education. While there may have been other key issues involved in the failure of this project, any such project in the future must have an engaged and supportive citizenry.

The appropriate strategy for engaging citizens will depend on the purpose. A clear challenge for Austin's future economic development strategies will be how to effectively engage the community in understanding and supporting the initiatives. The fact that the citizens were willing to tax themselves to support the creation of a major teaching hospital is positive evidence that the need for community engagement is understood. For a community as sophisticated and tech-savvy as Austin, how it employs technology to effectively engage citizens in a range of applications will have lessons for the nation as well.

Comprehensive regional planning

The Greater Austin Chamber of Commerce has effectively demonstrated how to create a regional approach to economic development. The counties in the region do not have economic development offices. The economic development focal points in the region are the cities. Counties get involved with regard to the need to provide incentives.

The chamber works with the individual city economic development programs in a supportive role. As the chamber's senior vice president of economic development Charisse Bodisch described, "we support our community partners in the five-county region by driving prospect leads, providing research assistance and working with them on individual prospects as a liaison with state offices."[82]

In some parts of the country communities within the same region compete head-on in a "competitive model." There can be a feeling that if a prospect chooses community A over community B, then community B is a "loser." In addressing this economic development culture Charisse points out how the Austin region is different.

> Prospects and their consultants who are used to the "competitive model" in other areas are pleasantly surprised with the regionalism demonstrated by our communities. Our communities are considered our Regional Partners. If a company locates in Austin, San Marcos, Round Rock or any of our communities we all win. We have hosted prospects over lunch in one community and representatives from surrounding communities were also at the table providing supporting comments of the community under consideration. The regional partners collaborate not only on economic development, but on transportation, air service, education and other initiatives that make us all stronger as a whole.[83]

Jose Beceiro served as the Greater Austin Chamber's director of business retention and expansion from 2006 to 2007, and then director of clean energy economic development from 2007 to 2013. He was a founding board member of the Pecan Street initiative from 2009 to 2013, and was associate director of research relations with the University of Texas Cockrell School of Engineering from 2013 to 2015. In April 2015 he became director of strategic corporate partnerships at Texas State University. From this broad perspective, he was asked to comment on the relationship between the economic development roles of the Greater Austin Chamber of Commerce and the city of Austin's economic development department.

> The Chamber and the City represent different units of analysis. The Chamber is trying to focus on the entire region for economic development. They want to make available to companies a whole range of options and opportunities to locate new facilities. For example, a general manufacturing and assembly company may want to locate in a less expensive suburb of the city where cost of labor and land could be less expensive. The Chamber is focusing on housing, affordability and transportation infrastructure issues. They collaborate

with the City on strategic initiatives. However, when new companies relocate from higher cost markets such as the North East or California this can have the unintended consequence of lowering affordability, driving local families to the suburbs and disrupting the traditional culture of Austin.[84]

It is likely that issues such as the one raised by Beceiro led the city of Austin to highlight the challenge of "Collaborating Regionally "in its comprehensive plan. This challenge is described well in the plan.

> As the biggest city in Central Texas, Austin has a duty to provide regional leadership and invite its regional partners to collaborate on solutions. Issues such as transportation, water resources, growth and development, environmental protection, climate change, and economic prosperity are regional in scale and scope. We need a platform for regional governance and coordinated comprehensive planning for our collective future. How can Austin lead the way to forge a productive dialog and set of agreements?[85]

If the Austin region can successfully meet this challenge, it can truly be a role model for much more than just how to create jobs.

Concluding Comment

At the outset of this chapter we posed two questions: (1) Has Austin's success come from better execution of the traditional model of economic development? or (2) Has Austin's success resulted from a rethinking of the traditional economic development approach? The Austin story has elements of both better execution and rethinking.

When Kozmetsky and his colleagues articulated the technopolis model, this was clearly rethinking that moved beyond traditional economic development practice. As the chamber took the lead on economic development with Opportunity Austin after 2000, its outstanding success came from superior execution of ideas that were part of leading economic development thinking. However, the challenges of the current business environment are moving the economic development players in Austin toward a rethinking of the existing model.

Issues that have not traditionally been viewed as business or economic development issues are forcing this rethinking. We see less emphasis on the independent actions of separate organizations pursuing their separate agendas and much more focus on collective efforts toward shared objectives with respect to transportation infrastructure challenges, workforce development, public education, and engaging populations that are more difficult to engage. This rethinking reflects the fact that no single organization has the answers or the resources to address these more complex problems. Collective action is essential. The collective action required goes beyond traditional collaboration and requires each organization to examine how it can best contribute to achieving goals shared by all the key economic development players. The more recent strategies of the chamber, the ATC, the city, the ATI, and Pecan Street, all have moved in this direction.

CHAPTER SIX

Dubuque, Iowa: Masterpiece on the Mississippi

Why Dubuque?

A primary message of this book is that the "rethinking" of economic development must be grounded in five key premises. First, the economic development strategy and practice must flow from an answer to the question: What type of economy and community do we want to create? This requires that the vision, goals, and strategies are aligned with the values of the community that comprises the economic unit.

Second, the approach to answer this question requires broad community engagement of the community in developing of the strategy that will guide the economic development process.

Third, the leadership of the economic development process must be centered in a "broad-tent" multistakeholder organization that is separate from electoral politics.

Fourth, the approach to developing and growing jobs must rely more on "organic" means rather than on "buying jobs" through lavish financial incentives. To use a baseball analogy, building a strong economy in a jurisdiction must rely on building a strong "farm system" rather than relying on "free agency." In the economic development realm this involves shifting resources from business attraction to business retention and growth and to new business creation and entrepreneurship.

Fifth, the term "economic development" is too narrow to adequately describe what is required.

As I scanned the environment looking for a place that illustrates these principles, I found no better example than Dubuque, Iowa. I discovered Dubuque somewhat by accident. In the fall of 2012, I was attending a meeting of my professional society, the Society of Industrial and Organizational Psychologists, where the topic was "Sustainability." I got into a discussion with a colleague from Bowling Green, Ohio, named David Dubois. Dr. Dubois told me of his work with a California consulting firm called True Market Solutions that assists organizations embrace sustainability as a platform to drive innovation and value creation. David told me about a session this organization was planning in Dubuque, Iowa, and invited me to attend.

The thought of going to Dubuque, Iowa, in the middle of January was not the most appealing option I could imagine. But the fact that I had been doing some consulting with a colleague in Iowa, Bob Haug, who at that time was director of the Iowa Association of Municipal Utilities, meant I could perhaps connect with Bob and that the two of us could make the trip to Dubuque.

The session in Dubuque was truly eye-opening. It was held in the beautiful new riverfront convention center and aquarium on the Mississippi River. The river was totally frozen this time of the year and had an eerie beauty. The presentations by City Manager Mike Van Milligen and many of his colleagues were even more interesting. They described a city that had made a commitment to sustainability as their vision, and each presenter demonstrated how sustainability became the lens they used to look at all city issues and decision making on concerns that ranged from flood control to landfill management, to city performance metrics, to riverfront development, to affordable housing, and to job creation. They also discussed ways in which they had engaged citizens in planning and decision making, and how they were converting a former industrial area, the millwork district, into workforce housing in repurposed buildings.

I did not know as I was listening to these presentations that I would be writing this book in 2015. However, as I began to develop the ideas for this book in mid-2013, it quickly became clear that the message I had heard from the people of Dubuque illustrated most of the core principles I would advocate in this book.

As the planning for the book continued and I began to do more research on Dubuque as a possible case example, I quickly realized this "Masterpiece on the Mississippi" had also been discovered by many others. The following list of honors and recognition the city has received speaks not only to its many accomplishments but also to the systemic breadth of its achievements. The list includes:

- Named one of the "100 Best Communities for Young People" by the America's Promise Youth Foundation in 2007;
- Named 15th in the "Best Small Places for Business and Careers" by *Forbes* magazine in 2007;
- Received its first "All-American City Award," one of 10 cities so named, in June 2007. Received this award again in 2012 and in 2013—an unprecedented three times in six years;
- Named the "Most Livable" small city by the U.S. Conference of Mayors in June 2008;
- Named the eighth best small metro area in which to launch a small business by CNNMoney.com in 2009;
- Won *American City and County Magazine*'s Crown Community Award for partnerships and collaboration that resulted in IBM's decision to locate a new global technology service center in the city in 2009;
- The Dubuque/IBM project was selected as the "Economic Development Deal of the Year" by *Business Facilities* magazine in 2009, while *Site Selection* magazine selected the IBM location project as a "Top Deal of 2009";
- Selected number one in terms of projected job growth of all cities under 250,000 population by *Forbes* magazine in 2010;
- Selected the best small city in which to raise a family in the country by *Forbes* in 2010;
- "Dubuque Works" was awarded first place in the workforce solutions category by the Mid-America Economic Development Council in December 2011 for the collaborative efforts of seven workforce partners to overcome barriers to employment;
- Received the City Cultural Diversity Award by the National League of Cities in 2012;
- Named the 14th Best Small Place for Business and Careers by *Forbes* in 2013;
- Named number one in job growth in Iowa for the period 2010–2013 by Iowa Workforce Development, accounting for 10 percent of all the net new private sector jobs in the state with only 3 percent of the state's population;
- Named 21st in the list of the "Top 100 Leading Locations" for business location by *Area Development* magazine in 2014;
- Was number one in the country among metro areas with 50,000–200,000 population for the number of economic development projects in 2014;
- Named one of the 10 Best American Cities to Work in Technology by SmartAsset.com in 2014;
- Named one of only five U.S. communities in the Smart21 Communities of 2015 list by the Intelligent Community Forum in October 2014.

What Is the Job Creation Story?

Unlike many communities, the focus in Dubuque is less on the number of jobs created and more on employment growth coupled with the "quality" of employment measured by average salary level. Simply creating jobs is an insufficient goal if your vision is to build a viable, livable, and equitable community. Quality of life requires the creation of "good jobs" that can be filled locally by qualified local employees who will enable employers to be productive and competitive and who will contribute to the larger community.

Between 2010 and 2013, Dubuque, with 3 percent of the state's population, contributed 10 percent of the net new job creation in Iowa. Between 1983 and 2013, total employment in Dubuque County increased by 36.3 percent. From 2000 until 2012, the per capita income increased in Dubuque by 32.8 percent compared with 29.9 percent in the United States. Median household income in Dubuque increased from $39,582 in 2000 to $50,885 in 2012. This 28.5 percent exceeds the national increase of only 21.4 percent. Median household income in Dubuque was 6 percent below the national median in 2000 and that gap has been narrowed to only 1 percent by 2012.

These results demonstrate significant progress toward one of the city's five-year community goals—economic prosperity. Economic development in Dubuque is not an end in itself but rather a means to a larger purpose. That purpose is defined by the city's 2029 vision statement:

> The city of Dubuque is a progressive, sustainable city with a strong diversi-fied economy and expanding global connections. The Dubuque commu-nity is an inclusive community celebrating culture and heritage and has actively preserved our "Masterpiece on the Mississippi." Dubuque citizens experience healthy living and retirement through quality livable neighbor-hoods with an abundance of fun things to do and are engaged in the com-munity, achieving goals through partnerships. Dubuque city government is financially sound and is providing services with citizens getting value for their tax dollar.[1]

With respect to the economic outcomes desired for residents and busi-nesses, the city plan makes these very explicit and demonstrates that Dubuque has asked itself the question "What type of economy do we want to create?" The desired outcomes for a successful economic development effort in Dubuque include the following:[2]

- Young professionals want to live here;
- Our children want to stay or return to raise their families;
- More retail, service, and entertainment opportunities are created—keeping dollars in Dubuque;
- Insulation from economic cycles through diverse businesses is provided;
- A variety of job opportunities for residents is created;

- A variety of educational opportunities and internships for those jobs are provided;
- Entrepreneurial opportunities are enabled to start and grow businesses in the community.

A Brief History of Dubuque

To understand the vision and community goals, it is helpful to review a bit of the history of Dubuque. The area was originally settled by the Mesquakie Indians.[3] The area was important in the French-Indian fur trading culture. The first permanent white settler was the French Canadian Julien Dubuque for whom the city was named. He arrived in 1785 and in 1788 was granted rights by the Mesquakie tribe to mine for lead. Following the Louisiana Purchase in 1803,[4] control of the land, including Dubuque's mines, shifted from France to the United States. Julien Dubuque died in 1810.

[He] was buried upon the land on a high bluff near the present town of Dubuque; and so great was the veneration entertained for him by the Indians, that for many years after his death they kept a fire burning upon his grave and watched it by day and night.[5]

Following his death, the Indians operated the lead mines and resisted efforts by white settlers to move into the area. It was not until treaties with the Indians were formalized by the U.S. government that settlers moved into the area and established a mining community. The Indian treaty was concluded September 2, 1832, and took effect in June 1833.[6] This opened the area to settlers and enabled the mining community, which became the city of Dubuque, to grow. Life in Dubuque was typical of many frontier towns.

It was a typical mining town, with dram shops where armed men congregated to drink and fight. Although it is usual to attempt to make the village previous to 1834 appear intensely wild and wicked, it was not so in reality, because the lawless were held in check by men like Langworthys McCraney, John King, Milo H. Prentice and others who united to secure good order and morals and were immensely aided by the first ministers and the first religious congregations. But moral suasion was supplemented by a set of orders or resolutions drawn up by John King and adopted by the citizens as a guide of law and order to serve until the usual courts could set in operation.[7]

As this description of early Dubuque points out, the idea of community engagement was established early in the history of the city. Another precursor of the current community ethic can be found in the first newspaper in

Dubuque, which was also the first newspaper in Iowa and the first west of the Mississippi and north of St. Louis. It was called the *Dubuque Visitor* and it appeared in May 1836. Its editor was John King and its motto was "Truth Our Guide—The Public Good Our Aim."[8] This motto could easily serve as the motto for the city's current comprehensive plan that emphasizes ethics, transparency, and responsiveness to citizens.

With its location on the Mississippi River, following the decline of lead mining, Dubuque became a city whose industry was dominated by fabricating products from wood and food processing. Timber from Wisconsin was transported down the river to Dubuque where it was converted to boats, windows, and doors. In addition, its location in the farm belt and its access to rail and water transportation enabled Dubuque to grow a large meatpacking industry.

The availability of jobs in Dubuque attracted a large number of immigrants who had initially settled in the crowded eastern section of the United States and who desired a better quality of life than they were experiencing there. The primary immigrant groups were Irish and German. The Irish settled in the southern part of Dubuque and the Germans in the northern sections of the city. English settlers settled in between these two groups.

In 1920, Dubuque was one of the first U.S. cities to choose through a citizen referendum the council-mayor form of government.

The economic crisis of the early 1980s

Over 30 million doors and 55 million windows were produced in Dubuque by CARADCO. The company was formed in 1856, and by the end of 1894, it was one of the largest millwork firms in the country dedicated to manufacturing sashes, doors, and blinds. Employment at the plant rose to 300 employees. Production continued at the plant until 1976 when Scoville, which purchased the company in 1968, relocated window production to Illinois due to the poor condition of the historic Dubuque facility.

This former CARADCO facility has now become a showplace in Dubuque as its "Millwork District" has become a shining example of historic preservation and repurposing old buildings. The CARADCO building has become the home of the Schmid Innovation Center—a one-stop shop for new business creation and also houses the Greater Dubuque Development Corporation (GDDC)—the principal economic development organization in Dubuque. In addition, the former factory building now houses 72 upscale residential units, a food co-op, and offices for arts and not-for-profit organizations in Dubuque.[9]

The Dubuque Packing Company, a former meatpacking company founded in 1891 by a merger of the Dubuque Packing and Provision Company and the Dubuque Butchers Association, operated in Dubuque from 1891 until 2001. By the 1950s the workforce reached 3,500. Annual sales supported a payroll of $20 million. By the end of the 1970s, thousands of people were dependent on "The Pack" as the plant was called, and its wages were among the highest in the city as a result of the collective bargaining agreement. By 1980, workers on the line earned an average of $25,000 in annual wages plus an additional $11,000 in benefits, including an average of five weeks of vacation per year.

In 1981, the company, citing changing market conditions, high wages, and inefficient equipment, closed the hog-processing operation, and in the next year, on October 16, 1982, closed the entire operation. The loss of the hog operations in 1981 resulted in the loss of 1,400 jobs and the closure of the entire operation cost Dubuque another 1,200 jobs, which raised the city's unemployment rate to 17.3 percent.[10]

Millwork and the meatpacking business were the major industries in Dubuque for many years. However the city's economy achieved a degree of diversification when another major business chose to locate operations in Dubuque in 1945. The iconic John Deere Company built its first tractor factory that it had ever built as a "greenfield" site. Tractor production ramped up through the late 1940s and 1950s and John Deere added an industrial division to its farm machinery business.

Dubuque became the design and engineering center for John Deere's construction and forestry equipment divisions and remains so today. By 1964, the plant had grown from its original 600,000-square foot factory to over 1,165,000 square feet and employment reached 3,800. By 1969 the Dubuque Works became a primary industrial factory and design of most industrial products was also consolidated to Dubuque, which brought more technical and engineering talent to the community. As rapid growth of the industrial products continued, the Dubuque Works expanded to 5,250,000 square feet and an employment base of 8,270 people.

The global recession that had contributed to the loss of the millwork business and the packing plant also hit John Deere very hard. The Dubuque Works lost the industrial training center and slowing production schedules led to the layoff of over half the United Auto Workers workforce. Six years later the foundry was closed.[11]

The impact of the recession in Dubuque was devastating. Mike Blouin, former president of the GDDC, put it this way:

Thousands of those very good paying blue-collar jobs disappeared. They weren't coming back. There were "for sale" signs on every block in the entire city with no buyers.[12]

In all, Dubuque County lost 7,500 jobs between 1979 and 1982. More layoffs came after that. People left the city in droves.[13]

Quite a few of the people I interviewed for this chapter summed up the doldrums of the early 1980s by saying that there were newspaper headlines, bumper stickers, T-shirts, and a billboard in Dubuque that asked "Will the last one out of Dubuque please turn out the lights?" The executive editor of the local newspaper, the *Times Herald*, Brian Cooper, took issue with this recollection, at least the part about there being a newspaper headline with this message.[14] It seems that this may be an example of the dictum that if a falsehood is repeated often enough it is perceived as the truth. So despite the fact that there was no such billboard in Dubuque and no newspaper headline asking those who were leaving to turn out the lights, few would deny that the phrase expressed the sentiment of a large number of Dubuquers when in the early 1980s the city's unemployment rate was for a short time the highest in the nation.

The community responds

Communities respond to crises in different ways. Some go into a death spiral and never recover. Others use the crisis to propel positive change. This is what happened in Dubuque. Later in this chapter we will look at how the community responded to this crisis in some detail, highlighting especially the work of the GDDC, the Community Foundation of Greater Dubuque, and city leadership. For now, though, we will look at the score-card of what the community has accomplished over the past 30 years from 1984 to 2014.

At the peak of the crisis in 1983, the Dubuque metro area had an average employment level of 37,600 people. That was a decline of more than 6,000 jobs from 1980.[15] As of May 2015, the employment level was 60,400, an increase of 60.6 percent or 1.89 percent per year. Iowa's statewide employment increase during this same period was 52.6 percent or 1.69 percent per year.[16]

The job growth story can be viewed in two phases. The first, the decade of the 1980s, started very strong. After the recession, which hit its low point in Dubuque in 1983, the remainder of the decade was a struggle to return to the 1980 levels. Job growth from 1980 to 1990 was –.006 percent. The second phase (1990–2015) saw a job growth of 36.4 percent. With the exception of the 2001–2002 slowdown following 9/11 and the recession of 2008, there has been very consistent growth in employment. In addition, the quality of jobs created can be seen by the fact that the average hourly wage in Dubuque County is $22.67 per hour—more than twice the average hourly wage in the United States as a whole[17] and almost $3.00 higher than the mean average hourly wage in Iowa.[18]

What we see in Dubuque is steady, mostly organic job growth that has resulted from a carefully planned strategy persistently and consistently implemented over a 31-year period. During this period there have been ups and downs that Dubuque has endured as the city encountered the business cycle swings that have impacted all jurisdictions. Compared to the state of Iowa and the nation, Dubuque has tended to weather recessions such as 2001 and 2008 better than other regions. This was validated by a 2014 ranking of Dubuque as number nine in the country on "economic strength indicators" and number seven nationally in terms of "recession-busting factors." The president and CEO of the GDDC Rick Dickinson commented on the changes in the structure of Dubuque's economy:

> Before 1983 it was a matter of having all of your eggs in two baskets. Twenty-five percent of all the people that worked in Dubuque worked at the Dubuque Packing Company or John Deere. That base of people's jobs was reduced by 75% or, in the case of the Pack, were completely gone. The reason we have weathered the storm so well this time is because our economy is diversified. If you added up the top ten employers in Dubuque today, including the county, John Deere, the public schools, and IBM, they barely add up to 25%. And today (2013), we have 60,000 people working in the metro area of Dubuque, compared to 36,000 in 1983. And it's a nice cross-section of manufacturing, service, financial services, and so while no one is recession proof, we're far more resilient than we were.[19]

How did they do it?

The short answer to the question "How did they do it?" is through community leadership, citizen engagement, planning, and strategic partnerships. The "secret sauce" for Dubuque, as it was for Austin, is collaboration, placing the needs of the community above self-interest and a willingness to do what it takes without concern for who gets the credit. Also central to the ability to create the climate in which these achievements could take place is the honest belief that no single individual or organization has the answer to what must be done to enable Dubuque to move toward its vision—it requires "collective impact."[20]

The Dubuque transformation story is much more than a "job creation" story although job creation is one of the beneficial outcomes. When asked "What has allowed Dubuque to accomplish what it has accomplished?" Tom Woodward, CEO and president of Woodward Communications, Inc.—the parent company of the primary Dubuque newspaper the *Telegraph Herald*—shared six community characteristics that help explain the success. These are:

1. The community DNA—It is the Midwest DNA that is characterized in part by privately owned family businesses which lead to a lot of local decision making.
2. Leadership—There are dedicated community leaders who have provided both time and money. These include Rick Dickinson and his team at the GDDC and the city government's commitment to economic development and the city's funding of economic development initiatives, and the fact that the private business community is at the table of GDDC.
3. Business planning focus—People are honest with themselves and they face the facts. There are a lot of smart people at the table and a focus on the key issues —workforce, land use, education and training, life amenities, and parks and entertainment.
4. Execution—We execute and produce results—we have quantifiable metrics for things that matter—we measure.
5. Collaboration—People have the ability to network and build partnerships.
6. Stewardship and accountability—We take seriously our obligation to protect and improve the assets that have been entrusted to us. We hold ourselves and each other accountable.[21]

These six characteristics provide a glimpse of the context and character of the community. Another CEO, Russell "Rusty" Knight, president and CEO of Mercy Medical Center—Dubuque, adds a seventh: generosity.

Dubuque is a phenomenally generous community. I think the reason is that we are fortunate to have a lot of family owned businesses. The owners are unbelievably community-oriented and generous. I get a lump in my throat talking about it because these people donate so much to so many causes— hospitals, colleges, charities. . . . You cannot underestimate the value of having the presidents and faculty of our colleges in the town. They volunteer their time to serve on Boards and are very community minded people. Their institutions are important to them but so is the community. They want the whole community to succeed. That attitude is typical in Dubuque.[22]

The Transformation of Dubuque—Part 1

The low point of the economic crisis came when unemployment hit 23 percent and for a short time gave the city the dubious distinction of having the highest unemployment rate in the nation. This fact as well as the human pain and misery this situation caused galvanized the community to take action.

Creation of the GDDC

Doug Horstmann, president of Dubuque Bank and Trust and former chairperson of the GDDC, described the origins of the GDDC:

> Initially there was an economic development department in the city. Then it shifted to the Chamber of Commerce. Then a group of major business leaders came together in 1984 and said "This is not working." Why don't we all chip in a bunch of money to create a separate organization that can drive economic development. This was the origin of the Greater Dubuque Development Corporation.[23]

Horstmann went on to point out that it was important that the organization be independent of the city government because "You don't get the buy-in of the business community when it is located in a political unit."[24]

Also commenting on this period, Rick Dickinson, current president and CEO of GDDC, recalled:

> There were organizations—city economic development office, the chamber of commerce—that were concerned with economic development but they were spread out like a dog's breakfast. There was no focus. There were leaders in the community, such as Bruce Merriweather who was head of what became U.S. Bank, and Nick Schrup II, President of American Trust, who said we have to bring people together. They started GDDC as a big-tent organization where everybody had a voice, and no one had control. The Board included the mayor, organized labor, the president of the Council of Governments, representatives of the Board of Supervisors and private sector employers. The budget was approximately $180,000 and it had an office manager and two clerical people.[25]

From 1984 until 1990 the organization had modest success. Three new businesses located in Dubuque and five existing businesses announced expansions.[26] While these successes were welcome, the resources of the GDDC at the beginning were insufficient for the challenge. Turning around an economy that had been so devastated was not a short-term initiative; it would require a rethinking of how the GDDC would operate. It also required some new leadership behavior from its key partner, the city of Dubuque.

Legalized gambling comes to Dubuque

A key decision made by the city in 1986 has turned out to pay great dividends to the community in a number of ways.

> A pari-mutuel dog racing facility was launched by a community bond issue. The city owns the facility and they contracted with a not-for-profit group to operate the facility. This group—the Dubuque Racing Association—consisted of 21 board members who are citizens from Dubuque and they run the organization. In time it became a full blown casino. The group has been quite generous to the city over the years. Each year they pay a fairly generous lease payment to the city to cover the cost of the land and the facility and then at the end of the year they distribute half of their profit to the city and the other half to charity. Last year (2014), the charity contribution was slightly over $1 million.[27]

Rick Dickinson pointed out that the community in the early 1990s still lacked focus and agreement regarding the approaches required to move the city forward.

> Up until the early '90s we were still chewing on each other's ankles. City Council meetings were like a precursor to the Jerry Springer show. They were a political food fight. Three things happened in the early '90s that changed things. Part of it was that the people of Dubuque had had enough. First, in 1992 a new mayor was elected—Terry Duggan. He served three terms. He was a realtor who loved this town and he ran the council meetings like a business meeting. The people also elected talented people for the Council. Second they hired talent to run the city. Mike Van Milligen (hired as City Manager) was a unique talent. He understands that citizens are customers. He eliminated anything that was restrictive with respect to private sector development and businesses attempting to grow. He worked with business. He surrounded himself with like-minded people and changed the culture of the city. Third, the people supported the talent they elected and the talent they hired. And Dubuque has never looked back since.[28]

Arrival of a new city manager

Mike Van Milligen assumed the duties of city manager in January 1993 following a national competitive search. He had started his career after graduating from college as a police officer in Carbondale, Illinois. While working as a police officer, he got his master's in public administration. He then moved to Skokie, Illinois, as head of budget and planning and was then promoted to assistant village manager. After 10 years in that position, Mike, believing he was ready to be a city manager, applied for the position in Dubuque.

After arriving in Dubuque, because of his planning background, Mike decided that the first thing he should do on his first day at work should be to examine the city's comprehensive plan. Here is how Mike described that day:

> My first day in office, I thought I should read the comprehensive city plan. So I pulled it off the bookshelf and it was dated September 1936. It immediately made me wonder and think that all the things that happened here in the '80s happened to the city because they had no plan. The things happened to them instead of them happening to the things. Fortunately the Council had also realized this and had begun a very rigorous approach to develop a new comprehensive plan and they were moving into the third year of a five-year process to develop the plan. Two years after I arrived, the council in 1995 adopted the first comprehensive plan since 1936.[29]

After the plan was approved by the council, the city launched a number of studies that were aligned with key priorities in the plan. The range of studies included the riverfront, downtown, industrial parks, and utility extension. All of these were areas that would require potential capital investment combined with external fund-raising. These studies launched a number of activities that consumed much of the city's focus and resources for the next five years or more.

Mike Van Milligen describes perhaps the most significant of these initiatives—the riverfront initiative. This initiative labeled "Americas River Project" opened in 2003.

> In early 2000 the little Dubuque County Historical Society—just like the historical society in every city, a group of nice people who had an interest in preserving the history of their city—had this executive director, Jerry Enzler, who was looking for an opportunity. The City, with the leadership of GDDC, had gone through an asset mapping process. You will say, "of course"

but it was not "of course."—Guess what the group decided was the Number One asset we figured out we had in Dubuque? It was the Mississippi River. The City had turned its back on the river. It was the garbage dump, a dumping ground; it was the place of dilapidated and decaying buildings. You would not go down to our riverfront for any reason.

This group came up with a $25 million plan to build a National Mississippi River Museum and Aquarium. I was in the room when they announced the plan and thought this is a great plan. I still get chills when I think about it. This $25 million plan turned into a $400 million plan. The Museum was $100 million. Not one nickel of debt. They raised every single penny. Now it is one of the 125 Smithsonian affiliated museums in the country. The city acquired a 90 acre campus on the river now called the Port of Dubuque. The City built a convention center. We worked with a private developer to build a hotel and indoor water park. We took the concrete flood wall and buried it, then built a beautiful river walk. Then McGraw-Hill, a company that was already in town, decided they wanted to build a headquarters building here. Flex-Steel Industries built a beautiful office building. Then Diamond Jo Casino built an $80 million dollar land-based casino and the city built a massive parking deck as part of that project.

In 2003 that was a real turning point when the community realized wow, we can do that! Little Dubuque can build a project of that magnitude— $400 million! That really does good things for your psyche. We can do that![30]

Launch of the Community Foundation of Greater Dubuque

Another key event in 2003 was the opening of the Community Foundation of Greater Dubuque. The mission of the foundation is to strengthen communities and inspire philanthropic giving. The second part of the mission is the role of the foundation to enable members of the community with philanthropic interests to have a way to easily and efficiently support the issues they care about either through immediate donations or through their will or estate plan. The principal donated to the foundation remains permanently in the foundation. The earnings from these funds are used to support the core foundation staff and benefit local charities. Donors direct the funds as they see fit, but the foundation staff provides valuable information on the focus and performance of various charities to assist donor decision making.

Why in a book about economic development and job creation are we devoting time to talk about a community charitable foundation? The answer is very simple. Unless a community is a place where people want to live, you will not have a viable workforce. Without a viable workforce, businesses will not be attracted to the area, and existing businesses will not choose to expand there. Beyond that, key economic development initiatives will succeed or fail depending on citizen acceptance. The foundation through its community leadership mission plays a significant role, usually behind the scenes, to increase the likelihood of success of a wide range of initiatives that impact job creation and especially workforce development.

When the foundation doors opened, Nancy Van Milligen was named president and CEO. At the beginning, the "Foundation was a post office box and an idea."[31] Currently the foundation has assets of $65 million. Since 2003, the foundation has provided grants totaling approximately $25 million to local charities. In addition, the foundation seeks external funding through grants and contracts that enable it to fulfill the first part of its mission—to strengthen communities—beyond what is possible through the work of charitable organizations that receive grants from the foundation.

Van Milligen joined the foundation at a time when community foundations across the country were transitioning from simply holding funds of donors and making grants to assuming more of a community leadership role and serving as conveners and catalysts for solving systemic problems in communities. Her background equipped her well to assume this broader role. She had a master's in public administration, she had taught at the college level, and she had been engaged in working to improve the statewide system for foster care in Iowa. Nancy and her husband Mike, the Dubuque city manager, had "fostered" 14 children. As a "customer" of the foster care system, she was able to see the system from the user perspective while her educational background enabled her to also see the larger system perspective.

One of her actions at the state level had been to encourage the creation of 17 citizen-level boards across eastern Iowa to engage foster parents and provide them a voice in how the system should be operated and improved. She also had a background as a VP of development for a local college, which helped prepare her for her role in working with donors at the foundation. Other than with foster care, she also had statewide commission experience on early childhood education as well as the Iowa Commission on Volunteer Services where she learned how to encourage effective public–private collaboration. These experiences helped her develop a total "large-system" perspective that has been applied very effectively in Dubuque.

Once on the job, Nancy drew on this varied background in terms of how she approached it. Her experience and views regarding the importance of community engagement and citizen engagement received further validation as a result of a "missed opportunity" in Dubuque. In 2005, the city had an opportunity to secure a professional, minor-league baseball team. In order to attract the team the town would have been required to partially finance and construct a new stadium. To move on this opportunity, it was necessary to take the issue to the citizens of Dubuque through a referendum to approve the stadium financing. There were significant time pressures on gaining a decision because of the team's scheduling and other business issues faced by the team owner. A vote was held and the citizens rejected the proposal to fund the stadium construction. Nancy's "take-away" from this experience was that the proposal failed because the community was not engaged before it was asked to vote.

This experience not only confirmed her previous experience regarding the power of engagement, but also propelled her to act. Nancy Van Milligen describes her efforts to engage the people of Dubuque in the process of inventing their future:

> So I went to the Chamber and said would you work with us to do a community visioning process—to really ask the community what they want to have happen? A lot of things were in the works, the riverfront, a lot of change. The Chamber agreed. So we launched Envision 2010. Part of the magic was its simplicity.[32]

The Community Foundation of Greater Dubuque partnered with the Dubuque Area Chamber of Commerce to launch a very broad community engagement process. The work began with the formation of an eight-member steering committee involving the two lead organizations and community and business representatives. The steering committee met for three months to plan the initiative. It designed a process, a logo, and a toolkit that would be used by members of the community to hold a meeting and solicit ideas from other community members.

Eric Dregne, who is now the VP of strategic initiatives for the foundation, joined the steering committee. At the time he joined, he was the general manager of the Younkers Department Store, the largest department store in Dubuque. Eric describes the Envision 2010 process:

> It was an effort to find out where the community wanted to go. What we did was ask the simple question "What should be next for Dubuque?" We pushed that question out to the community. We did a lot of marketing[33] to make sure that people would get the toolkits. In the toolkit we asked people to do three things: (1) think about what should be next for Dubuque, (2) gather a group of people to talk about it, and (3) write down the group's answers and turn them in to the committee.
>
> We got a few thousand people to participate and received over 2,300 ideas. We also had nights where people who did not want to engage their

friends could show up and we would facilitate the conversation. We then formed a 21-person selection committee to narrow the list. The group was representative of the community in terms of diversity and age. They were charged with narrowing the list and they narrowed it to 100. We then took that back out to the community where they narrowed it through a voting process to 30. And then the committee narrowed it to 10—the 10 big ideas that will move the community forward. The committee criterion for selecting the top 10 ideas was "big ideas with broad acceptance that will have a long-term impact on the growth and quality of life of the greater Dubuque community"!

The chosen ideas were things like expansion and improvement of our library system, expansion of the second phase of the River museum, development of the millwork district, Crescent community health center (once a donor realized that the community was behind this issue the donor stepped forward with a million-dollar endowment to make it happen). Some of the ideas were new; others had been out there but had never gotten the traction needed to make it happen.[34]

The complete list of the 10 items that resulted from the Envision 2010 process:

- America's River Project, Phase II
- Bilingual education curriculum
- Community-wide wireless
- Community health center
- Indoor–outdoor performing arts center
- Integrated walking, biking, hiking trail system
- Library services expansion
- Mental health and substance abuse services
- Passenger train services
- Warehouse District revitalization

Eric Dregne described what happened next:

In January 2006 the 10 ideas were announced at a widely publicized community meeting attended by over 600 people. We announced that in two weeks we would have a second meeting where people who were interested in these ideas should attend. At that meeting, we had 10 tables and we had a very intentional handoff. We had batons and we passed the baton to the table and they took the baton physically and literally. At that point the tables had two tasks: choose a team leader and figure out when your next meeting date would occur.[35]

Complete or substantial progress has been made on all the initiatives and most of the implementation teams have now been disbanded. However, in cases in which complete implementation has not yet occurred, such as passenger train service to Chicago, considerable work triggered by Envision 2010 continued. For example, in January 2010, the Illinois governor committed $60 million to create a Chicago–Dubuque passenger route. Further discussions were under way to consider expanding this idea to include high-speed rail between Chicago and other cities, which could help Dubuque in the future. The revitalization of the Warehouse District was not a four-year project although significant progress was made by 2010. That work continues today and the Warehouse District is becoming a showplace for Dubuque in terms of mixed-use development and repurposing vacant historic buildings.

A summary of the results of Envision 2010 was produced by the Community Foundation. In addition to presenting the implementation status of the 10 big ideas, the document captured 10 other lessons learned and presented them as "Envis10n . . . So Much More Than 10 Ideas."[36]

1. **Dubuque's Envision 2010 Served as a Catalyst for Dozens of Other Community Projects:** These included Every Child/Every Promise, Accessdubuquejobs.com, Kennedy Mall revitalization, Mystique Community Ice Center, Distinctively Dubuque, Sustainable Dubuque, Dubuque 2.0, the Petal Project, Young Professionals of Dubuque, Project Hope and the beat goes on. . . .

2. **Great Leadership Does Make a Difference:** Envision 2010 created a portal for the emergence and development of new talent and leadership for our community.

3. **Process Matters:** Envision 2010 was not as much about the accomplishment of the 10 ideas in their purest sense, but more about trusting that the community would ultimately decide where our community was headed.

4. **The Journey is More Important than the Destination:** Envision 2010 taught us that our goals are perpetual and they evolve and change with the needs of our community.

5. **Public and Private Partnerships Are the Key to Success:** Our deliberate actions to achieve real things have shown again and again that when we work together anything is possible.

6. **Imitation Is the Sincerest Form of Flattery:** Envision 2010 proved its sustainability as a, replicable model for other communities. The Envision 2010 process has been recognized, honored and emulated by cities in Iowa, the Midwest and the nation.

7. **Let's Get Excited:** Envision 2010 energized, excited and ignited a community hungry to get involved and answer the question "What's next for Dubuque?"

8. **Failure is Not an Option:** The goal was not an ending but a launching pad to what is possible. The community decided what it needed to do to make our dreams/ideas a reality, what worked for our community and what didn't and how we needed to adapt and evolve our wants to what was the best fit for our community.

9. **It Does Not Matter Who Gets the Credit:** From America's River to All-American City we know how to make things happen. We don't care who gets the credit—we care about getting it done.

10. **Dream Big and Big Things Happen:** The 10 ideas were all lofty and creative goals and we did not let circumstances limit our possibilities. Great things happen when you dare to dream big.

The Transformation of Dubuque—Part 2

In 2005 the citizens of Dubuque elected a new mayor. Upon his election Mayor Buol asserted: "The next five years will define the next 50 for Dubuque." His platform was based on "engaging citizens as partners." As a member of the city council the mayor had been supportive of the launch of Envision 2010 which was a citizen-led initiative, supported by the then mayor and council, but not initiated or led by city government.

In 2006, Mayor Buol with support from the council stated that "cities that get out in front on sustainability as a top city priority will have competitive economic advantages in the future."[37] After making this announcement and after signing the U.S. Conference of Mayors Climate Protection Agreement in support of the Kyoto Protocol, Mayor Buol formed the Sustainable Dubuque Commission and charged the commission to come back to the council in 18 months with a comprehensive definition of what sustainability would mean for Dubuque. Members of this 40-citizen group represented most of the key stakeholders in the community, including local government, schools, utility companies, religious organizations, neighborhood associations, youth organizations, nonprofit organizations, the business community, and environmental organizations. Their product was a vision statement, a logo, and a set of driving principles for what came to be called "Sustainable Dubuque."

In a conversation with Mayor Buol, I asked what led him to make sustainability a core city focus. He explained:

> When I was running for mayor, I already had grandchildren. I saw the consumption patterns where we were using 25% of the world's resources and thought about what will happen when others in the world want their part. People kept talking to me about social and cultural issues and about air

quality, water quality and availability. Then I started talking to businesses and about how they will operate in the future and what they will require. If a business is doing something sustainably, they will probably be ahead of others in their sector.

I made the statement to the Council in my first goal-setting session in 2006 that I really believe that cities that get out in front on sustainability will have a marked economic advantage in the very near future.[38]

I also asked him about the need to convene a commission to "define" sustainability for Dubuque. He shared his thoughts that truly revealed his fundamental belief about how one should govern when in public office:

I really felt that if we were going to do anything significant, we better get the community to buy-in. They had to lead or be a major part of the discussion. You can make all the policy you want, but if citizens don't want it—long term it is not going anywhere! Everybody should have a voice—you don't have to agree, but you have to listen and understand their perspective. Ever since I first ran for the Council I was always focused on engaging citizens as partners. When we involved them to develop the sustainability plan, they hit it out of the ballpark![39]

This philosophy led to the community-developed vision adopted by the council, which states:

Dubuque is a viable, livable and equitable community. We embrace economic prosperity, environmental integrity, and social/cultural vibrancy to create a sustainable legacy for generations to come.[40]

This brief and powerful vision statement became the "lens" that city policy makers use to consider all new proposed policy decisions. The statement reflects many of the values of the community, and these values are defined more specifically in the 12 principles that further articulate the vision (Table 6.1).

To serve as the focal point for Sustainable Dubuque, the city hired Cori Burbach who has the title "sustainable community coordinator." Cori was the first person in Iowa to have such a title. She participated in the commission that developed the sustainability vision for the city. Cori was ideally suited for the role of coordinator as she has a very engaging personality and brings tremendous energy to the role. She talks about how the commission approached its task:

Table 6.1 How Dubuque Defines Sustainability

Dubuque is a community that values . . .

Community design	*The built environment of the past, present, and future which contributes to its identity, heritage, and sense of place*
Smart energy use	*Energy conservation and expanded use of renewable energy as a means to save money and protect the environment*
Resource management	*The benefits of reducing, reusing, and recycling resources*
Regional economy	*A diversified regional economy with opportunities for new and green markets, jobs, products, and services*
Green buildings	*A productive and healthy built environment*
Community knowledge	*Education, empowerment, and engagement to achieve economic prosperity, environmental integrity, and social/cultural vibrancy*
Healthy local foods	*The benefits of wholesome food from local producers, distributors, farms, gardens, and hunters*
Community health and safety	*Systems, policies, and engagement to ensure that all residents have access to healthy and safe lifestyle choices*
Reasonable mobility	*Safe, reasonable, and equitable choices that enable access to opportunities to live, work, and play*
Healthy air	*Fresh, clean air, reduced greenhouse gas emissions, and minimized health risks*
Clean water	*Water as the source of life, and seeks to preserve and manage it in all forms*
Native plants and animals	*Biodiversity through the preservation, restoration, and connection of nature and people*

Source: Table created by the author from the principles and their definitions in the publication: City of Dubuque, *Creating an International Model for Sustainability* (Dubuque, Iowa: Author, October 20, 2014).

> From day one, this is not just an environmental issue. The question the mayor asked during his campaign was what type of community do we want to create? What would cause your children to decide to live here? So this has always been about a broader issue such as "quality of life." But we framed it as sustainability.[41]

This vision not only serves to guide decision making by city government, the private economic development organization also aligns its practices with this vision. When asked to comment on how the GDDC supports Sustainable Dubuque, Rick Dickinson described how they integrate sustainability into their economic development practices:

With Sustainable Dubuque we are "reactive" to political directive. We try to find a way to position political issues in ways that work for our business community. We are proactive on the issues of the day that our clients are dealing with. We feel that Sustainable Dubuque is a great brand for us in recruiting companies and for recruiting talent.

With regard to sustainability for businesses, we run seminars for companies with vendors of fixtures and lighting, we have utilities give seminars on ways to conserve energy and do energy audits in order for businesses to save money through energy conservation. We don't get into discussions regarding whether climate change is real. But we do get into discussions about how to conserve energy, which reduces emissions which also reduces our carbon footprint.

We look for things that will improve the workplace, while simultaneously improving our community. And you get the added benefit that if you believe in climate change these things will benefit that as well.[42]

When asked to elaborate about how he "sells" sustainability to employers who are his clients, Rick provided some very pragmatic ideas:

One size does not fit all. But becoming more productive and more efficient does fit all. For example, we have entered into an agreement with the U.S. EPA to be one of the initial participants in Advanced PM 2.5. We have had four consecutive years of reductions in particulate matter even though our economy has grown during that period. We have two motives. We do not want our companies to have restrictions on the type of equipment they can install based on the particulate matter. We also do not want to limit the types of companies we can recruit to the area. The other side of it is that we want cleaner air for our children and families to breathe. This reduction in particulate matter has come from shifting our energy sources for generating electricity. John Deere used to have a coal-fired generating plant as a backup. Now they have a gas-fueled plant.

When we work with businesses we do not take the regulatory approach —"You should do . . ." We look for ways that sustainable practices can reduce resource consumption and help us become more efficient, improve productivity and reduce costs. What might we do with alternative practices? For example, converting from gas to diesel, bio diesel or compressed natural gas as alternatives. We approach it in an assistance way. . . . We are saying "If you do this, this might happen." We bring in this best practice by company A, B or C to demonstrate how they have done it. We want to share this and let you decide if this might be beneficial to your business.

Sustainability basically is quality of life.[43]

IBM Comes to Dubuque

On January 15, 2009, during the recession triggered by the global financial crisis, the *Telegraph Herald*, Dubuque's major newspaper, announced some very positive news. IBM and city leaders would hold a press conference to announce that Dubuque had been chosen as the site to locate its first major new nonmanufacturing operation in a smaller U.S. community in over two decades. This announcement was the culmination of an extensive effort by the GDDC and other city leaders to woo IBM to Dubuque. The *Telegraph Herald* headline boldly announced "1,300 Jobs" and pointed out that the location of this global service technology center would bring 1,300 jobs with an average wage of $45,000, and an annual payroll of $58.5 million. IBM's total investment would be $120 million.[44]

Speaking in 2013, Rick Dickinson called it the most significant economic development event in Dubuque since 2008.

> It was the most impactful thing because the tools that we prepared in order to successfully recruit IBM have also been in place for a number of other successes.[45]

Smarter Sustainable Dubuque

The location of the global service center was only the beginning of IBM's relationship with Dubuque. Mayor Buol described what came next:

> IBM had been looking for some time for a community where they could integrate their technology to build an integrated smarter city. After they selected Dubuque for their Service Center, they had heard about our public-private partnerships and so we got a call from their Watson Research Center. They wanted to partner with us on something. It just came down to sustainability and smarter city as the focus. They knew from their previous experience with us that we could bring people to the table who were engaged and that we could get things done.[46]

Dave Lyons added further details to this discussion. Dave was trained as an attorney but has had an impressive career in public service and as a private consultant. He was the former insurance commissioner for Iowa, former director of the Iowa Department of Economic Development and former VP of the Farm Bureau. As director of economic development he was ahead of his time in moving the state away from direct incentives to earned incentives, and then to primarily using state funds for infrastructure support. When he assumed the director's position, 70 percent of Iowa's economic development support went to direct incentives for firms moving into the state or expanding. By the time he left the position, 90 percent of the incentives were earned incentives but a larger part of the budget was spent on infrastructure support than incentives of any type. As VP of development for the Farm Bureau, Dave was responsible for establishing the early ethanol plants that were beneficial to Iowa's corn farmers, as well as the biodiesel plants and wind energy development in which Iowa was an early leader in the country.

Following IBM's expression of interest in a partnership between the city of Dubuque and its Watson Research Center, Mayor Buol and Mike Van Milligen engaged Dave Lyons in a consulting role to be the city's primary point of contact with IBM. Dave provides his perspective on the IBM–Dubuque relationship:

> IBM was interested in Dubuque for very traditional reasons. They had not made a significant investment in the U.S. for a very long time. They decided it was time to change that investment pattern and locate a Global Service Center in the U.S. They did a nation-wide search for a site and they chose Dubuque. . . . Through its normal process Dubuque got on the list. We met all their traditional economic development site selection criteria and in addition, Dubuque had this "feel" to it. So Dubuque was selected.[47]

Mike Van Milligen described how IBM went about the due diligence process that led to its selection of Dubuque, as well as what happened next:

> When the VP of IBM made the announcement that we were selected, he said you have made a lot of promises to us, but we believe that you can deliver based on the partnerships that you have here in your community. And believe me, they looked at every nook and cranny in the community. They had three major site visits; they had sub-teams investigating different aspects. They also said there is a synergy here with our corporate philosophy. We are about creating a Smarter Planet and you have made Sustainability your Number One priority. So we match philosophically. They also liked that there are 322,000 college students within 100 miles of Dubuque.
>
> IBM announced they were coming to Dubuque on January 15, 2009. In March I had a phone call from the VP of IBM who ran the Watson Research Center. He said "I want to come to visit you for a couple of days." I asked "Why?" He said, here in New York all that I am hearing is people talking about Dubuque. We did all this research and we chose Dubuque and everyone here thinks it is a great idea. I have to come and see this place for myself.

I said "Fine"—so we hosted him for three days. At the end of the visit he said "Mike, I have bigger plans for Dubuque."

A couple of weeks later we had this massive conference call. We had 50 people in a room with this massive video screen and he had 10 people with him in New York. This question was what types of partnerships can we create for the Watson Research Center in Dubuque. It was an all-day brainstorming session. . . . He called me a few days later and said "Mike, here is what we are looking for. We have been looking for one city in North America where we can create a Smarter City model for a Smarter Planet. You are it. I would like to come to Dubuque and announce it."[48]

To differentiate the joint initiative with IBM from the existing Sustainable Dubuque initiative, this joint effort was labeled "Smarter Sustainable Dubuque." The IBM–Dubuque partners chose to focus initially on water conservation. This project exemplified the key principles that underlie the partnership in terms of the "interests" of the partners. Dave Lyons described the approach:

We turned the relationship with IBM into a partnership where the city was able to get what it needed, which was to harness data faster and better to solve problems. It gave IBM the opportunity to have a living laboratory. The city was big enough that the results would have statistical relevance and it was small enough that they could get answers quickly.

We did smarter water based on the theory that water is a precious re-source since cities waste 40–50% of their water. Leaks do not have a billable address. IBM is very interested in this as part of their city services management process. The research challenge was to link data with water. This would enable us to tell how much is being manufactured, how much is being lost, where it is being lost, when it is being lost, etc. This has to be a community engagement process if it is going to work as information must go to people who actually use the water. We need a dashboard that will let the user have the information required to make decisions regarding their water use. . . . The dashboard allowed people to choose one of three settings. One allowed people to see the comparisons between water use at different times in terms of money. This is how much is wasted and how much it is costing you. The second option was waste in terms of gallons. And the third was in terms of the carbon footprint. You have to give people information tailored to them that is actionable. To make it actionable, we had to tell them where we thought the leak was. So a homeowner would get a note saying you have a leak and we think the leak is in the shower.[49]

One of the key people involved in the implementation of this project was Chris Kohlmann. Chris is the information services manager for the city of

Dubuque. Chris commented on how involvement in this project, working with the IBM team, helped her and members of her department transform their thinking:

> In 2009 when the project started with IBM I was still thinking in the old paradigm and I was probably dismissed from more meetings than I was invited to. I was coming up with all these reasons why we should not do it—e.g. capacity, human capital; technology is not aligned with us, etc. However, as we began to work with the researchers on the project [my view changed]. . . . What we gained were new thought processes around data. Finding new ways to think can be more valuable in the long run than new "stuff."
>
> We continue as a department to go through a transformational shift. . . . With our focus on engagement, our staff needs to be attuned to the needs of our internal customers as well as citizens. . . . How do we engage people around data? . . . We need to focus on lean processes to be more agile and able to shift gears more quickly when something does not work. . . . A lot of our partnership with IBM has led us to shift our metrics from outputs to outcomes. With water the obvious issue is the environmental piece—number of gallons saved. However, in Dubuque, water is abundant and cheap. So what will move the needle and get people's attention? When we began to focus on leaks, it was an example of shifting our focus to the system.
>
> What citizens want is to have choices. Some want to save money and some want to save the environment and some want to do both. The information about leaks provided people with the information that enabled them to do both. . . . We got an eight-fold increase in leak detection because we made it easier for them to find a leak. The other thing was it hooked people up to the grant which provided up to $100 to use to fix the leaks in their house.[50]

Smarter Sustainable Dubuque projects have moved beyond the water project into other areas of city services, which have helped the community become more viable and more livable—two key aspects of the Dubuque vision. Mike Van Milligen summarizes the efforts quite concisely:

> We did a pilot project around water conservation and the pilot homes cut water usage by 7%. We did a pilot project around electricity usage and the pilot homes reduced electricity consumption by 3–7%. We just completed a project around recycling. We are two years into a four-year pilot around transportation. Through this project we were able to completely redesign our transit system and we have increased our ridership by 28% through the data we have obtained. We are now contemplating the next project and it will be about a still larger concept.[51]

Dave Lyons, who has spearheaded these projects as a consultant to the GDDC, the lead organization for working with IBM on Smarter Sustainable Dubuque, captured the essence of these projects with the design specification stated as:

> How do I give people what they need (information that is specific to them and that is actionable) so that they can do what they want?[52]

There is another key facet to this story regarding Smarter Sustainable Dubuque. Nancy Van Milligen, CEO of the Community Foundation, picks up the story here:

> One day Eric and I went to a meeting when IBM was talking about putting these black boxes in people's basements (i.e., the data feedback boxes for the water project) and how consumers having better information could change their behavior.
> Eric and I looked at each other. Our work has shown us that information isn't enough; that if information alone will change people's behavior then no one would smoke cigarettes. We push hard not to do things "to" people but rather to do things "with" people.
> We knew we needed "community engagement."
> We were able to obtain a $200,000 grant with the Knight Foundation totally for the purpose of engaging and informing people around this Smarter Sustainable Dubuque effort. . . . We (as the private Community Foundation) could do some things that the City could not do. We were very effective in the water pilot. We had people singing on buses, asking people to journal their actions, getting colleges to compete against each other, etc. These activities helped consumers internalize the information and allowed us to have better results and actually, be very effective in the water pilot.[53]

Eric Dregne elaborated on the engagement initiative led by the Community Foundation, which was labeled Dubuque 2.0:

> We were at a meeting with a group of community leaders and raised the question of whether this (the IBM smart city concepts) would really work. That is, whether the system and just the data shared with people would be enough to get people to change their behavior and have a more sustainable lifestyle. We gave examples that if it were true that people were that data driven, no one would smoke. With gas selling at $4.80 a gallon we would not be driving the way we are right now. So there must be more to it than just the data. The data is important but it may not be sufficient. So we asked the question, if we are going to do this project who is going to engage the

community and what process will we have to help understand and care about the data that will be coming out of this little black box that will be in their basement on their computer desk? Why would they even let you do it if they were not engaged?

I think we brought to IBM the engagement process as well as the entrepreneurial or progressive spirit to try this stuff and put water meters in 22,000 homes. We put this same pitch to our local utility that this worked so well with water let's see if it would work with electricity. They agreed to do 1,000 homes. There was another project to help us redesign our bus routes. All along, Dubuque 2.0's role was to talk about these projects and get information out. We hosted community cafés to talk about sustainability. We had a number of different topics. We didn't limit the conversation to water meters. The idea was just to get people thinking about the bigger picture. Then when the water meter conversion was happening they could say, "Oh yeah, this is just part of the sustainability thing. Overall it is good."[54]

Particularly in the case of Smarter Sustainable Dubuque, we can clearly see what makes Dubuque a special place. Dave Lyons clearly articulated what this "secret sauce" really is and how it originated following the crisis of the 1980s. Dave has been intimately involved in many of the key initiatives in Dubuque as a private consultant. Living in Des Moines and having served in a number of statewide roles, he has had the opportunity to closely examine other Iowa cities as well.

In the '80s recession, Dubuque was hammered. It was at the tipping point. What happened was that the community formed a very interesting alliance —an organic one and a virtual one—between the for-profit sector, the non-profit sector and the governmental sector. People did not know what to do, but they realized that the problems were so big they could not be solved by any sector acting alone. It was a "fight or flee" time.

They formed a very close communication process that continues until today. It operates like an interlocking Board of Directors in a holding company. There are separate operational units but the boards are interlocked. Everyone knows what is going on and it can act very quickly. The non-profit, for-profit and governmental leaders talk and innovate together. It allowed them to solve some of the critical problems they had in the '80s in terms of diversification of industry and transportation issues. This tripartite infrastructure allows Dubuque to react earlier to opportunities than a community like Dubuque could normally do. It also allows them to pursue opportunities more flexibly. They recognize that the City is in a somewhat unique place—it is too big for small city solutions and too small for big city approaches.[55]

Luring IBM to Dubuque really put the city on the national map in terms of economic development. *Business Facilities Magazine* selected the Dubuque/IBM project as the Economic Development Deal of the Year and *Site Selection* magazine honored the IBM Project as a "Top Deal of 2009."[56] Rick Dickinson, president and CEO of the GDDC, describes what happened after the word of the IBM deal spread across the economic development communities in the country:

> With IBM coming here it is not about the number of jobs—it is about the brand. IBM brought a brand to Dubuque that we could not have bought for love or money. It was the best brand in the world.
>
> After the IBM decision to come here we had a flurry of activity from other cities trying to understand why IBM chose Dubuque because these cities knew they were better than we were. When we told them that the secret sauce was that we work well together, we have civility in our community, we collaborate and support each other and that sustainability is part of the ethos of our community, they looked at us and said we don't want to hear that. We want the silver bullet.[57]

The Economic Development Lead Organization—The GDDC

The cornerstone economic development organization of the "organic" alliance that was created after the 1980s recession is the GDDC. The GDDC is led by its president and CEO, Rick Dickinson, who reports to and is guided by a 42-person board of directors. The board is led by an annually rotating chairperson and an executive committee composed of 17 of the 42 board members who focus on the day-to-day business. The full board meets quarterly. Members of the board come from large and small private sector businesses, from government—city, county, state, and council of governments, education—both K–12 and higher education, and organized labor. Board members are the top persons from the organization they represent.

Greater Dubuque is a private organization funded by five-year capital campaigns. The current "Next" campaign runs from 2012 to 2017. The funding goal was $8 million and the organization raised $9.5 million. The GDDC budget is approximately $2 million per year with two-thirds coming from the private sector and one-third from the public sector.

Each capital campaign also resets the goals for the next five years. For example, the NEXT goals for this campaign include the following by 2017: $700 million in new construction; to achieve an employment level of 60,000 jobs with an average hourly wage of at least $18.00 per hour;

and to grow the population to 96,500. The results reported in the 2014–2015 annual report are summarized in Table 6.2.

The GDDC has five primary activities. Rick Dickinson, president and CEO, provides an overview of these activities:

> Basically, we do five things here. Our first priority is business expansion and retention. That should be a "no-brainer" but it is not. Most organizations like our own—that is not their focus and they would be almost embarrassed to even say it. Our first priority is taking care of the people that are here. Based on the input from existing employers regarding their needs we developed our second priority program, which is Workforce Solutions. Our third program is business recruitment. We believe we are better at recruitment because of our business retention program. We have a better understanding of the product we are trying to sell since we can see it through the eyes of the people who are already here. Plus, any companies that consider coming here will contact existing employers to see what it is like here. They want to know "Do they take care of you?"
>
> Our fourth and fifth programs are new to us. Fourth is Sustainable Innovation and fifth is Startup Dubuque. Dave Lyons leads both these efforts.[58]

The GDDC has relocated to the historic Millwork District of Dubuque and has its office in a repurposed and renovated "green" building. Not only is it a beautiful and functional building, but it also speaks to GDDC's integrity with respect to sustainability as an "ethos" by serving as a living example of this ethos in practice. In addition, in similar quarters next door, it has established its business incubator and virtual one-stop support program for assisting new business creation under their Startup Dubuque banner.

Table 6.2   Progress on 2012–2017 NEXT Goals

Goal	2017 target	2014 level	Comments
Population growth	96,500	96,370	
New construction	$700 million	$540 million	
Employment	60,000	59,000	700 new jobs added in Q1 2015
Average hourly wage	$18.00	$24.61	As of March 2015

Source: Created by the author based on statistics reported by the Greater Dubuque Development Corporation in its 2014–2015 Annual Report: Greater Dubuque Development Corporation, Momentum: reaching the NEXT level (Dubuque, Iowa: Author, undated), www.greaterdubuque.org/media/user-files/subsite_88/files/2015_Annual Report.pdf.

The GDDC is ideally configured to carry out its mission in Dubuque. First it is a private sector organization, separated from partisan electoral politics. Its funding strategy combined with its separation from politics enables the organization to establish priorities and remain focused on longer term initiatives rather than be "whip-sawed" by the urgencies of the moment or the "hot political issue" of the moment. It can ask the question, "What type of economy do the citizens of Dubuque want us to create?" and then develop and execute programs that support this economic development vision. While the GDDC is separated from politics, the organization has a very close personal and organizational relationship with both the mayor and city manager. GDDC supports the mayor's initiatives, for example, Sustainable Dubuque and Smarter Sustainable Dubuque, and the city manager and the mayor pay attention to and listen to the needs of local businesses as articulated by the GDDC.

Unlike the Chamber of Commerce, which is the public advocate for business, the GDDC works behind the scenes and seeks to build community consensus through its diverse board on key issues. Rick Dickinson points out that the GDDC would never show up at a council meeting or critique any public official or endorse any public policy. Instead, it advocates for specific projects behind the scenes that enhance Dubuque as a place to do business or that meet the needs of employer A, B, or C. However, it would not advocate even behind the scenes on any partisan issue like "right to work" or whatever happens to be the political issue of the day.

GDDC's business retention and expansion program

The business retention and expansion program of the GDDC is led by Dan McDonald. Dan is assisted by two existing business specialists, Bill Baum and Rob Apel. Together they exemplify their mantra to "focus like a laser beam on existing businesses." The primary approach they use to carry out this focus is their nationally recognized Info-Action program. The basic goals of this program are quite straightforward and simple—obtain information on what businesses need to grow and then take action to make sure they get what they need. Rick Dickinson pointed out that in the Info-Action meetings there is a need to separate the "top of the mind" issues from the "deal breakers":

Top of the mind issues are the things you read in the newspaper as typical business community complaints, e.g. "the taxes are too high, we need to be a right to work state," etc. These are the knee-jerk issues that have an impact on businesses but they are emotional. Deal breakers are workforce, space, relationships, things that are fundamental to the way the business operates.[59]

The key to the success of this program is sustained, successful implementation. Dan Mc Donald describes their approach:

> It is not glamorous, it is not sexy, it does not garner the news headlines. . . . What we have done consistently, and I mean consistently, as tempting as it is to get off that, is to meet with nearly 350 businesses per year. This year we will have met with 345. We are not just stopping in to say "howdy." We sit down, establish rapport and make sure that we have a relationship that whenever issues come up they will let us know. When issues come up, most of them are man-made issues. We can't control what happens in the marketplace, but we can make sure that we remove any and all barriers that are non-free market related that if removed can improve the company's ability to grow.
>
> It would perhaps be logical to meet only with "primary sector industries"—a manufacturer, located here doing interstate commerce, selling outside the area and bringing money back into the region. But we decided over a decade ago to also meet with what we call "indicator companies"— presidents and CEOs of all the large financial companies and service companies. They see things that we do not typically see. We also meet with small entrepreneurial companies. Some time ago I met with a company that had two employees. We met in a broom closet somewhere. Today they have 50 employees and are selling products all over the country.[60]

A key tool that is used in these Info-Action meetings is a software tool called Synchronist. This tool is used by over 30 states and jurisdictions including Austin, Texas, in its business retention activity. Dubuque was the first location in Iowa to adopt the software but it is now used across the state. Within the state of Iowa there are approximately 1,200 business retention calls done per year. The GDDC does 340 of those calls. Dubuque, with only 3 percent of the state's population, does 28 percent of the business retention calls. This is a measure of how much emphasis Dubuque places on business retention.

> The software allows the GDDC to create a database and track trends with respect to the concerns of the business community. It was from an analysis of this data that the GDDC decided to create its Workforce Solutions program as this was a strong need pointed out by the business retention visits with CEOs. Talking about the software Dan McDonald notes "The software is a tool, but it is secondary to getting out from behind your desk and actually meeting another human being and saying how can we help you."[61]

It is this "we care" and "we are here to help you" attitude that seems to permeate everyone at the GDDC and the mayor's and city manager's offices.

City Manager Mike Van Milligen commented on these meetings and their importance as well:

> Every Wednesday morning from 10:30 to 12:00 Rick, his staff, my economic development director and I meet. . . . Someone needs a pothole fixed, someone needs a stop sign, someone is contemplating a $30 million expansion of their business. The CEOs want to have these conversations (with GDDC in the Info-Action sessions) because someone is listening and things get done.

These comments were echoed in my interviews with business leaders. I asked the business interviewees to rate the effectiveness of the city in responding to business concerns. Byron Taylor, the former general manager of John Deere Dubuque Works, who had recently retired from this position, had this to say:

> I had a great experience with John Deere as a company and Dubuque as a community. Both are entrenched with their values and have a real commitment to their citizens and to their employees. . . . I would rate city government as a double plus (that would be equivalent to a 5 on a five point rating scale where 5 was the top grade). When we would have a business issue and we have had a couple, I could engage the city and county governments and have always found them to be receptive. And I have found them to help in ways that were unexpected. . . . We had an interruption of service due to a cut in a fiber-optic line. We got immediate service—that is the type of commitment and service we see from the city, the development organizations and the civic organizations.[62]

Russell M. Knight, president of Mercy Hospital, spoke of how the Info-Action process is also used by the GDDC board as important data to guide its strategic planning initiatives:

> In their Info-Action process they ask "What is working?" "What is not working?" "What do you worry about?" Then they do a nice job of compiling that information from all their respondents and identifying issues and concerns. They then can say "We are really worried about the tax structure" or that "Transportation is not acceptable—we need to be lobbying to have it improved." They do a good job of getting that information from everybody and using it to look ahead and use the data as input to a strategic plan to address the issues and concerns.[63]

When Dan McDonald was asked to share evidence of how this business retention focus works, he shared this observation:

> We have two new industrial parks—on the south side is the Dubuque Technology Park and on the west side is the Dubuque Industrial Center-West. We have approximately 30 businesses in those two parks. Ninety-two percent of those businesses were existing business expansions. Over a 15-year period that is the way it is supposed to work and the way it does work.[64]

When asked to talk about their use of financial or other incentives to promote business expansion Dan explained their approach:

> In economic development the dirty little secret is that the big time money too often goes to the glitzy, shiny stuff. The number of business expansions that require financial incentives is far less than the number of opportunities that come through site selection firms. Many of the 30 firms [in our business parks] did not get a dime of funding. The ones that did received "pay to play" money. For example, we have tax increment financing. In order to get that tax refund over a 10-year period, (1) you have to build that $6 million facility and (2) you have to pay your property taxes in order to get the rebate. It is not cash-on-the-barrelhead like these big headlines you see.
>
> The other major tool is our State of Iowa 260e jobs training program. The way that works is if you are adding 30 employees to your payroll, we will take a part of your employee withholding tax that goes into a pot in Des-Moines and refund that to you to offset training costs and salary while new employees are in training. However, if you are not meeting your payroll, there is no rebate. You actually have to pay-in to get it back.
>
> We can provide a number of tangible or intangible benefits. From an airport issue to a zoning issue to developing links to a college or university for a taxpayer subsidized service, we try to make a problem disappear. Iowa State University provides the engineering extension service . . . and we connect the names and faces and serve as brokers to link service providers with clients.[65]

GDDC's Workforce Solutions programs

Workforce Solutions is a key program for the GDDC. The program evolved from employer comments obtained during the Info-Action meetings with business leaders. This workforce program is led by Sarah Harris VP of Workforce Solutions. Sarah and her GDDC team focus on the current and emerging workforce needs of employers in the Greater Dubuque region. Sarah describes the philosophy that guides their work:

> Workforce development is a community effort. Collaboration has served us well. If you can get all of your partners together and get everybody on the same page with regard to workforce and put all your egos aside and work together to identify and solve the problems that is the way to be successful. Data is a huge piece of the issue. You can't develop strategies for perceived problems; you have to know what the problem really is. And you have to listen to people. We do that really well.

The GDDC Workforce Solutions program has three key initiatives. First is HR-Action. This program is similar to the Info-Action program conducted by the GDDC business retention program. With HR-Action Sarah meets with approximately 150 human resource executives per year to gather information from them regarding their current and future workforce issues, needs, and concerns. She also uses the Synchronist software to document and capture the qualitative data from the interviews. This allows her to analyze trends and compare what she hears from HR executives with what Dan McDonald and his business retention team learn from CEOs with regard to workforce issues.

The second workforce initiative positions GDDC as a data hub for workforce data. While the HR-Action program gathers qualitative data, the data hub initiative seeks to obtain, analyze, and review quantitative information. The GDDC contracted with Economic Modeling Specialists International, a firm that brings together data from 90 different state and federal databases and enables Sarah to query these databases to define projected workforce gaps, for example, the 10 job titles paying over $20 per hour with the greatest gap between the number of jobs available and the number of qualified candidates to fill those jobs within a given region. Not only do these databases enable Sarah to identify "gaps" that need to be filled, but they also allow her to monitor changes in workforce data that enable GDDC to evaluate the impact of their actions in terms of closing previously identified gaps. Sarah provides additional insight into how this data hub initiative can help her work with partners to develop data-based strategies to address community workforce needs:

> I see us as a data hub for workforce development. We now have a subscription to the consultant's database so we can pull data and do analyses ourselves. . . . When you look at the top 50 occupations [in Dubuque and the six contiguous counties] that pay over $17 per hour there will be a gap

of 7,471 over the next 10 years. The data tells us that even if we can train every unemployed or underemployed person in our region we will still not be able to fill all the positions we need to fill. We must go outside of our region and maybe outside of our country to recruit people to the region to close these gaps. This is great data to have because it enables us to go to our stakeholders and point out what we need to do.[66]

The third workforce initiative is Dubuque Works. This initiative mirrors the comment made by Sarah that workforce development is a community effort that requires collaboration. Dubuque Works is coordinated and led by the GDDC and involves three major funding partners and 12 program partners. The structure of Dubuque Works is shown in Figure 6.1. Sarah Harris describes the goals of Dubuque Works:

> The program has three goals: Human Capital—the partners identify and address the recruitment, retention and relocation needs as defined by employers; Skill Development—partners build workforce capacity by enhancing training to meet employer demand; and Collaboration and Evaluation—partners combine collaborative workforce efforts with quality research to generate evidence-based practices that improve performance and outcomes for local employers.[67]

As shown in Figure 6.1 the major inputs to the process in Dubuque Works include the goals of the initiative, funding for programs, and data inputs that identify the gaps that the partners must work to close. Once the gaps are identified, partners discuss and decide how, collectively, they will address these workforce needs. Each partner manages and directs its

Figure 6.1 Organizational Structure of Dubuque Works (Based on interviews with Sarah Harris, June 8, 2015 and August 31, 2015 and on *Dubuque Works: 2014–15 Annual Report*)

own programs, but as a collective group, the partners assure that they align their efforts in order to close the gaps that are identified.

In some cases the programs generate their own funds, such as Access Dubuque Jobs.com which is an Internet site that links jobs with applicants. Over 150 local companies pay an annual fee to list their jobs on the site. The site attracts over 80,000 visitors per month and more than 1,000 jobs are posted per month. Over 3,800 résumés are posted by job seekers per month. This site is sponsored by the Telegraph Herald Media Company, a division of Woodward Communications, and a portion of the income from the site is provided to the GDDC to support other Dubuque Works programs.

Within Dubuque Works some of the programs are collaborative partnerships led by Dubuque Works program partners as well as community partners beyond the core Dubuque Works members. For example, a key partner in Dubuque Works is the Community Foundation of Greater Dubuque. This organization has its own funding resources and supports and facilitates initiatives such as Project Hope, which is an initiative with several subprojects all designed to reduce poverty by increasing access to education and employment. One of the subprojects under Project Hope is Re-engage Dubuque. This is a very successful and creative effort to connect young people aged 16–21 who dropped out of high school to schooling that will give them a high school diploma or High School Equivalency Diploma and employable skills.

Another key partner in Dubuque Works that funds its own project is the Dubuque Area Chamber of Commerce. The chamber funds and leads a career academy that is geared to helping local college students prepare for success in the workforce. The students receive counseling on business networking, résumé writing, and interviewing skills, and are connected with local CEOs and human resource executives in local companies who give practical career advice. In addition, the program provides a way for local companies to attract talented college students to their businesses.

Another set of programs within Dubuque Works are programs that are funded by GDDC through private funds raised from key partners. An example of this would be newcomer services. Sarah Harris pointed out that by talking to employers such as IBM she learned that there was a "gap" in services to new arrivals to the community. The community did not have a good way to welcome new people, especially those with international backgrounds, and help them imbed themselves into the community.

Sarah identified potential partner organizations in the community who dealt with some aspect of this issue and brought them all together in a room. Sarah describes what happened:

We had the people in the room who carried out the work in their respective organizations. I stated to them that your boss has given permission for you to say what is not working (with respect to this issue of welcoming newcomers). I then asked them if there is anything you are now doing that is not working that you would like to move off of your plate. One person stated that "I run the trailing spouse program and when someone moves here and their spouse comes as well, I try to help them find a job. I distribute their resume to employers and nothing ever happens. It takes my time but it does not work."[68]

The group of partners continued this discussion, identifying other ways that resources were wasted on things that were not working. They then shifted the discussion to what could be done collectively to create a better outcome for new people coming to the community. One of the resulting ideas was to create a "community concierge" who would drive new residents around the community, introduce them to people and opportunities, and serve as a point of contact for questions and issues.

The final set of services are those performed by Dubuque Works partners that are funded totally or in part through grants. One of the key benefits of the collaborative partnerships in Dubuque Works is that the partners can creatively align various funding sources—federal and state funds such as Workforce Investment Act funds, some of which require local matching—with private funds to more flexibly address key workforce gaps than could be done by any single organization working alone.

Figure 6.1 shows that it is through the collaboration and alignment of the various programs operated by the Dubuque Works partner organizations that results are achieved. The results tracked by GDDC as well as partner organizations are then fed back to the partner organizations along with other data so that programs can be revised, added, or deleted as appropriate.

It is common in the workforce development field for service providers to measure their results in terms of activities. It is much more difficult to be able to track outcomes and relate them to the programs to identify cause and effect. One reason for this is that the problems in the workforce development field are very complex, and it is very difficult for any one organization working alone to be able to track how their individual efforts impact outcomes such as reducing the unemployment rate, moving people out of poverty, increasing the average hourly wage, or increasing the competitiveness of area businesses. However, through collective action such as that demonstrated by Dubuque Works, all the partners can align their individual efforts on the "specific workforce gap issue" defined by the collaborative, and increase the total impact they can make on the key outcome.

Through its "data hub" activity, GDDC is working to increase its capability to track these outcomes and more effectively determine cause and effect between workforce initiatives and changes in the outcomes that ultimately help Dubuque area employers be more competitive, and help Dubuque area citizens lead more fulfilling lives.

Rick Dickinson summarizes the approach that guides the GDDC workforce initiative and all of the GDDC programs that have produced so much success over the years:

> Sooner or later you have to get something done. We have had fits and starts— but we always ask "Did we get something done?" If we did not, we change direction and work until we get it done. There are a ton of people in Dubuque who share that philosophy.[69]

Other Key Roles in the Dubuque Transformation

The initiatives that have enabled Dubuque to make sustained progress have required a blend of public and private funding. External public funding has come from a combination of state and federal support. Dubuque has been extremely successful in attracting these funds and in skillfully blending different programmatic funding to achieve the city's goals and adhere to the guidelines and constraints of the federal and state funding agencies. The individual from the city's perspective who is most responsible for these efforts has been Teri Hawks Goodmann, assistant city manager for strategic partnerships—a unique position in Iowa city government.

Starting in 2007, creating this position enabled the city to take advantage of Teri's skills developed over a long career in the political arena and her vast relationship network at the city, state, and federal levels. Her fundraising prowess was on display as she led the $188 million campaign for the Dubuque riverfront development in 1997–2003.

One of Teri's key partners is Kelley Deutmeyer, executive director of the East Central Intergovernmental Association (ECIA). This council of governments organization is a full-service organization that administers programs in the areas of community development, economic development, housing, employment and training, transit and transportation, and planning. Kelley and her staff administer a range of funding programs, including the Economic Development Administration, the Small Business Administration, and the Workforce Investment Act programs. Working with Teri they collaborate on grant writing and securing funding that supports programs for key Dubuque organizations such as the Community Foundation, GDDC, the Chamber of Commerce, and the ECIA.

Future Challenges for Dubuque

In this chapter we have highlighted many of the strengths that enabled Dubuque to successfully overcome the difficulties it experienced when its unemployment rate led the nation. There are many lessons that other jurisdictions can learn from the strategies and approaches that helped make Dubuque a worthy role model for cities and regions across the country and the world. Like all jurisdictions in an uncertain world, Dubuque faces a number of challenges that will test its resilience. Some of these are known; some are probably unknown. Six of the known challenges are described below.

1. Competing for talent

When I asked Maurice Jones, the economic development director for the city of Dubuque, to tell me how the economic development profession has changed, his response echoed the responses to this question I heard from virtually every economic development professional I interviewed for this book:

> When I started in economic development it was about attracting the companies, now you have to attract the people.[70]

What Maurice was referring to of course is how cities, counties, and states attract and retain the young professionals who are critical to starting, growing, and attracting businesses, and who can choose to live virtually anywhere. This challenge is one of the reasons Maurice was hired by the city from the Chicago area, and also because of his previous work in Louisville, Kentucky, to help enhance Dubuque's vibrancy by expanding retail, restaurants, and nightlife venues in Dubuque. In addition, he is responsible for helping implement the Arts and Culture Master Plan, which is the number one policy priority in the city's 2014–2016 comprehensive plan.

As Dubuque attempts to become a more diverse community, it is necessary for all institutions in the community to consider how they need to prepare for this change. One institution that is critical to helping Dubuque in this transition is the K–12 school system. As the school population becomes more diverse, the school system employees also need to reflect this change.

Stan Rheingans, superintendent of the K–12 school system, reflects on the difficulty in attracting and retaining a diverse staff in Dubuque:

> We have and are trying to diversify our staff, which is a hard sell in Iowa. Teacher pay in Iowa tends to lag behind Illinois, Minnesota and even Wisconsin. There is great competition for the minority candidates. . . . The issue for us is not only recruitment but also retention. We might recruit someone for two to three years and then they move on due to their desire for a more active social scene and where they feel they fit in better.[71]

Despite the staffing challenges, Stan has made considerable strides in aligning the school system with the community's vision, including its economic development goals, and in striking the proper balance with respect to the way the school system interacts with the community.

> Business leaders understand more and more that strong education is economic development. You must have a strong K–12 education system not only to produce graduates who might be their future employees, but also to entice other businesses. When IBM came to town they wanted to be sure that their employees could send their children to school here and feel good about the experience. . . . I would hope that all of us in the school district would see that building good relationships between the school system and the community drives positive outcomes for our students and that we see that all of our futures are intertwined. I would hope that all students, when they walk across that stage at graduation, would feel that they have not just a good education but that they will have doors open for them that will enable them to achieve to the maximum of their potential. Our students cannot afford for me to be territorial with respect to our relationships with the community.[72]

In Dubuque both a challenge and an opportunity are also posed by the fact that there are 322,000 college students enrolled within 100 miles of the city. A major strategy the city is undertaking is to find ways to engage and retain many of these students following graduation. Programs like the Chamber of Commerce's Career Academy address this opportunity. However, beyond efforts to attract these students to remain in Dubuque, the city is also engaging them to help plan how to create the environment that will entice them and their peers to settle in Dubuque. Finding better ways to attract talented people at all employment levels remains a key challenge for Dubuque, and will probably be the basis for the next Smarter Sustainable Dubuque pilot program with the IBM Watson Research Center.

2. Building a more diverse and vibrant community

From the mayor and across the city, leaders acknowledge that Dubuque must become a more inclusive city. Through its initiative called Inclusive Dubuque launched in 2013, the community has begun a very comprehensive strategy to address this need. The mission of Inclusive Dubuque is "to advance equity and inclusion to meet the economic and cultural needs of a diverse community." Nancy Van Milligen, president and CEO of the Community Foundation of Greater Dubuque, points out why the challenge in Dubuque is different from the challenge of inclusivity in other parts of the country:

> It is hard for me to get our large urban foundation partners to realize this, but we never experienced the civil rights movement like Atlanta or Baltimore did. So much of our situation is still unknown. So many people have never experienced diverse cultures before. . . . I had a young farm boy from a nearby town say to me "Ms. Van Milligen, I have never met a black person in my life."[73]

The Community Foundation is, according to the Collective Impact paradigm, serving as the backbone organization for this initiative. While the city's leadership is united on the need for this strategy, it is moving the community into uncharted waters as the comment from the farm boy points out. One of the opportunities that Dubuque has in confronting this challenge is that it has framed the challenge as much broader than a black/white racial issue. It is truly a challenge to move Dubuque into a global culture mind-set in which a community is educated and informed about how diversity will enable it to perform more effectively in a global economy. As the community learned when IBM brought a number of international families to the community, there is work to be done to make Dubuque a welcoming community. That same approach is helpful when it is applied to all racial and cultural groups.

In typical Dubuque fashion, the city is using data, partnerships, engagement, and strong leadership to inform and educate its citizens regarding the need to change. If we think about this challenge using the values map presented in Chapter 2 what Dubuque is attempting to do is to create a values shift for an entire community and enable the community to activate values such as empathy, equity/rights, equality/liberation, and human dignity. It is a courageous and necessary effort that will position Dubuque to be an even better place to live, work, and grow a business.

3. Nurturing and retaining the next generation of community leaders

The transformation of Dubuque has been led by a strong group of community leaders who have placed the "common good" over personal self-interest. Private sector leadership and commitment to the community has been crucial because these leaders not only provide knowledge, experience, and vision, but are also able to bring significant organizational resources to support the various community initiatives. Dubuque particularly has benefited from the fact that it has been able to retain the headquarters of key businesses whose leaders have been very generous in their community support. Other Iowa cities that have seen their major businesses sell out to global businesses have lost that "homegrown" business loyalty to the community and have suffered as a result.

The challenge is to develop and retain the next generation of business leaders, political leaders, and nonprofit leaders who will build on the foundation that has been laid and steer Dubuque into the future. John Schmidt, who has been one of the strong community leaders, raises the issue:

> In 1984, this community came together and created the Greater Dubuque Development Corporation and they put the seeds together that we have been living off of for the past 25 years. This next group of leaders cannot just rest on the ground that has already been plowed. They need to keep planting new seeds. I think there are some younger leaders out there. . . . The challenge is are we doing enough to push this community leadership development process forward?[74]

Another dimension of this challenge is to assure that citizens continue to elect people with talent and knowledge to city and county government positions. Mayor Buol and the city council have helped differentiate Dubuque through its sustainability brand. Engaging citizens to define the dimensions of that brand has helped build broad community support for this vision. Can this support be sustained if there is a change in political leadership? Mayor Buol addressed this challenge:

> Long term I think about whether the next city council will maintain that vision. . . . We really need to get our sustainability project out from under the government—out in the community with a strong partner. I have talked with so many mayors who say that when two or three members change on the city council things can just go into the "tank." There is ownership in the community (for this vision) but it does not show up at the ballot box. We had some candidates in the last election who knew nothing about city government and how it was operating and they were able to get 40% of the

vote against three of our strongest city council members. This was because of low voter turnout. I have been preaching this—if you care about this city— you have to vote![75]

4. Renewing the vision and maintaining community ownership and support

Dubuque has been extraordinarily successful at uniting a community around a common vision. But visions must be renewed, and commitment to the vision must be nurtured as time passes. As the city grows and becomes more diverse, will the community be able to achieve the "unity from diversity" that it seeks, or will it tend to fragment as the memories of past economic crises that helped unite the community fade away? Will the next generation of leadership maintain the commitment to community engagement as a way of crafting a new community vision? Will newly elected officials be willing to put self-interest aside as their predecessors have done and subordinate their private agendas to the welfare of the community as a whole? Dubuque has made impressive strides in putting initiatives in place that work to sustain and reinforce the values that will lead to future success. It will be up to the next generation of leaders to learn from the past and build on this foundation.

5. Strengthening the ecosystem for entrepreneurship

Dubuque has done an excellent job in retaining businesses and helping existing businesses grow. Creating a focus for entrepreneurship and new business starts is a relatively recent focus. Through the initiative called Startup Dubuque, this has become a community focus. Dave Lyons, who is serving as a consultant to the GDDC, is leading this effort as he has been doing with regard to the city's partnership with IBM on the Smarter Sustainable Dubuque initiative.

Dave describes the approach being pursued in the Startup Dubuque effort:

> Startup Dubuque takes all comers—as opposed to venture capital companies that look at a business plan and quickly select those opportunities that only need some money to kick-start the business. Our model will do a triage process once the "entrepreneur" arrives to determine the amount of support needed—day care for kids, transportation needs, business plan support, etc. We will accept both entrepreneurs from elsewhere who want

to start a business in Dubuque, as well as local people who have an interest. The return on investment for the infrastructure is greatest if we grow the effort organically. We have a "virtual one-stop" shop sized for a community like Dubuque. We have the Service Core of Retired Executives (SCORE), the U.S. Small Business Administration funded Small Business Assistance Center (SBA), and the Northeast Iowa Community College involved as partners. A call comes into the Greater Dubuque Development Center (GDDC) and is then put into the triage process to decide what is needed and to follow up.

We know that entrepreneurs need to guide themselves. We have formed the committee, they are nurturing the process, the one-stop shop has been formed and now we have some customers who can tell us what they need. Now we can talk about the networking, the technology, etc.

In terms of where we are in the process, if there were 100 steps in the process to build this program we are still in the single digits—we are very early in this process.[76]

Dave and the GDDC have made an excellent beginning in this process. Through the generosity of Dick and Carrie Schmid, the city has been able to create the Schmid Innovation Center to house Startup Dubuque. Building an ecosystem that will support a healthy start-up culture in Dubuque will take time, but they have built a logical, systematic plan. With Dave Lyons's track record, the odds for success are high. He is well aware of some key challenges ahead, such as identifying and engaging mentors, recruiting entrepreneurs, and developing sources of capital to fund start-up businesses at all stages of their development. Others in the community have been involved in these discussions. Local business leader John Schmidt speaks to the issue of engaging investors and developing funding models for financing start-ups:

We have looked at several different models, but it is time that we start moving on some of these. It seems we need to get off the dime. There is some patient money out there that would be willing to flow into start-ups if we get some visibility and bring some key people into the effort. William C. Brown Publishing probably spawned several businesses. That skill set was out there. A similar thing happened in the insurance world here. It seems that we do have some capabilities here that maybe we should continue to try to leverage. That is what they have done remarkably well in California haven't they?[77]

6. Maintaining community support for infrastructure investments

A key role for the city is providing and maintaining the infrastructure that will support growth and economic development. In some cases the city will build and maintain the infrastructure, in some cases the city will partner with other public or private organizations to provide the infrastructure, and in other cases the city will work to persuade private organizations or investors to build, own, operate, and maintain infrastructure projects. As it identifies community needs and considers alternative strategies for meeting the infrastructure needs, the city must also maintain a solid financial position. One measure of this is the bond rating applied by rating agencies to debt incurred by the city, which significantly impacts the city's costs of borrowing to meet its capital requirements.

As the city's leadership attempts to balance these complex decisions at the same time the leaders are increasing its transparency in all dealings, including financial management, there is a challenge to explain the financial decision making to citizens. Dubuque recently confronted this challenge when it chose to build a new water resource reclamation plant. Rick Dickinson, CEO of GDDC, described the reasoning behind the decision and the challenge:

> The existing facility had to be rebuilt. The choice was whether to build it in a sustainable way or do you build it as another facility that meets minimum standards but that continues to incinerate our waste and pollute our air and put fly ash and feces into our atmosphere. Or do you convert it to an anaerobic digester that captures the methane and converts it to electricity to run your facility and produce renewable compressed natural gas (CNG) to run our city vehicles. This is what the city did. It is more expensive at the beginning, but it pays off in the end. Are you able to explain to your citizens why it makes economic sense to pay more on the front end and be more cost effective over the long term?[78]

The Dubuque and Austin case studies describe the success of two cities that are quite different in many ways. However, the lessons we can learn from these stories share much in common. In the next chapter we will build on these two examples as we describe our recommended new framework for transforming local economic development. Many of the best practices gleaned from Austin and Dubuque will be reflected in this new framework.

CHAPTER SEVEN

A New Framework for Local Community and Economic Development

In my opinion, those people who have been marketing without a clear understanding of the kind of community they have and the kind of community they are building have largely failed.[1]

Our analysis of both the literature on economic development and the analysis of successful practices have led to the conclusion that growing jobs requires a focus on growing and building communities. In this chapter our discussion will integrate the community-building efforts of local governments with the more focused economic development initiatives of the proposed development corporation. This new holistic economic development framework requires that the private sector development corporation operate in an integrated, close working partnership with the public sector governments within its defined "place" in order to build a successful economic development effort. If the "place" is defined as a city or town, the partnership is with the city or town government. If the "place" is defined as a county, the partnership will be with the county government. Each local system must determine the definition of "place" that will serve as the focus of the economic development system. The essential element in the designation of the "place" is that it is a geographical unit to which its citizens have a strong emotional attachment and sense of connection.

Mac Holladay, the CEO of Market Street Services, a private sector economic development consulting firm, is the source of the opening quote above. Having worked for many years in the public sector as an economic development professional before moving into the consulting world, Mac has a unique perspective on this necessary public–private collaboration. From his broad experience base, he describes his view of the priorities of the new framework for local economic development:

> There are three legs to the economic development stool—entrepreneurship and innovation, existing business expansion, and recruitment. We have had the order backwards for a long time. I worked for four different governors and I have been to more ribbon cuttings and ground-breakings than any human should have to suffer through. The fact of the matter is that most of the new jobs come from expansion not from relocation.[2]

Mac speaks from the point of view of a very successful practitioner and consultant. We can view the same question from the standpoint of an academic researcher who is a leading scholar on economic development practices, Dr. Maryann Feldman:

> The initial event or entrepreneurial spark that gives rise to prosperous regions is not deterministic nor do they automatically set in motion path dependencies that automatically yield successful places. What matters most is human agency—the building of institutions and the myriad public and private decisions that determine what I call the character of place—a spirit of authenticity, engagement and common purpose.[3]

In this chapter we will focus on building a framework that will guide policy maker decision making in improving the effectiveness of local economic development. We define "local" as city, county, or region (multicounty). We are convinced, based on our analysis, that a focus on local economic development rather than state or national is the appropriate unit of analysis. In the next chapter we will focus on actions that can be taken at the state level to support, enable, and assist local economic development. However, state-level economic development initiatives will succeed or fail in large part based on what happens at the local level.

Before we move to the discussion of the framework, it is helpful to reflect on what we mean by the term "economic development." Maryanne Feldman presents a definition that sets the appropriate context for our discussion of the key elements for success of local economic development.

> Economic development is the expansion of capacities that contribute to the advancement of society through the realization of individual, firm and community potential. Economic development is measured by a sustained increase in prosperity and quality of life through innovation, lowered

transaction costs, and the utilization of capabilities towards the responsible production and diffusion of goods and services. Economic development requires effective institutions grounded in norms of openness, tolerance for risk, appreciation for diversity, and confidence in the realization of mutual gain for the public and the private sector. Economic development is essential to creating the conditions for economic growth and ensuring our economic future.[4]

A key distinction that she makes in this definition is that economic development and economic growth are two separate concepts. Economic development is the driver and enabler of economic growth. We have reviewed other models (e.g., the Deming Chain) that show how quality and productivity improvement drive firm success and job growth. Economic development creates the "fertile soil" that accelerates firm-level productivity growth that leads to job creation. This definition is also consistent with our focus on the "agricultural model" rather than the "selling model" as the appropriate framework for economic development.

Building an Effective Local Economic Development System

This chapter will present our recommendations for a new framework for local economic development from two perspectives. The first is the structure of a local economic development system and the second is the set of principles that describe key aspects of how the system can operate to be effective. We consider the local economic development system to include the private local economic development corporation and its partnership relationships with local government and other public and private sector entities.

Structure of the local economic development corporation

This new economic development framework is based on the assumption that the primary frontline economic development organizations within the state are the local economic development systems, which we will describe. There will be as many of these local economic development systems as there are defined "places" in the state that have the local leadership and resources to create the recommended economic development corporation and its associated relationships. Currently, local economic development organizations, if they exist, may exist as city or county government departments, as public/private corporations, or as private sector organizations (e.g., development corporation, chamber of commerce) focused on city, county, or regional economic development.

In this section we will describe an alternative "ideal" local economic development system structure that is anchored by a private local economic development corporation. The proposed structure of this corporation is shown in Figure 7.1. We view this organization as a private, not-for-profit corporation that is supported by a combination of public and private funds.

We recommend that two-thirds of the funds come from a private sector capital campaign that is repeated on a five-year cycle. The additional one-third funding is derived from the local governments within its defined "place." This funding is designed to cover the core staff of the organization and its operating budget. Programmatic funding for key program initiatives, for example, workforce development and entrepreneurship development, may come from state and federal program funding or from private funding as well. In addition, the organization may be able to generate revenue from programs such as the job posting website run by the Greater Dubuque Corporation, which provides funds to cover part of its workforce development programming.

In Chapter 9 we will address the challenge of transitioning from what exists today as the local economic development organization toward this ideal organizational structure.

The organizational structure depicted in Figure 7.1 consists of a board of directors that is responsible for governance, fund-raising, strategic planning, and overseeing the performance of the corporation. It has the

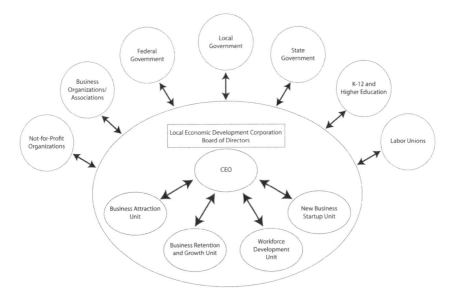

Figure 7.1   Local Economic Development Corporation Framework

traditional fiduciary responsibilities of a not-for-profit board of directors including hiring and reviewing the performance of the president and chief executive officer. The organization has four operating groups. These are focused on the three principal strategies for job creation—attraction, retention and growth, and start-ups. The fourth operating group focuses on what many economic development officials will say is the most important issue today, which is recruiting and developing talent. This is commonly called "workforce development" although some organizations prefer other titles for this function.

This economic development corporation operates in an environment that is defined in part by the seven circles in Figure 7.1. These circles represent the key external partners for the local economic development corporation. It is not a coincidence that a number of the circles correspond to the key partners identified in the technopolis wheel depicted in Chapter 5. The circle labeled "local government" refers to the public sector government bodies that are contained in the geographic area served by the corporation that we refer to as "the place." If the place is a county, the key partners would be county government and major city governments in the county. If the place is a city, the primary public sector partner would be the city government. State government is a partner with respect to developing alignment between the state and local economic development priorities. While the local economic development corporation does not report to the state government, it may receive funding through grants or contracts that help align its work with state initiatives. The state government may also provide technical assistance and coordination with state resources such as intermediary organizations that support entrepreneurship, technology commercialization, technology extension programs, management and leadership consulting, and training.

The federal government is a partner for local initiatives through both state-level executive branch policies and programs, grants, and contracts, and through assistance in compliance with federal regulations. The local corporation and its local public sector partners may also lobby their federal congressional delegation and their staff directly in order to obtain federal support and assistance for priority projects and to keep them informed of local needs and priorities.

Business organizations and business associations are key partners for the core economic development initiatives. They are customers for services provided by the corporation and its resource partners, and they are sources of funds during the corporation's capital campaigns. Not-for-profit organizations are partners who can bring both financial and nonfinancial resources in terms of expertise, information, communication resources, and volunteer staff to participate in community priority initiatives such as workforce development, support for entrepreneurial initiatives, and assistance to new people and firms moving into the community.

The education community, both K–12 and higher education, represent key partners for a number of reasons. The K–12 system partners with the corporation with respect to aligning curricula with the workforce needs of the community. However, beyond that, the community offers a wide range of learning opportunities for students in the form of internships, student project opportunities, engaging business and labor representatives to help develop career awareness, and so on. The higher education community offers a range of partnership opportunities with the corporation that can assist all facets of the core economic development system—workforce development, business retention and growth, business attraction, and entrepreneurship development.

Organized labor is a key partner with the corporation with respect to union–management cooperative ventures, area labor–management committees, and political assistance in dealing with state and federal legislative bodies. The labor unions bring knowledge and resources that make them valuable partners with respect to workforce development as well as business attraction and retention of existing businesses.

Key principles that will guide the local economic development corporation and the local economic development system

The operation of the local economic development system is guided by nine key operating principles. These principles have been derived from the previous chapters in this book and especially from the two case studies of local economic development initiatives—Austin and Dubuque.

Leadership system

We refer to the "leadership system" rather than simply leadership. This is because the leadership system embraces more than the individuals who visibly lead the local economic development process. In communities, leadership is distributed across various sectors—government, education, business, health care, not-for-profit, and so on. However, the key leadership roles that must be engaged in order to establish an effective economic development system or transform an existing economic development system are leaders that can be characterized as first-level influencers.[5] These individuals are people who have had recognized success in their "own" sector, and they also maintain extensive personal and professional links to their peer leaders in other sectors. They can effectively span the boundaries of their sector with credibility and influence. This is essential in organizing and setting the vision for the economic development system and for raising funding to sustain the organization. First-level influencers may serve on advisory boards, but often will remain in the background rather than occupy formal leadership positions. However, their engagement and involvement are crucial for building a successful economic development system.

Another key element of the leadership system is the engagement of second-level influencers.[6] These individuals are people with strong informal communication links to the first-level influencers and who have their own boundary-spanning communication links across sectors. They are outward looking and open, rather than being closed and provincial, in their perspectives. These individuals are likely to occupy active leadership roles in key organizations and are the people who can "get things done."

The leadership system requires a structure. The recommended structure is a "big-tent" board that comprises first- and second-level influencers who represent the key constituencies in the community. The board of the Greater Dubuque Development Corporation (GDDC) is an example. This board represents both the customer groups served by the economic development system and the key partner organizations that must provide the resources and expertise to enable the system to function.

A final element of the leadership system that becomes more crucial over time is the process for developing community leaders. This leadership development system must assess, recruit, develop, and recognize the community leaders of the present and the future.

Vision and strategy for the place

Before we can define a vision or strategy we must define the "place." In this book we define "local" economic development to include either city, county, or region (multicounty). In developing a vision and strategy we must more clearly define the unit of analysis. In our Austin case example, the formal economic development strategy called "Opportunity Austin" focused not just on the city, but also on a five-county region surrounding and including the city. This spirit is exemplified in a comment by Julie Huls, president and CEO of the Austin Technology Council (ATC). Julie's comments also exemplify the mission clarity and mutual respect between the ATC and the Greater Austin Chamber of Commerce.

> We have nothing to do with bringing in new companies. That is the Chamber's lane. They have done incredible work at national recruiting. Our piece

of the pie is in making sure that companies that are already on the ground have what they need to stay and grow. That does not mean that you have to be headquartered in Austin. There were three announcements recently of companies that will be expanding here and they are all headquartered outside of Austin.[7]

The Dubuque case also focused on a multicounty region. The importance of the definition of place is to increase the extent to which the citizens have an emotional attachment to the "place" and are willing to put the welfare of the "place" above their narrow self-interest.

Part of what is required for citizens to take ownership of the economic development effort is that they truly care about the "place." One way to determine the attachment of people to a place is to ask: How do you answer the question "Where are you from?" when you are traveling away from home? Another clue to defining the place is to examine the "laborshed" for a particular location. "Laborshed" refers to the geographic area from which a place draws its commuting workers. Another issue in defining the place is the resource concentration of the area in terms of population, employers, tax base, and so on. The place must include sufficient resources to sustain the economic development system. In our discussion, the term "place" refers to a geographical region. When we use the term "local community" or "community" we are also referring to the place.

Once the place is clearly defined, the most important question that can be asked with regard to an economic development strategy is: What kind of economy do we want to create? Our case example for Dubuque provides the clearest example of how a community might go about answering that question. Based on his interaction with citizens both as a council member and then in his campaign to be elected mayor, Roy Buol articulated a vision for the community in one word—"sustainability." However, rather than try to define that himself or have the city council define it, he and the council convened a citizens group to create the definition. The result of this process is an example of how citizens could be engaged to answer the question: What kind of place do we want to create?

This process assured that the values of the community were reflected in the vision for the community. From that point on it was up to the community leadership to use "sustainability" as the lens through which to focus strategic planning and decision making. It is beyond the scope of this book to discuss strategic planning methodologies. However, developing a strategic plan for the "place" is essential. The importance of a plan that is systematically and regularly updated was described well by Mayor Buol of Dubuque:

It has been our planning focus that changed things. We have our five-year goals and a 20-year vision of where we want the city to be. As long as you keep your eyes on the vision, the goals will come into clarity and your immediate priorities will be very clear for you. That has been the key to our collaboration.[8]

The Austin case example also provides a perspective on strategy development in that the economic development community—the Greater Austin Chamber, the University of Texas, the Austin Technology Incubator, and the Austin Technology Council—have understood the importance of building economic clusters around fundamental community technology strengths. Jose Beceiro, director of Strategic Corporate Partnerships at Texas State University, provides a view of how the clean tech cluster is emerging in a different way from other Austin clusters:

What you are seeing in Austin is a convergence of technologies that are being applied in new ways. Clean-tech is about applying advanced technologies to existing infrastructure to improve the quality and reliability of that infrastructure—whether it is an electric utility grid, a water system, or a natural gas network. MCC and SEMATECH were taking industry sectors that were not really present in Austin and driving a stake in the ground and saying we will be a "computer hub" and we will be a "semiconductor hub." There was semiconductor research going on in the Engineering School at UT but we did not have a cluster of semiconductor firms prior to the arrival of SEMATECH. Before MCC we did not have a significant software industry in Austin. They acted as accelerators of these two industry sectors. Pecan Street is acting as an accelerator of clean-tech, but it is really taking existing technology sectors and realigning them and reapplying them to new applications.[9]

Engage and inform individual and organizational partners

Economic development is not an end in itself. It is a means to improve the quality of life of citizens and businesses as well as that of future generations. This requires that the economic development system view individual citizens and businesses as partners and develop and adopt methods to engage and inform them. Engagement with businesses and citizens is essential in order to understand their needs and assess the impact of the economic development activities. Informing all partners is necessary to enable them to understand the external forces impacting the community and the reasons behind the strategies and plans that are being implemented to promote economic development, and to enable individual and organizational partners to align their decisions with the community strategy.

Dubuque is at the forefront of a movement within the public sector to transform the way governments interact with citizens. In the past, citizen involvement meant things like citizen participation in public hearings or community forums. Typically, in such processes, government agencies would develop a policy or regulation and then either submit it in writing to citizens for comment or hold public meetings where citizens could react to the proposal in person. Such attempts to involve citizens are not examples of "citizen engagement."

The fundamental difference between involvement and engagement comes down to who holds the power. In the involvement scenarios, all the power still rests with government. With citizen engagement there are various degrees of engagement that represent different degrees of power-sharing with citizens. Dubuque has made increased citizen engagement in the city's governance process an explicit priority. In the case of Sustainable Dubuque, a committee of 40 citizens was empowered to define the meaning of sustainability for Dubuque. With one exception, the recommendations of the citizen-led group became the policy of the city. Essentially, community engagement extends the notion of partnerships from an organization-to-organization relationship to also include the government-to-citizen relationship. Government and citizens view each other as partners.

Benefits of this strategy include increasing citizen ownership of the governance process, increasing trust in government, improved service delivery, and developing a more informed citizenry. Helping citizens develop the skills to act as partners is also a significant part of building this government-to-citizen relationship. Fortunately for Dubuque, it has an organization that has built considerable expertise in fulfilling this role. In a number of major citizen engagement initiatives—Envision 2010, Dubuque 2.0, and others—the Community Foundation of Greater Dubuque has performed admirably. Expanding the role of the Community Foundation from its narrow philanthropic mission is an example of building an institutional asset that can enable the economic development system to implement its strategy.

Assess and build community assets

The idea of building community assets moves us to the next element in the discussion of operating principles for the local economic development system. In most strategic planning models, there is a requirement to conduct a SWOT analysis. This refers to an assessment of the community's strengths, weaknesses, opportunities, and threats. Strengths and weaknesses refer to conditions that the community can control or influence. Opportunities and threats tend to be events or conditions or forces that are external, and the community has little ability to influence or control them. In building strategies the economic development system builds on its strengths and takes advantage of its opportunities, while it must take action to improve in areas of weaknesses and take defensive action to minimize or mitigate threats.

In this framework, community assets are things that the community can control or influence. The community can use assets that are strengths as it builds its economic development strategy. Assets may be geographical features, institutions, facilities, or intangibles such as a spirit of collaboration or expertise. We saw in the Austin and Dubuque case examples a number of examples of community assets.

Key assets for Austin included the city being the site for the state capital, the University of Texas, a strong music scene that attracts talent to the area, a strong base of technology companies, and the existence of considerable angel investment capital. Another key asset in Austin is the presence of the municipal electric system, Austin Energy, that not only provides very competitive electric service but also is a key funding partner of many community initiatives including economic development. In Dubuque, examples of assets were the Mississippi River, the dog track and casino that provide revenue to the community (similar to the funding role provided by Austin Energy in Austin), the waterfront convention center development, a number of colleges, generous corporations that are headquartered in the city, and the presence of IBM's global service center and the smarter city's collaboration with IBM. However, when the city began its transformation, the Mississippi River and its waterfront had not been considered assets and had been neglected. Part of the transformation involved considerable effort and fund-raising to convert this neglected asset into a tourist attraction and a major source of citizen pride and commercial real estate development.

The way in which assets impact economic development strategy was addressed by Mac Holladay, whose firm Market Street Services assisted Austin in developing its formal economic development strategy called Opportunity Austin. Here is what Mac had to say about asset building:

> As we worked on the first strategy—Opportunity Austin 1—they were distressed that I did not include in their portfolio of what they might do anything that related to bio-science. I told them specifically, you have a wonderful chemistry department here at the University of Texas but you don't have a medical school. You can't play in this (the bio-science) space. What they have done now is create a medical school by taxing themselves—and also getting help from Michael Dell. Now they have that new asset. Part of

what needs to happen in communities is asset building. This is a way of focusing on the quality of place as well as the workforce.[10]

As this comment points out, lack of certain assets limits the range of strategies that are viable. On the other hand, availability of the asset can open up strategies that were previously not viable. Now that Austin has a medical school it can accelerate its business cluster building activities with respect to bio-health businesses, for example, bio-health incubator, growing the bio-health ecosystem for entrepreneurship, and focusing on hybrid strategies that leverage the existing information technology cluster into the bio-health area. The fact that the Austin community was willing to tax itself to create this community asset is an excellent example of community engagement in the economic development process.

Sometimes solving a problem in the community can lead to asset creation. This was illustrated in Dubuque by the way in which its focus on planning and equity enabled the city to take steps to deal with flooding in one of the poorest neighborhoods in the city. Past flooding had resulted in six presidential disaster declarations since 1999. Rick Dickinson, president of the GDDC, describes how solving this problem created an asset that makes the community more desirable not just for residents of the immediate neighborhood, but also for the entire community:

> How do you take a centuries-old storm water management system that lacks sufficient capacity and that has resulted in the flooding of thousands of residents just in the last decade alone? How do you convert that into something that is more functional and that positively impacts the neighborhood? It would have been less expensive to tear up the old one and just put in a larger tube underground to collect the storm water. The decision the city made was to "daylight" that facility, to make it an amenity within the community, enhance the lowest income neighborhood in our community, and spend extra money in structure and design and green space to make it not just a storm water collection system, but also a linear park that will benefit everyone in the community for generations to come.[11]

This is an example of how the city made a decision, through citizen engagement, to prevent future flooding crises. It is also an example of how the city is guided by its core values and its vision. This "Bee Branch" project is a win for the environment, a win for the people of Dubuque, and an economic win in the long run, with the design and funding recommended by citizen task forces. Even though the initial cost was greater than a "bigger tube in the ground," it will save money over time.

Community information, measurement, and analysis systems

Community data and information play multiple roles. Economic and community development depend on data and analysis to assure that strategies are grounded in fact-based reality. Data are also a key community resource that, if captured, stored, and shared, are a valuable economic development asset. Data and information are also essential for assessing results and providing feedback, making it possible for the economic development system to continuously improve itself.

As a tool for strategy development, data provide the lens that enables the leadership of the economic development organization and the broader community to look at itself objectively. Mac Holladay gives an example from his experience in working with a large number of local economic development entities of how the data lead the strategy development process in perhaps unexpected areas.

> When a community examines itself holistically and thinks seriously about the kinds of companies it wants to grow, create or in some cases recruit— they are forced to look at everything. In one city, we had to deal with race relations because they had abandoned the public schools, but you cannot go forward without them. Race and leadership ends up being one of the four or five goal areas for this city. The tactics of economic development might be one of the five goal areas. Part of it is understanding that if you don't have a great place, you cannot move forward.[12]

Community assessment data can be used to build understanding. This understanding can help create a consensus among the community leadership of what must be done to close the gap between where the community is on the key data elements and where members of the community want it to be in order to become the community citizens aspire to. Julie Huls, president and CEO of the Austin Technology Council, explains how better measurement data enable her to focus improvements on the Austin tech community:

> We try to have a very in-depth understanding of the nature and impact of the tech businesses in Austin. Tech has a 21.5 billion dollar impact on our economy. However, we did not have a good understanding of what this "new-tech" community really looked like. We needed to drill deeper. So we are gathering this data and we will integrate this data into the economic development decision making of the broader community. That way those institutions—e.g., City of Austin, Chamber, colleges and universities, workforce development institutions, etc.—that are making decisions and

investments to support the Austin tech community will have a better understanding of how they can benefit tech.[13]

The effectiveness and speed with which data can lead to action depend
in large part on the collaboration, trust, and relationships that define the
culture of the community. Dave Lyons, former insurance Commissioner
for Iowa, former director of the Iowa Department of Economic Development, and a consultant to the GDDC, pointed out that the relationships
formed in Dubuque among key leaders of community organizations in
response to the 1980s' economic crisis represent a major strength of the
city.[14] He characterized the relationships as like an interlocking board of
directors that enables all the leaders to know what is going on and facilitates their ability to act quickly. The fact that the nonprofit, for-profit,
organized labor, and government sectors all talk and innovate together
allows them to react earlier to opportunities than a community like
Dubuque could normally do. In a culture with these characteristics, data
can be a powerful resource.

Taking advantage of this strength depends on the availability of effective
data-capturing mechanisms. Organizations like the Community Foundation and the GDDC that are actively scanning the environment capture
the data and through their broad-based community networks allow these
data to serve as an early warning system. Through data-gathering programs
and methods such as Info-Action, HR-Action, community cafes, and a
range of other engagement strategies, the city can detect concerns before
they become crises and identify opportunities before other cities have
detected the signals. However, having the information within the community is of little use unless it can be converted to action. Because of the trust,
partnerships, and communication mechanisms among the key players,
early warning information can be converted to timely action.

The early warning mechanisms do not only apply to human systems in
Dubuque. As a result of the work with IBM in Smarter Sustainable
Dubuque, the city has developed capabilities it will be expanding to have
early problem detection in its physical systems. Making use of the "Internet
of things" the city is monitoring physical systems through data sensors that
enable it to anticipate failures and better schedule maintenance and component replacement before there are actual failures.

Still another perspective on the importance of data is the way in which
data from the city, state, or county serve as a value-adding resource for citizens and local businesses. Acting as an "information utility," a government
entity can open its data to citizens and local businesses in ways that enable
citizens to do things they otherwise could not do. This can spur

entrepreneurship and it can improve quality of life for citizens. The smart city project in Dubuque with IBM provides data to citizens that enable them to detect water leaks, conserve water, save money on their water or electric bill, and save time in using the public transportation system. These demonstration projects have given rise to the observation voiced by Dave Lyons that the design question underlying the smart city projects is:

> How do I give people what they need (information that is specific to them and that is actionable) so that they can do what they want?[15]

The information recipients may be city leaders, businesses, or individual citizens. Data are the new enabling resource in the information economy.

Community partnerships

The organizational model that we propose for the local economic development corporation is a public–private partnership. This partnership is evident in the composition of the board and it will be evident in the discussion on community and economic development tactics. It is hard to imagine a local economic development system that makes better use of partnerships than Dubuque. By examining the views of some of the Dubuque leaders about how to make partnerships effective, we can draw lessons that will benefit any local economic development entity. They use partnerships as a vehicle to attract resources, address workforce development challenges, engage citizens, and deliver services.

To the community leaders of Dubuque, the term "partnership" is not a vague, abstract idea. Rather it is a conscious strategy that defines the daily work of many, if not most, of the key community leaders. Whether it is leaders of private sector organizations, public sector organizations, or nonprofit organizations, leaders in Dubuque actively develop, cultivate, and grow partnerships as a key part of their daily work activity.

Dubuque has a position filled by Teri Hawks Goodmann entitled assistant city manager for strategic partnerships. Other cities would typically hire a lobbyist to do what Teri does for Dubuque. Her title, which is unique among cities in Iowa, is evidence of the emphasis placed on the importance of partnerships in Dubuque. When Mayor Buol speaks about sustainability, he always talks about the need to engage citizens as partners. This is not just empty rhetoric from a politician. He truly understands the implications of these words and his sincerity is reflected in the way the city views citizens and in the way citizens respond. When asked to describe how the city has been so successful in bringing in resources to support the strategic plan the mayor said this:

It is really the same approach that we have in doing things in Dubuque—it is about building partnerships. It is the long-term relationships that we build that are the ones that really produce results. As a community we have really engaged our federal partners, our [federal] legislators and their staffs and we have done the same thing with our state legislators. We bring the federal staff to Dubuque so they can see what we are working on and they can see what we are planning. . . . We keep these relationships very strong and that is the role of Teri Goodmann. . . . They understand that when they help Dubuque with a project, we are going to do it right and they are going to get the credit for it and they are going to have a best practice going forward. There are a lot of things we have done that have allowed them to say "Look how Dubuque does it." . . . Those partnerships that we maintain (with federal and state officials) are every bit as critical as the partnerships we build and maintain locally. We work very hard at those long-term partnerships and that is a rare commodity in today's world. But they have proven to be very successful.[16]

Mayor Buol continued regarding how to maintain partnerships:

Partnerships are about creating "win-win" opportunities. They are hard, especially when you have controversial things come up in your city. But we have been able to navigate that mine-field without having anything blow up underneath us.[17]

City Manager Mike Van Milligen echoed the mayor's comments about the importance of partnerships:

For partnerships, you have to be willing to work together. You have to bring lots of people to the table. You can't worry about who gets the credit. . . . Partnerships are fragile—they have to be nourished.[18]

Core economic development processes—The tactics of economic development

The local economic development corporation structure shown in Figure 7.1 depicts four operating units. Each of these units "owns" one or more core economic development processes. A process is a sequence of actions, repeated over time, that are designed to provide value to "customer(s)."[19] Customers of the economic development corporation are individual citizens, individual organizations (for-profit and not-for-profit) and "the place," that is, city, county, or region.

Let's look at one of these operating units—the business retention and growth unit. The primary function of this unit is to engage in actions that will lead to increased business and job growth within firms and enterprises that are currently located in the local place. The core business process that defines the work of this group is a process we can label "Assessment-Action." This is a process in which staff members plan and conduct assessment visits with the senior executives of business organizations and gather information about the company, its plans, its products, its customers, its employees, and its challenges. The major process steps in the Assessment-Action process are:

1. Enter the firm profile into the Assessment-Action software;
2. Schedule visit to the firm;
3. Conduct structured assessment visit with the firm's leadership;
4. Enter findings in the Assessment-Action software;
5. Repeat steps 1–4 daily; and
6. Hold (weekly) meetings with key decision makers for the "place" to review major business concerns and initiate actions to address them.

This is a simplified version of the process by which the staff of the development corporation conduct assessment visits to firms in the local area. Each week, the results of these visits are summarized and analyzed, and a meeting is held with the partners who are able to take action to address the firm's needs and concerns identified in the visits for the week. Processes 1–5 above are the assessment steps and process 6 is the action step.

In Dubuque, for example, the staff who conduct the firm visits meet weekly with the president of the GDDC, the city manager, and the city's director of economic development. In these meetings, issues are discussed and actions are planned to deal with the major business concerns identified that week which limit their productivity and ability to grow revenue and create more jobs, and which are under the control or influence of the GDDC or the city or county government.

Each of the other units within the economic development corporation similarly must define its key business process or processes and implement them consistently to achieve the planned outcomes.

Continuous improvement

In Chapter 3, one lesson we learned from the past is that, to deliver sustained success, all organizations must focus on continuous improvement. The economic development corporation is no exception. To put it simply, the methodology for continuous improvement is the plan-do-study (or check)-act (or PDSA cycle) that was introduced by Dr. W. Edwards Deming.[20] A number of elaborations of this improvement strategy have been developed with perhaps the most rigorous being the Six Sigma methodology[21] that has been popularized by a number of organizations including the General Electric Company. Basically, what is required is that the organization adopt a continuous improvement methodology and apply it systematically and repeatedly. This approach is really applying the scientific method to performance improvement. It requires the leadership of the organization to understand the cause-and-effect relationships between the actions taken by the organization and the results those actions create. By rigorously and systematically analyzing these relationships, the organization can continuously improve its performance.

Continuous improvement is a methodology that enables an organization to improve itself. Economic development organizations need continuous improvement. However, because they are dealing with a set of challenges that exceed the capabilities of any single organization, regardless of how well financed and supported, economic development organizations also need an improvement paradigm that enables them to improve the effectiveness of their collaboration with other organizations in order to focus the "collective resources" of a number of organizations on the economic development challenges. This improvement paradigm is called "collective impact." We will use the case study from Dubuque to introduce this idea.

Because the economic crisis in the early 1980s was too significant for any single organization in the community to address alone, Dubuque was forced to adopt a strategy of "collective impact." Business leaders, government leaders, leaders of the faith community, and the non-profit sectors all came together to collaboratively craft responses to the crisis. Everyone pitched in and no one worried about who would get the credit. New institutions were created, new community leaders emerged, and adoption of "collective impact" enabled Dubuque to pull itself like the proverbial phoenix from the ashes of an economy that had been devastated.

The phrase "collective impact" was not invented in Dubuque. It was the title of what has become an influential article published in the *Stanford Social Innovation Review* by John Kania and Mark Kramer in 2011.[22] The authors were not writing about Dubuque and the leaders of Dubuque had no knowledge of this work until it was discovered by Nancy Van Milligen and Eric Dregne through their work in the nonprofit management field. The academic model proposed by Kania and Kramer lists five conditions required for collaborating organizations to achieve success in dealing with problems that are too complex for any one organization to tackle alone.

The five conditions are:

1. A shared agenda—The collaborating organizations must have a shared vision for change;
2. Shared measurement systems—A shared agenda means little unless the partner organizations agree on how their joint efforts will be measured and evaluated;
3. Mutually reinforcing activities—This enables the collaborating organizations to each identify the set of activities it can best perform and then coordinate and focus the activities of the partners on the target outcomes through mutually reinforcing activities;
4. Continuous communication—The CEOs of the partner organizations need to regularly communicate, build trust, share what each other is doing, and engage in joint problem solving to improve effectiveness;
5. Backbone support organizations—Collective impact requires a separate organization and staff with its own funding that fulfills the roles for the partners of project manager, data manager, and facilitator. The backbone support organization should bring a highly structured methodology for group decision making and process management that it uses in facilitating the activities of the collaborative.

As knowledge of this "formal model" has been shared in Dubuque among the key partner organizations, there have been a number of reactions, ranging from "this is what we have been doing since 1984" to "this is the model that we fully embrace" to "this is a way to package many of our initiatives in order to explain them more effectively." Like many "models," there is a tendency for individuals to selectively focus on "pieces" of the model that reinforce their existing beliefs.

Anyone who looks at what is happening in Dubuque, however, will conclude that leaders in this city understand that all the model's elements have validity and that most have become a way of life in Dubuque. It is possible to nit-pick whether one organization is really fulfilling completely the role specified as a backbone organization, or whether an organization is blurring the backbone versus participant role, or whether the backbone organization is focused sufficiently on having a structured process that holds each participant accountable for results and that enables effective group decision making.

The reason that collective impact, whether this label is applied or not, has had such a successful application in Dubuque has less to do with whether each of the participants has conformed to all the specifications in the model but rather how each organization trusts and respects each other, how all are aligned through the city's comprehensive plan, and how all share the common agenda of making Dubuque a better place.

The extent to which this formal model is being integrated into the con-versation and practices in Dubuque can be seen in the March 2015 issue of the city's publication *City Focus* entitled "Outcomes," which shares its performance results with citizens.[23] This document includes a definition of the formal collective impact model, defines certain organizations as backbone organizations, and positions the approach as a key strategy for driving large-scale social change. It is fair to conclude that what has long been an "implicit" strategy in Dubuque is quickly becoming an "explicit strategy."

In the new economic development framework proposed in this chapter, we believe it is essential that the economic development corporation *not* view itself as the agent working by itself to create the desired economic development outcomes. Rather it must view itself as a backbone organiza-tion working with groups of partners and collaborators who jointly must work together to create broad understanding, engagement, and alignment to "collectively" achieve the type of community that the citizens of the place want to build.

This idea of broad community collaboration is built into the governance system of the economic development corporation through the broad-based board. Each of the operating units can apply collective impact by serving as the backbone organization for their function and by engaging a targeted set of collaborating organizations and applying the collective impact paradigm to guide their operation.

Tracking results

Ultimately, the purpose of an economic development system is to pro-duce improved economic development outcomes. In her definition of eco-nomic development, Dr. Feldmann pointed out that the results can be measured in terms of a sustained increase in prosperity and quality of life. Both of these are outcomes that most communities would aspire to achieve. However, the specific definitions of "prosperity" and "quality of life" might differ from community to community. It is possible to provide a generic set of metrics for various aspects of economic well-being or prosperity as well as quality of life. A number of different organizations have developed such lists of metrics.[24] However, since each community must define what they are trying to become, each community will also have to define a set of metrics that correspond to their vision and goals.

Even though leaders of economic development organizations know that they need to customize their measurement indicators to align with their vision, most like to see examples of metrics that other jurisdictions might be using. In that spirit we provide in Table 7.1 some sample metrics for three dimensions of economic development—economic outcomes, social outcomes, and environmental outcomes.

Table 7.1   Sample Results Indicators for a Local Economic Development Corporation

Economic results indicators*	Social results indicators	Environmental results indicators
Change in average annual wages	Percentage of owner-occupied housing	Change in number of miles of hiking/biking trails
Change in labor force participation rate	Percentage of renters paying less than 30% of income on rent	Number of LEED-certified buildings by certification level
Change in unemployment rate	Percentage of residents without health insurance	Change in number of rides on public transportation
Change in number of businesses by size	Change in property and violent crime rates	Change in number of megawatts of installed solar photovoltaic energy capacity
Employment growth by target sector	Change in downtown capital investment	Change in number of gallons of water use per capita
Number of jobs created through business expansion and growth	Change in number of physicians per capita	Percentage of monitored days with good air quality
Change in amount of venture capital investments	Number of acres of parkland compared to benchmark places	Change in pounds of waste per capita sent to the landfill
Change in volume of small business administration loans	Child poverty rate	Percentage of new residential buildings that meet energy star standards
Change in capital investment due to firm expansion	High school graduation rate	Percentage of businesses that have obtained ISO 14000 registration
Change in number of new business start-ups	Change in percentage of population between ages 25 and 34	Change in the number of energy audits conducted for residences and businesses

*Table prepared by author based in part on data adapted from Market Street Services.

In developing and using performance metrics, it is helpful to keep several principles in mind:

- A family of measures or metrics is preferable to single metrics;
- Resources migrate from aspects of performance that are not measured to aspects of performance that are measured, so it is important to measure the right dimensions of performance;
- Most metrics that are useful will take the form of a ratio;
- Interpreting the meaning of metrics is enhanced by viewing the metric over time or as compared to a benchmark, for example, the performance of other local economic organizations and state or national benchmarks.
- It can be helpful to include in the set of metrics some performance indicators that enable comparisons with other local economic development organizations as well as indicators that are specific to the unique goals of the place.

The local economic development corporation's success in implementing these principles at the local level will be significantly enhanced by a supportive state department of community and economic development. In Chapter 8 we will describe the second key element of the new framework for economic development. This is the transformed version of the state department of community and economic development.

CHAPTER EIGHT

A New Framework for State Community and Economic Development

It is clear that the transition to a new economic development model is already under way. The call to regionalize workforce development as a way to solve the employment and skills crisis was the focus of a recent book by Edward E. Gordon.[1] The previously discussed National Governors Association[2] report discussed initiatives in Tennessee, Colorado, and New York to regionalize their economic development approach. A Brookings Institute report added Michigan to this list.[3] Referring to the actions of Governor Rick Snyder of Michigan, Brooking's Jennifer Bradley's writes:

> In his state of the state speech, Snyder pledged to make the state's regions the drivers of state economic development policy, with state agencies in their service. "We have a number of very strong regional groups that are capable of taking the lead in the field." This is a very mild-mannered way to describe a significant inversion of state policy. States usually don't even recognize their regions, seeing instead a fractured map of hyper-local jurisdictions, commissions and boards. And they certainly don't tell them, "You show us the way, because you know best."
>
> Under Snyder, the Michigan Economic Development Corporation (MEDC) will station representatives in Michigan regions to make sure that state programs and policies complement, rather than complicate, local efforts. . . . MEDC will take on the role of "clearinghouse—a best practice center," helping one region replicate the successful strategies of another when it comes to opening up markets for export or luring foreign investment. Again, this is something new—a vision of metropolitan areas as a

group of linked entities that all contribute to the state and to each other. This usefully ignores old regional turf wars.[4]

This strategy effectively applies the quality improvement model derived from Dr. W. Edwards Deming that we discussed in Chapter 3. In this case, the State Department of Economic Development in Michigan is inverting the organizational pyramid and treating the regions as the customers of the state's MEDC. In her blog Bradley refers to allowing the regions to lead, not only in terms of the growth and retention of existing businesses and new business start-ups, but also in terms of business attraction and foreign trade—two areas that traditionally have been led by state economic development agencies.

In commenting on the approaches of the governors of Michigan, Colorado, New York, and Tennessee, Bradley points out that these pragmatic governors are trying to work with the regional governance, not the governments.[5] By regional governance she is referring to organizations like the board of directors of the local economic development corporation that we described in Chapter 7—collections of business, labor, civic, philanthropic, and government leaders.

Another Brookings blog provides additional evidence of not only how momentum is building for a move to a new economic development framework, but also how difficult this change is and how it is encountering a number of obstacles.

> Now, however, cities and metro areas are moving away from these traditional economic development strategies to a new model of economic growth that can lead to long-term prosperity. This model focuses on enhancing existing market assets and capabilities to boost trade, increase the value of advanced industries and create incomes and opportunities for workers, no matter where they live in the region. While landing a big brand name firm (invariably with sizeable public incentives) still grabs headlines, we are seeing more attention paid to business formation, talent creation and the role of place making and infrastructure in both.
>
> With this new model comes a broader cadre of leaders that reflect the evolution underway in economic development. The task of fostering quality jobs, incomes and opportunities falls beyond the work of municipal economic development staff, chambers of commerce, and business attraction and retention agencies. Hence we have witnessed an explosion in the number and range of players in regions—from elected officials to employers, business groups, universities, community colleges, entrepreneurs, and nonprofit executives—who are working in partnership to tackle the challenge.[6]

Some interesting findings from a five-year research initiative launched in 2011 by Brookings and the Rockefeller Foundation address the challenges metropolitan regions face in moving toward the new economic development framework. This project worked with 22 metropolitan regions and 7 states employing strategies designed to grow and retain high-quality jobs in innovative, productive industries in ways that expand opportunity for all.[7] The project, called the Project on State and Metropolitan Innovation (PSMI), is an example of the type of research that is needed to shed more light on the advantages and difficulties in attempting to implement broad-based systems change in economic development. In this report Pete Carlson summarizes some of the perceived benefits and challenges derived from day-long interviews with 13 leaders from some of the research sites. Some positives were:

1. The project strengthened and expanded new efforts to develop and deploy new approaches for expanding economic growth and opportunity;
2. Partnerships developed have created a collaborative capability that will extend beyond the duration of the project—in some cases bringing together public and private leaders at the sites who had never before worked together or focused on regional issues;
3. The projects have produced positive ripple effects within the regions that extend beyond the direct interventions;
4. Since the goal of PSMI is long-term change, the real impact will not be known for several years as significant change in economic development practices takes time to produce results.[8]

Some of the challenges highlighted included:

1. "Galvanizing" leaders who can work across programmatic and jurisdictional boundaries are critical to the process and are in short supply;
2. The work is long-term and systemic, but the funding is short-term and programmatic;
3. Sites are challenged to secure sustained funding for "backbone" organizations and intermediaries who are critical to sustaining the work;
4. Systems change requires a holistic approach, but moving on too many fronts can overwhelm the effort. Focusing on single projects is more feasible, but will not produce systems change;
5. Entrenched interests and systems resist change and shifting resources within public programs that are established is difficult;
6. "A natural process of entropy arises from inevitable changes in leadership, the economic and political landscape, and priorities in organizations and funders increasing the challenge of sustaining long-term efforts."[9]

This field research has created findings that reinforce a number of the principles that we drew from our case examples in Austin and Dubuque—for example, the benefits of separating the economic development organization and program funding from dependence on elected political leaders; the importance of dedicated funding to "backbone" support organizations; the criticality of first- and second-level "influencers;" the importance of new shared mental models that break old "paradigms" with respect to how economic development operates, for example, placing the emphasis on growing existing businesses and entrepreneurship over job attraction and lavish public incentives; and inverting the organizational pyramid with respect to the relationship between state and local economic development entities.

What Are the Key Roles of the State Economic Development System?

What is the state-level economic system? It is clear that the traditional view that it is primarily the executive branch state department is much too narrow. As we pointed out in Chapter 4 in the description of the Maryland economic development system, it is necessary to look not only at the executive branch organization, but also at the legislative branch and higher education system. The key challenge as we think about the roles is how to achieve as much coordination and alignment as possible among these entities.

Figure 8.1 depicts the key roles of the executive branch state community and economic development department in the new economic development framework. We do not intend that this diagram include all facets of the state department role. There are political, administrative, ceremonial, and functional roles that are outside this discussion. In Figure 8.1 the intention is to highlight those roles we believe to be critical in an inverted pyramid structure where much of the statewide economic development leadership is delegated to the local (regional, county, and metro) economic development systems that we described in Chapter 7.

Our description of this organizational framework begins with the backbone units (represented by triangles in Figure 8.1) and then proceeds from the bottom of the figure to the top where we find the "frontline" local economic development systems. This depiction is meant to illustrate that the lower part of the Figure 8.1 shows the foundation and support structure that enables and assists the "frontline" organization's efforts to accomplish its goals.

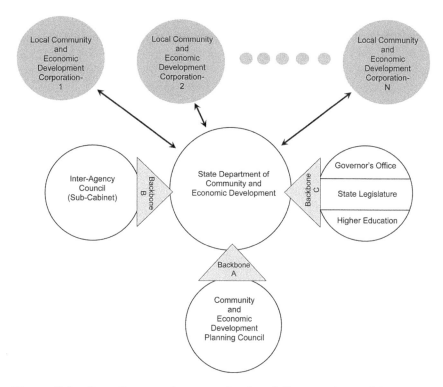

Figure 8.1 State Support Structure for Local Community and Economic Development Corporations

Backbone organization

At each of the organizational interfaces we have depicted a backbone unit, labeled backbone A, B, or C. Within the state department of community and economic development these three backbone units reside in a small organization that resembles an internal consulting group. The members of this backbone organization are highly trained individuals who provide "backbone" support to the "collectives" depicted in this diagram, for example, the interagency subcabinet and the planning council.

The backbone organization is an essential element of the collective impact paradigm that we briefly mentioned in Chapters 5 and 6. The importance of the skills provided by this organization was also noted in the Brookings evaluation of its PSMI.[10] In our discussion we refer to the "backbone unit" as a unit of 1–3 individuals who improve the effectiveness of the collaborative relationships between the state department of economic development and the various "collectives" depicted in Figure 8.1. The sole function of these units is to serve as "process consultants" to enable and accelerate performance improvement by the subcabinet of state government, the economic development planning council or the three key state entities, the governor's office, the legislature, and higher education organizations. Typically in state government, the leader of commissions or interagency groups would be provided with administrative support. That is not what backbone organizations represent. These are highly skilled individuals who are not typically found in state government organizations.

A key transformational change proposed in the new framework is for the state department of community and economic development to create and fund this backbone organization. To have a better understanding of the backbone roles, we need to examine the collective impact model in more detail and specifically the role of the backbone organization. The initial formulation of the collective impact model identified five conditions of collective success:[11]

- Common agenda
- Shared measurement systems
- Mutually reinforcing activities
- Continuous communication
- Backbone support organizations

The authors summarized the roles of a typical backbone organization into three: project manager, data manager, and facilitator. Each of these three roles carries with it a specific set of skills that are required to fulfill the role. A follow-up article by three practitioners of the collective impact methodology elaborated on what backbone organizations do. These authors listed six key activities of effective backbone organizations that reflect different stages of maturity of the initiative: (1) guide vision and strategy, (2) support aligned activities, (3) establish shared measurement practices, (4) build public will, (5) advance policy, and (6) mobilize funding.[12]

If we translate these generic activities to the roles envisioned for backbones A, B, and C, what would these roles and activities be? Table 8.1 addresses this question. What we observe from Table 8.1 is that these roles will require dedicated staff who operate for the most part in the background performing essential tasks that are designed to achieve, over time, major system change—transforming a centralized bureaucracy that has operated in a top–down fashion to an organization that exists in large part to support local community and economic development systems.

Backbone staff members need to be highly skilled professionals with skills in group facilitation, performance measurement, process management and improvement, data management and analysis, project management, and interpersonal communication. Many, if not most, of the skills required

Table 8.1 Roles of State-Level Backbone Organization*

Roles	Backbone A†	Backbone B‡	Backbone C§
1. Guide vision and strategy	Support creation of state vision and goals to achieve economic, social, and environmental performance and support attainment of local economic development systems goals	Support development of the subcabinet mission and purpose with regard to aligning state agencies with the local economic, social, and environmental development goals	Coordinate input from governor's office, legislature, and higher education into the formation of the state vision and state goals
2. Support aligned activities	Facilitate alignment of goals and activities across sectors represented by planning council members and engage their constituencies in supporting local economic development systems	Enable the interagency council and individual members to have the information to enable them to align policies and activities with state economic development goals and strategies	Inform staff of governor's office and legislature regarding the local economic development system goals and ways they can be supported. Assist research universities to align research, commercialization, and technical assistance initiatives with state industry clusters and economic development goals
3. Establish shared measurement practices	Facilitate development of state-level measurement systems that embrace the metrics from local systems and enable council members to align their organizational metrics with the state metrics as feasible	Assist agencies in aligning their measurement systems with state and local economic development goals and metrics as feasible	Inform staff of governor and legislature of measurement system alignment progress and develop ways they can encourage and accelerate progress

Table 8.1 (Continued)

Roles	Backbone A[†]	Backbone B[‡]	Backbone C[§]
4. Build public will	Facilitate council members' ability to capture and spread economic development success stories and engage grassroots support within their sectors for key policy issues	Assist agencies to develop understanding among their staff regarding the importance of alignment of their actions with economic development strategies and how to do it in ways consistent with the agency's core purpose	Enable governor's office and legislative leadership to be able to share success stories and to inform the public of the progress being made to enhance community and economic development at state and local levels
5. Advance policy	Support development of legislative proposals and executive action that will accelerate progress toward state and local goals	Enable efforts by agencies to help shape state and federal economic development policies that support economic, social, and environmental outcomes	Support data and information gathering to enable governor's office, legislature, and universities to craft policies based on facts
6. Mobilize funding	Coordinate communication with federal legislative delegation and their staff, private investors, and foundations regarding support needed for research and local community and economic development asset building	Coordinate communication with agency heads regarding funding streams that can jointly support the state's economic, social, and environmental outcomes	Coordinate communication with legislature, governor's office, and research universities regarding state-level funding needs and needs of local economic development systems

[*]Table created by author.
[†]Backbone A—Support for the state community and economic development planning council.
[‡]Backbone B—Support for the interagency community and economic development council.
[§]Backbone C—Support for coordination with governor's office staff, legislative leadership and staff, and leadership and staff of higher education institutions regarding community and economic development programs.

of the backbone staff are not the traditional skills one would find in a state economic development organization.

The set of skills in the backbone organization represent a coherent performance improvement methodology such as that provided by DMAIC in the six-sigma methodology.[13] DMAIC is an acronym for a process improvement strategy with five key elements—define, measure, analyze, improve, and control. This methodology brings structure and rigor to the process improvement and performance improvement processes that are typically lacking in traditional organizations. Structure and rigor are precisely what the backbone organization brings to this role.

In an era of tight budgets, it is often difficult to justify funds to support individuals like the backbone organization members who are not in the spotlight and whose contribution can be viewed as intangible because the "collective" and its leaders are the ones who get the credit for successes. While it is likely that the improvements stimulated by the backbone organization will pay for themselves many times over, they should not be hired for this reason alone. More important is how they will be able to transform the state department over time to become a much more effective organization. *It* is abundantly clear from academic research and from field studies that the role of the backbone is essential in order for lasting system change to occur. Without the backbone support, old ways of thinking and old ways of doing things will persist. The role of the backbone organization is to challenge the status quo, overcome inertia, be a "paradigm breaker," and bring additional rigor to the economic development improvement initiatives.

Sustained funding for this function is required from the state department of community and economic development. However, it should be clearly noted that their success will be entirely dependent on the support they receive from the governor and top agency executives.

Community and economic development planning council

As a means of engaging the private sector, many states have established economic development councils as Advisory to or as a board of directors for the state department. Typically, the governor acts as chair of this council. In our recommended structure, the governor appoints a private sector leader to chair this council. This leader must fit the qualifications of a first-level influencer that we discussed in Chapter 5. We strongly recommend that the membership of the council be a broad-based group of first- and second-level influencers who not only represent the business community but are individuals with power and influence who are also able to make informed decisions regarding improving the quality of the "place" as well as the quality of the "economy." This requires the engagement of economic leaders, social and educational leaders, and environmental leaders.

This council should be charged with the responsibility to develop an overall economic development vision and goals for the state. The process should begin by engaging the key sectors of the state including the private sector, higher education and K–12 education, not-for-profit organizations, state government agencies, and organized labor, as well as the local economic development organizations. The vision answers the question "What do we want to be as a state?" Fully engaging key sectors in this process will likely require an extensive multimonth iterative effort. The product of this process should be a vision statement that has broad community awareness and support.

Next, the council should develop a broad set of goals that support and will move the state toward the vision over the next three to five years. In developing these goals, the constituencies represented by members of the planning council should also be engaged, along with the local economic development systems. In defining the goals, the council must address the question: What can we be in five years? The vision typically would have a time frame much longer than the vision. In Dubuque, for example, the vision the leaders developed was for 20 years. However the goals are typically three- to five-year goals that are revisited and adjusted as planning assumptions change.

It should be stressed that the vision and goals are not the governor's vision and goals, but rather they represent the state's vision and goals. Adopting this mind-set will be difficult or even impossible for some occupants of the governor's mansion. However, for those who understand the significance of gaining statewide understanding and "ownership" for the vision, the impact will be significant. In the long run, this will also be the most politically rewarding point of view. In this new framework, the governor and the legislature become the stewards of the citizens' vision. This is the essence of democratic governance.

At this point, the role of the planning council becomes one of monitoring plan implementation by the state department and local economic development system. Another role of the planning council is to continually "look over the horizon" to identify emerging opportunities and threats. Finally, the planning council should be asked to recommend strategies that can only be implemented at the state level to improve the overall "ecosystem" within the state for community and economic development. This will include financing mechanisms, attracting investment capital, supporting university research and commercialization, and funding of state-level intermediary organizations that stimulate enterprise creation and growth and community and workforce development.

State department of community and economic development

We noted in the discussion of Figure 8.1 that it is not meant to encompass all the functions of the state department of community and economic development. State departments have functions that address federal-to-state issues, state-to-state issues and relationships, and relationships between the state and the world. As we have seen earlier, however, some of the issues such as building export markets and other foreign trade issues that were formerly the exclusive role of the state department are increasingly being shared with or totally carried out by local economic development groups. This is particularly the case in the larger metro areas.

In the present discussion, we will limit our focus to those functions of the state department we believe are most important for community development, talent development, and job creation. In these activities a key role of the state department in the new inverted framework is to act as the translator and interpreter between the state vision and goals defined by the planning council and the vision and goals established by the local economic development systems that are operating on the frontlines of the economic and community development initiatives.

In order to effectively play this role, we recommend that the state department assign a state department employee to each of the local economic development systems. These people become the key translators of the needs and desires of the local systems to the state department and become the link between the resources of the state department and other state-level resources to the local system.

In order to make this liaison role more effective and promote greater alignment between the local and the state vision and goals, we recommend a combination of the initiatives being used in New York and Michigan. These two methods involve partnership agreements (Michigan) and competition among regions for state funding (New York). It appears in our review of these methodologies that New York's approach is somewhat less consistent with the philosophy of "bottoms up" than Michigan's. While both approaches can have merit, we prefer the partnership strategy as it seems more in keeping with the "inverted pyramid" philosophy in which the state does not drive or dictate to local economic development systems what their goals and focus should be.

The Michigan approach to aligning state and local goals makes use of partnership agreements of two types. The first type is interlocal agreements. These are agreements between "public entities to jointly exercise powers." These agreements enable collective action between public agencies that allow them to "provide services, share resources and reach a common goal they may be unable to reach separately." This type of partnership was made legal by legislation in Michigan through the Urban Cooperation Act of 1967. This authority was used to form the Michigan Economic Development Corporation—a partnership between the Michigan Strategic Fund and public agencies across Michigan.[14]

The second type of partnerships is "corporate partnerships." In Michigan, the corporate partnerships may be between any nongovernmental organization and the MEDC. These partnerships with private businesses and not-for-profit organizations state that both entities will cooperate and assist each other in implementing economic development strategies that promote economic growth.

Our recommendation of the partnership mechanism is a way to formalize the relationship between the state economic development organization and the local economic development corporation. This can also be the basis for the state to agree to locate a state staff member with the local organization, and it can clarify the role of that staff member. It is up to the partners to decide to what extent the agreement addresses alignment of goals, shared measurement systems, reporting relationships, and so on.

There is one aspect of the New York approach that we find especially valuable and may be possible to introduce voluntarily through the alignment mechanisms we have already discussed. This approach attempts to create measurement systems among the local economic development regions that permit comparisons and benchmarking. Since we pointed out that part of the state role is to serve as a clearinghouse of best practices among local economic development entities, shared measurement systems would be very beneficial.

In the New York approach, the state recommends or mandates that all regions measure a common set of metrics defined by the state. It is unclear how much input regions have had in choosing these metrics. However, in addition to the "shared set of metrics," regions are encouraged to develop custom metrics that fit their unique goals and objectives. There is an expectation that these measurement results are shared with the state and with other regions on a periodic basis.

New York dedicates a fund each year that regions can compete for based on initiatives defined by the state. While this approach has benefits, it should not be the way to fund the local economic development core operating budgets. Our new framework strongly encourages that two-thirds of the core local community and economic development corporation funding come from local private sector partners, with one-third coming from local city and county government. Competition for state funds, however, can be very useful to local economic development corporations in helping them build local assets and infrastructure that will accelerate their ongoing development. Competitive funds such as these should be used for one-time project funding rather than for recurring staff and operational budget items. Competitive funds can be most helpful as long as the justification for funds in the statewide competition is based on how the funding will accelerate progress toward local goals, rather than based on how the funding will only increase alignment with state goals. Ideally, state and local goals will be largely aligned voluntarily, so this conflict would not be an issue.

Interagency council (the subcabinet)

Enabling the local economic development organizations to achieve their goals of community and economic development requires that all state agencies with local programs that relate to community and economic development align their initiatives with the need of the local communities. Obviously, this must be done within the legal, regulatory, and budget constraints of their departments. This will involve forming agencies such as the state departments of planning, labor, housing, transportation, education, and health into a subcabinet of the governor's cabinet to focus on local community and economic development. This subcabinet should be led by the head of the state department of community and economic development and assisted by backbone support (Backbone B in Figure 8.1), which is also funded by the state department of community and economic development. The role of this subcabinet is to identify needs coming from the local economic development systems and find ways to collaborate across agencies to meet those needs. Since many of these agencies have "pass-through" federal funds they administer, part of this role is finding ways to more flexibly use and target the federal funds to the local needs.

Governor's office, state legislature, and higher education

The state department of community and economic development is a creation of both the legislature and the governor's office. As a result, the ability of the department to significantly "shape" either of these entities may be very limited. Nevertheless, having a systematic approach to the interactions with the governor and legislative leaders and their staff is vital.

The purpose of Backbone C, which will likely involve several backbone staff, is vital. A key part of the backbone staff's role is to engage the staff of the three entities shown in Figure 8.1—the governor's office, the legislature, and higher education—in the initiatives of the department. Specific areas of focus are to keep leaders and their staff informed of the needs of local economic development systems, engaging the leaders in overcoming obstacles and barriers to progress, and assisting the department's lobbying efforts in support of legislative initiatives needed by the community and economic development constituencies. By applying the backbone tools to these relationships, the impact that the department of economic development can achieve will be significantly enhanced. In addition, the department can be more responsive to the governor's and legislature's priorities.

In Chapter 7 and in this chapter, we have described the structure, operating philosophy, and modes of operation of the two principal elements of the new economic development framework. In the next and final chapter, we provide some thoughts that hopefully add additional clarification to this framework and defend the ideas against some arguments that might be raised against moving in this direction. We will close Chapter 9 with some additional hopeful signs that the transformation we are proposing is proceeding and is gaining strength.

CHAPTER NINE

Enabling the Transformation: What It Will Take

In this book, through case examples and through our description of a proposed new framework, I have made the case for transforming the existing economic development system into one that will more effectively identify and deliver the outcomes citizens need and seek. This transformation will be difficult. Recognizing this difficulty, I would like to end the book with a hypothetical dialogue with a professional economic development practitioner who is a bit skeptical of the changes we propose.

Through this dialogue, I would like to acknowledge the dedicated, competent economic development professionals who may hold dissenting views from those proposed here. There are many practitioners who have been devoting their professional careers to improving their world, but who are working in a flawed system they did not create. My hope is that these professionals will consider the case examples I have presented and the recommendations I am making, then reflect on their situation and hopefully join the growing movement that is transforming community and economic development in the United States.

My dialogue is with Bob—a highly ethical, widely respected, true economic development professional—

Bob: The approach to the new economic development framework seems to stress the ability to produce a planned economy. Where is the recognition of the "free market" forces that underlie regional and state economies?

Tom: The recommendation to create an economic development vision, goals, and plan does not make the assumption that all events are controllable. However, people must have the opportunity to work to create a future that allows them to move toward their vision as individuals and as communities. The free market will not produce this desired future. The situation is like a sailor in a sailboat on the ocean. The winds change in direction and velocity. But the sailor can adjust the sails to move toward the desired destination. Free market forces can be opportunities and they can pose obstacles, but communities can adjust their goals and strategies to fulfill their dreams. That is what the new community and economic development framework is all about.

Bob: Your recommendation to separate economic development from the elected political process is overwhelmed by the need to organize government functions and organizations to support the attainment of economic development outcomes.

Tom: When we say that the economic development system is flawed, we are not saying that the government systems are flawed. The reason the economic development system is flawed is that it is typically housed in a system (the elected political system) whose incentives and capabilities are not compatible with the incentives and capabilities that make economic development systems most effective. For example: (1) economic development requires community consensus and ownership of a vision regarding the type of economic system we want to create. The electoral political process is divisive, does not fully engage citizens, and creates winners and losers not consensus; (2) the incentive for elected officials is to respond to campaign promises and to pursue actions that will produce results that are visible during their term of office—two years or four years. Economic development requires constancy of purpose and a longer view, and it requires investments in building assets—infrastructure, education, and community branding that will likely not yield payoffs in the short-term; (3) The need of elected politicians for positive headlines has caused many jurisdictions to prioritize business attraction over the retention and growth of existing firms and the creation of new businesses through an emphasis on entrepreneurship and innovation. This may be done in spite of overwhelming evidence that most job creation results from the growth and retention of existing businesses and new business creation rather than business attraction.

Certainly there are elected officials who are not totally motivated by self-interest and who do work to create consensus, focus on long-term issues that will not benefit them during their term in office and who do focus on business retention and growth more than business recruitment. However, these elected officials are the exception rather than the rule. It is for this reason that both cities in this book's case examples have chosen to separate their key economic development organizations from electoral politics, although both have developed close working partnerships between the local governments and their private economic development organizations.

The need to separate the core economic development process from control by elected officials does not mean that elected officials and government are not essential to an effective economic development process. Conducting an effective business retention and growth process requires a close working partnership between the local economic development corporation (in the new framework) and the local government in order to address and remove obstacles to growth that hinder new job creation. Furthermore, the ability to create a "place" that will attract and retain a talented workforce also requires the engagement and effort of the total public sector as well as private economic development organizations working toward the common goal of workforce development. Escaping the "flawed system" requires a true, win–win–win partnership among the public, private, and not-for-profit sectors where each contributes what each is best able to do without worrying about who gets the credit.

Bob: How do you propose wresting the authority and control of local economic development from elected officials and transferring it to a private not-for-profit corporation guided by an unelected Board?

Tom: The short answer is that it will only occur when local community leaders and citizens decide that such a change is in the best interest of the community. The proposed new framework is more about creating a new organizational entity than eliminating what exists. The conversation that must take place within communities is about what type of community we want to create and what is the best community organizational framework to enable us to move toward our vision. In Dubuque and in Austin the two primary economic development entities are separate from the elected political process and are regional in scope, but both cities still have departments of economic development.

In addition, both cities are funding partners of the private economic development organizations. The issue is what is the best structure to enable us to create the type of community that we want to create. We believe that having a lead economic development organization that is separate from the elected political process but that can work in close partnership with local government is the best way to proceed.

Bob: The definition of "place" is an important issue in the regional approach to economic development. Counties and municipalities within each region will have difficulty surrendering to an identity that does not include their parochial interests.

Tom: This is an excellent point and it is certainly one of the challenges in regionalizing economic development. Different states, for example, Michigan, New York, Colorado, and Tennessee, have dealt with this issue in somewhat different ways. It appears that in most "regional definitions" the county remains a key entity. However, across the country, the resources and roles of county governments differ from state to state. A factor that complicates the definition of "place" is that the "laborshed" does not follow the boundaries of counties and municipalities.

It appears that how regions are formed is best dealt with through local conversations among municipality and county leaders and officials rather than have the regional boundaries arbitrarily defined by state government. The important issue is to achieve to the extent possible a feeling by people within the regions that they are willing to support regional community and economic development and are willing to put the interest of the region above their self-interest. Until regions can do this, economic development will suffer.

Bob: In a climate where many people view government as the enemy and where raising taxes is political suicide for elected officials, how do you expect to persuade jurisdictions to adopt a new community and economic development framework?

Tom: There are several aspects of the new framework that respond to the climate that your question accurately describes, at least in many parts of the country. The antigovernment, antitax sentiment is one of the arguments for moving away from total dependence on public funding of local economic development. In this climate it is difficult for state and local economic development agencies to have the funds needed to attract and retain the talent necessary to create effective organizations. This becomes a bit of a negative spiral as lack of talent leads to less effective government, which reinforces the antigovernment sentiment. This situation can only be changed through enlightened and courageous local leaders who are willing to publicly state that you cannot cut your way to excellence. Building excellent communities requires excellence in all sectors—public, private, and not-for profit. Mobilizing community leadership is one of the key factors in overcoming this "austerity" binge.

Another factor that underlies the antigovernment sentiment among citizens is a feeling that they do not have an effective voice in government. As a result, the way in which the new framework engages citizens in defining what type of economy and community they want to create helps build ownership of the vision and support for efforts that will help move the community toward that vision. Over time, as results are produced, trust builds, support builds, and the barriers begin to fall. But this process requires dedicated effort and sustained, consistent leadership over many years from all sectors to inform and engage citizens in broad-scale change.

Bob: What role does the news media play in slowing or accelerating the transformation to a new economic development framework?

Tom: The news media cannot be "cheerleaders" for change or they would lose credibility. Too often the news media serve to highlight failures and help play into the antigovernment, antipublic policy, even antibusiness chorus. Let me leave you with one example of how the news media can maintain their integrity but help the process by reporting on "good news" and by shining the light on misconceptions and flawed mental models.

An example is an editorial by Joe Nocera in the *New York Times* entitled "The Good Jobs Strategy." Nocera described his experience as an attendee at the Aspen Ideas Festival.[1] Like many of us who have attended many conferences we sit through hours of presentations from smart people who focus on different facets of the topic at hand. While there may be debate over various strategies and outcomes, most of the information we hear conforms to our expected range of academic discourse. Rarely does a presenter grab our attention to the point that we are moved to take action based on what we heard. After listening to a number of presentations focusing on the relative benefits and fears regarding how innovation will impact job creation, there was a presenter who really grabbed Nocera's attention—and that speaker was a young woman from MIT named Zeynep Ton.[2]

> Her big idea is that companies that provide employees a decent living, which includes not just pay but also a sense of purpose and empowerment at work, can be every bit as profitable as companies that strive to keep their labor costs low by paying the minimum wage with no benefits. Maybe even more profitable.[3]

Ton's presentation described her research findings showing that the less profitable companies not only paid their employees less but also were generally poorly managed. They provided very little training, scheduling was poor, and this management perspective resulted in a workplace in which there was poor job satisfaction and high levels of turnover. As a result they also had dissatisfied customers.

Nocera cites Ton's research findings that when executives are asked why they allow such conditions to exist, they said the only way they can guarantee low prices to customers was to operate with employees who were paid as little as possible, because labor was such a big part of their overhead costs.

What Zeynep Ton had discovered is that many executives and managers are operating and making decisions every day with a flawed mental model—that human beings are simply "costs" to be minimized rather than potential partners who, if appropriately trained, engaged, and compensated, can be the engine to transform the business model and create profitable and successful enterprises.

These flawed mental models pervade our society. The press can provide a valuable function by telling stories like this that shine the light on these destructive ways to understand and characterize reality. The press can also challenge why these flawed models persist despite overwhelming evidence that they are wrong.

In our case studies, Charisse Bodisch, senior vice president for economic development of the Greater Austin Chamber of Commerce, and Rick

Dickinson, president and CEO of the Greater Dubuque Development Corporation, have built their success on positive mental models. Charisse puts it this way: "Our secret sauce is the caring and sharing attitude."[4] Rick Dickinson had a similar response when asked by economic development officials from other cities who wondered how Dubuque was able to attract the IBM Global Service Center. Rick told them "Our secret sauce is that we work well together, we have civility in our community and we have the big 10 organizations that collaborate and support each other and that sustainability is part of the ethos of our community."[5] Rick said that his economic development colleagues did not want to hear that. They wanted to know what the silver bullet was that allowed Dubuque to attract IBM. These other economic development professionals just did not understand. They, too, were operating with flawed mental models.

Our hope with this book is that we have challenged your thinking enough that it will lead you to reconsider your mental model of community and economic development. The transformation is underway. We hope you will choose to reflect on these ideas and join or create the conversation in your community. We hope you will work to accelerate the move toward a new community and economic development framework that will better enable your community to achieve its vision for economic, social, and environmental progress.

Notes

Preface

1. Stiglitz, Joseph E., and Bruce C. Greenwald, *Creating a Learning Society: A New Approach to Growth, Development and Social Progress* (New York: Columbia University Press, 2014).
2. Ibid., 6.

Chapter One: The Jobs and Employment Challenge

1. Jim Clifton, *The Coming Jobs War* (New York: Gallup Press, 2011).
2. John C. Haltiwanger, Ron S. Jarmin, and Javier Miranda, *Who Creates Jobs? Small vs. Large vs. Young* (working paper 16300, Cambridge, MA: National Bureau of Economic Research, August 2010), http://ww.nber.org/papers/w16300
3. Aris Melissaratos, personal interview with the author, January 7, 2015.
4. Katie Glueck, *Politico*, June 1, 2013.
5. Emily J. Brown and Swati Ghosh, *Looking around the Corner: The Future of Economic Development* (Washington, D.C.: International Economic Development Council, 2014), www.iedconline.org
6. Erin Sparks and Lucas Pappas, *Redesigning State Economic Development Agencies* (Washington, D.C.: National Governors Association, undated).
7. J. Manyika, S. Lund, B. Auguste, L. Mendonca, T. Welsh, and S. Ramaswamy, *An Economy That Works: Job Creation and America's Future* (McKinsey Global Institute, June 2011), http://www.mckinsey.com/employment_and_growth/an_economy_that_works_for_us_job_creation
8. Erin Sparks, *Top Trends in State Economic Development* (Washington, D.C.: National Governors Association, August 2013).
9. Ibid.
10. Jed Kolko, *Business Relocation and Homegrown Jobs, 1992–2006* (San Francisco, CA: Public Policy Institute of California, 2010).
11. Sparks, *Top Trends in State Economic Development.*

12. Tifan Clark, *Incubator or accelerator, which is right for you?*, ideacrossing blog, August 21, 2013.

13. Seed-DB, April 18, 2014, www.seed-db.com

Chapter Two: What Type of Economy Do We Want to Create?

1. National Governors Association, *Growing State Economies: A Policy Frame-work* (Washington, D.C.: Author, undated).

2. William McDonough, "Driving Sustainable Transformation via the Power of Design," *The Guardian*, August 19, 2013, http://www.the guardian.com/sustainable-business/sustainable-transformation-power-design

3. Jay Rao and Joseph Weintraub, "How Innovative Is Your Company's Culture?" *Sloan Management Review*, March 19, 2013.

4. Brian P. Hall, *Values Shift: A Guide to Personal & Organizational Transformation* (Rockport, MA: Twin Lights Publishers, 1995), 21.

5. Benjamin Tonna, personal communication.

6. Milton Rokeach, *Beliefs, Attitudes and Values* (San Francisco: Jossey-Bass, 1968).

7. Ibid., 124.

8. Hall, *Values Shift*.

9. Ibid.

10. Ibid.

11. Peter Senge, Hal Hamilton, and John Kania, "The Dawn of System Leadership," *Stanford Social Innovation Review* 27 (Winter 2015).

12. David Brooks, "Class Prejudice Resurgent," *New York Times*, December 1, 2014, http://nytimes.com/2014/12/02/opinion/david-brooks-class-prejudice-resurgent.html

13. Ibid.

14. Aris Melissaratos, personal interview with the author, January 7, 2015.

Chapter Three: What Can We Learn from the Past?

1. www.historyplace.com/speeches/marshall.htm

2. Ibid.

3. Ibid.

4. Ibid.

5. Ibid.

6. V. R. Berghahn, "The Marshall Plan and the Recasting of Europe's Postwar Industrial Systems," in *The Marshall Plan: Lessons Learned for the 21st Century*, ed. E. Sorel and Pier Carlo Padoan (Paris, France: OECD, 2007).

7. This section is based on a paper by Robert B. Austenfeld, Jr. entitled "W. Edwards Deming: The Story of a Truly Remarkable Person," http://web.crc.losrios.edu/~larsenl/ExtraMaterials/WEDeming_shortbio_Ff4203.pdf

8. Ibid., 63.

9. We will learn more about the U.S. response to the Japanese technology challenge in our Austin case study in Chapter 5 where we will discuss the rise of U.S.

cooperative research initiatives to accelerate technology development in the micro-computer and semiconductor industries.

10. W. Edwards Deming, *Out of the Crisis* (Cambridge, MA: Massachusetts Institute of Technology, Center for Advanced Engineering, 1986), 23–24.

11. Ibid., 3.

Chapter Four: Overview of Current State-Level Economic Development Strategies

1. National Governors Association, *Redesigning State Economic Development Agencies* (Washington, D.C.: Author, undated), www.NGA.Org/Center

2. www.michiganbusiness.org. Reprinted with permission from the MEDC.

3. Ibid.

4. National Governors Association, *Redesigning State Economic Development Agencies*, 9.

5. Ibid.

6. www.Orbusinesscouncil.org

7. Ibid.

8. National Governors Association, *Redesigning State Economic Development Agencies*, 13.

9. Ibid.

10. http://www.bizjournals.com/baltimore/news/2013/05/01/maryland-ranks-first-in-us-for.html

11. William E. "Brit" Kirwan, personal interview with the author, October 29, 2015.

12. Gus S. Sentimentes, "Maryland Raises $84 Million to Invest in Tech Start-ups," *Baltimore Sun*, March 15, 2012.

13. Based on the nature of its mission, TEDCO's primary impact on the state is focused on those areas where technology businesses are concentrated. Another financing institution in Maryland is the Maryland Economic Development Corporation (MEDCO). The mission of MEDCO is to assist in the modernization and retention of existing businesses, and to attract new businesses to the state. When requested, MEDCO can also assist with local jurisdiction projects such as developing vacant or unused industrial sites. MEDCO provides assistance often in more rural areas where TEDCO would not be involved.

14. State of Maryland Office of the Governor, "Governor O'Malley Promotes Innovate Maryland, Tours Emerging Technology Center at Hopkins," press release, April 13, 2012.

15. Report of the Maryland Economic Development and Business Climate Commission, 2014 Interim Report, Annapolis, Maryland, February 2015.

16. Ibid.

17. Norman R. Augustine, address to "Maryland Rising" convocation, Owings Mills, Maryland, December 8, 2014.

18. Richard Bendis, personal interview with the author, November 3, 2015.

19. www.Tedco.md/John-m-wasilisin

20. Report of the Maryland Economic Development and Business Climate Commission, 2014 Interim Report, Annapolis, Maryland, February 2015.

21. Brian Darmody, personal interview with the author, October 5, 2015.

22. "Unprecedented Redevelopment Reshapes College Park," *TERP* (Fall 2015): 2.

23. William E. "Brit" Kirwan, personal interview with the author, October 29, 2015.

24. Jim Clifton, *The Coming Jobs War* (New York: Gallup Press, 2011).

25. Ibid.

Chapter Five: Austin, Texas: The Human Capital

1. This was particularly helpful in aiding Austin's recovery from the Great Depression when Lyndon Baines Johnson was elected as the U.S. congressman from Austin's district and who delivered more federal post-Depression funding to Austin than was received by any other Texas city. Johnson's support led to funding for a major dam construction and public housing and to the establishment of the Del Valle Army Air Base during World War II which became Bergstrom Air Force Base, now the site of Austin's International airport.

2. www.weareaustintech.com/pike-powers/

3. Bruce R. Scott and Srinivas Sunder, *Austin, Texas: Building a High-Tech Economy* (Boston, MA: Harvard Business School Publishing, June 20, 2002), 2.

4. Ibid., 2.

5. www.weareaustintech.com/pike-powers/

6. www.ic2.utexas.edu/about/mission-and-history/george-kozmetsky/

7. R. W. Smilor, D. V. Gibson, and G. Kozmetsky, "Creating the Technopolis: High-Technology Development in Austin, Texas," *Journal of Business Venturing, 4* (1988): 49–67.

8. Scott and Sunder, *Austin, Texas: Building a High-Tech Economy*, 2.

9. Ibid., 10.

10. Pike Powers, "Building the Austin Technology Cluster: The Role of Government and Community Collaboration," *The Human Capital*, pp. 56–57, http://www.kansascityfed.org/PUBLICAT/NEWGovernance04/Powers04.pdf

11. David V. Gibson and Everett M. Rogers, *R&D Collaboration on Trial* (Boston, MA: Harvard Business School Press, 1994).

12. R. W. Smilor, G. Kozmetsky, and D. V. Gibson, *Creating the Technopolis: Linking Technology Commercialization and Economic Development* (Cambridge, MA: Ballinger Publishing Company, 1988).

13. Ibid., 100.

14. Gibson and Rogers, *R&D Collaboration on Trial*, 101.

15. Ibid., 101.

16. Ibid., 120.

17. Ibid., 170.

18. Ibid., 158.

19. Ibid., 435.
20. Ibid., 431–432.
21. Ibid., 433.
22. Ibid., 61.
23. Powers, "Building the Austin Technology Cluster," 57.
24. Ibid., 57.
25. SRI, 1985. Quoted in David V. Gibson, Raymond W. Smilor, and George Kozmetsky, *Austin Technology-Based Industry Report, March 1991* (Austin, TX: The IC² Institute, University of Texas at Austin).
26. Powers, "Building the Austin Technology Cluster," 57.
27. Richard Florida, The *Rise of the Creative Class: And How It's Transforming Work, Leisure, Community and Everyday Life* (New York: Perseus Book Group, 2002).
28. Gibson and Rogers, *R&D Collaboration on Trial*, 475.
29. Ibid., 475.
30. Ibid., 483.
31. Ibid., 492.
32. Ibid., 493.
33. Ibid., 495.
34. Ibid., 495–496.
35. Ibid., 496.
36. Ibid., 496.
37. Ibid., 486–487.
38. Ibid., 531–533.
39. Powers, "Building the Austin Technology Cluster," 58.
40. Michael E. Porter, "Clusters and the New Economics of Competition," *Harvard Business Review*, November–December 1998.
41. Ibid.
42. Enrico Moretti, *The New Geography of Jobs* (Boston, MA: Mariner Books, 2013).
43. Ibid.
44. David V. Gibson and John S. Butler, "Sustaining the Technopolis: The Case of Austin, Texas," *World Technopolis Review*, 2 (2013): 64–81.
45. MIG, Inc., *Austin, Texas: Developing a Shared Economic Vision to Create an Innovation Economy* (Gainesville, FL: Envision Alachua, June 2011).
46. Market Street Services, "Opportunity Austin vs. Advance KC: A Winning Economic Development Strategy." Presentation to the Greater Kansas City Chamber Leadership Exchange, September 25, 2012.
47. Jose Beceiro, personal interview, May 6, 2015.
48. Ibid.
49. Market Street Services, "Opportunity Austin vs. Advance KC."
50. Ibid.; and Powers, "Building the Austin Technology Cluster," 58.
51. Market Street Services, "Opportunity Austin vs. Advance KC."
52. Ibid.

53. Jose Beceiro, personal interview, May 6, 2015.

54. Ibid.

55. Bureau of Business Research, *The Economic Impact of Austin Technology Incubator Alumni Companies on Travis County, 2003–2012.* Unpublished report prepared for the Austin Technology Incubator, January 2014, http://ati.utexas.edu/wp-content/uploads/ATI-impact_BBR-rpt_FINAL.pdf

56. Mitch Jacobson, personal interview, April 15, 2015.

57. Bureau of Business Research, *The Economic Impact of Austin Technology Incubator Alumni Companies,* 13.

58. Opportunity Austin 1.0 launched in 2004 and extended through 2008. Opportunity Austin 2.0 covered the period 2009–2013.

59. Bureau of Business Research, *The Economic Impact of Austin Technology Incubator Alumni Companies.*

60. Mitch Jacobson, personal interview, April 15, 2015.

61. Ibid.

62. Mitch Jacobson, personal interview, April 15, 2015.

63. Charisse Bodisch, personal interview, April 20, 2015.

64. Bryan Walsh, "Is This America's Smartest City?" *Time,* June 26, 2014.

65. Bryan Walsh, "SXSW: Using Big Data to Shrink Energy Waste," March 14, 2013, http://science.time.com/2013/03/14sxsw-using-big-data-to-shrink-energy-waste/

66. Walsh, "Is This America's Smartest City?"

67. Jose Beceiro, personal interview, May 6, 2015.

68. Mike Berman, telephone interview, September 23, 2015.

69. City of Austin, *ImagineAustin: Comprehensive Plan* (Austin, TX: Author, June 15, 2012), 28.

70. Joel Trammell, personal interview, April 17, 2015.

71. Julie Huls, personal interview, April 17, 2015.

72. City of Austin, *ImagineAustin: Comprehensive Plan,* 27.

73. Paul DiGiuseppe, personal interview, April 16, 2015.

74. Joel Trammell, personal interview, April 17, 2015.

75. Julie Huls, personal interview, April 17, 2015.

76. City of Austin, *ImagineAustin: Comprehensive Plan,* 5.

77. Julie Huls, personal interview, April 17, 2015.

78. Russ Garland, "Austin Ventures, No Longer a Texas Giant, Wrestles with Its Future," *Venture Capital Dispatch,* March 9, 2015, blogs.wsj.com/venturecapital/../Austin-ventures-no-longer-a-texas-giant-wrestles-with-its-future/

79. Joel Trammell, personal interview, April 17, 2015.

80. City of Austin, *ImagineAustin: Comprehensive Plan,* 24–25.

81. Ibid., 25.

82. Charisse Bodisch, personal interview, April 20, 2015.

83. Ibid.

84. Jose Beceiro, personal interview, May 6, 2015.

85. City of Austin, *ImagineAustin: Comprehensive Plan,* 5.

Chapter Six: Dubuque, Iowa: Masterpiece on the Mississippi

1. City of Dubuque, Outcomes, *City Focus: Highlighting Issues Important to Dubuque Residents*, March 24, 2015. www.cityof dubuque.org/cityfocus
2. Ibid.
3. www.cityofdubuque.org/706/Julien-Dubuque-Monument
4. www.history.com/topics/louisiana-purchase
5. Franklin T. Oldt and P. J. Quigley, *History of Dubuque County Iowa* (Chicago, IL: Goodspeed Historical Association, undated), http://www.archive.org/details/cu31924028913965
6. Ibid.
7. Ibid.
8. Ibid.
9. www.encyclopediadubuque.org/index.php?title=CARADCO
10. www.encyclopediadubuque.org/index.php?title=DUBUQUE_PACKING0
11. www.encyclopediadubuque.org/index.php?title=JOHN_DEERE_DUBUQUE
12. thinkdubuque.com/city-at-work.html
13. Ibid.
14. After some research, he discovered that the line did not originate in Dubuque; it was on a billboard in Seattle, Washington, in April 1971 when two local realtors were very pessimistic about the decline in the aerospace industry which impacted Seattle, the home of Boeing. Cooper in an editorial challenged his readers to produce photos or artifacts of this phrase in Dubuque. One reader produced a T-shirt that was created and sold in a local bar that did have this phrase printed on the front. But to date no one has come forth with photos of the "oft cited" billboard or a bumper sticker. And Cooper points out that there is nothing in the newspaper archives with an issue of the newspaper with this line as a headline.
15. http:data.bls.gov/pdq/SurveyOutputServlet, July 22, 2015.
16. Ibid.
17. Bureau of Labor Statistics, News release US-15-1353, July 17, 2015.
18. Bureau of Labor Statistics, May 2014 State Occupational Employment and Wage Estimates—Iowa.
19. Bryce Parks, "Dubuque: The Envy of America, Part One," *365ink Magazine*, January 3–16, 2013, 12, www.Dubuque365.com
20. John Kania and Mark Kramer, Collective Impact, *Stanford Social Innovation Review*, 9(1) (Winter 2011).
21. Tom Woodward, personal interview with the author, June 11, 2015.
22. Russell M. Knight, personal interview with the author, June 10, 2015.
23. Doug Horstmann, personal interview with the author, June 10, 2015.
24. Ibid.
25. Rick Dickinson, personal interview with the author, June 8, 2015.
26. Greater Dubuque Development Corporation Annual Report 2013–2014, www.greaterdubuque.org/media/userfiles/subsite_88/files/annual_reports/2014_AnnualReport.pdf

27. Mike Van Milligen, personal interview, June 9, 2015.

28. Rick Dickinson, personal interview with the author, June 8, 2015.

29. Mike Van Milligen, personal interview, June 9, 2015.

30. Ibid.

31. Nancy Van Milligen, personal interview with the author, June 9, 2015.

32. Ibid.

33. For example, the process began with a free community breakfast on July 8, 2005. More than 400 participants attended and were asked to think of 10 ideas for community projects to improve Dubuque by 2010. At the end of the session, participants were given the visioning toolkits and were asked to self-facilitate discussions with their friends and neighbors. Toolkits were also available on the project website.

34. Eric Dregne, personal interview with the author, June 9, 2015.

35. Ibid.

36. Envision: Ten Community Projects by 2010 (Dubuque, IA: Community Foundation of Greater Dubuque, undated). www.cfleads.org/resources/webinars/2011_webinar6/tools/Envision2010.pdf

37. Ibid., 6.

38. Mayor Roy Buol, personal interview with the author, June 10, 2015.

39. Ibid.

40. This vision was adopted in 2005. The 2029 vision presented earlier in this chapter represents an update and elaboration of the 2005 vision that was adopted in March 2015 by the mayor and the council.

41. Cori Burback, personal interview with the author, June 12, 2015.

42. Rick Dickinson, personal interview with the author, June 8, 2015.

43. Ibid.

44. *Telegraph Herald*, January 15, 2009.

45. Parks, "Dubuque: The envy of America, Part One," 11.

46. Mayor Roy Buol, personal interview with the author, June 10, 2015.

47. Dave Lyons, personal interview with the author, June 8, 2015.

48. Mike Van Milligen, personal interview with the author, June 9, 2015.

49. Dave Lyons, personal interview with the author, June 8, 2015.

50. Chris Kohlmann, personal interview with the author, June 12, 2015.

51. Mike Van Milligen, personal interview with the author, June 9, 2015.

52. Dave Lyons, personal interview with the author, June 8, 2015.

53. Nancy Van Milligen, personal interview with the author, June 9, 2015.

54. Eric Dregne, personal interview with the author, June 9, 2015.

55. Dave Lyons, personal interview with the author, June 8, 2015.

56. Greater Dubuque Development Corporation, *A Year of Delivery: 2009–2010 Annual Report* (Dubuque: IA: author), www.greaterdubuque.org.

57. Rick Dickinson, personal interview with the author, June 8, 2015.

58. Ibid.

59. Ibid.

60. Dan McDonald, personal interview with the author, June 8, 2015.

61. Ibid.
62. Byron Taylor, personal telephone interview with the author, June 10, 2015.
63. Russell M. Knight, personal interview with the author, June 10, 2015.
64. Ibid.
65. Ibid.
66. Sarah Harris, personal interview with the author, June 8, 2015.
67. www.greaterdubuque.org/gddc/workforce-solutions
68. Sarah Harris, personal interview with the author, June 8, 2015.
69. Rick Dickinson, telephone interview with the author, September 1, 2015.
70. Maurice Jones, June 12, 2015, personal interview with the author.
71. Stan Rheingans, personal interview with the author, June 9, 2015.
72. Ibid.
73. Nancy Van Milligen, personal interview with the author, June 9, 2015.
74. John Schmidt, personal interview with the author, June 11, 2015.
75. Mayor Roy Buol, personal interview with the author, June 10, 2015.
76. Dave Lyons, personal interview with the author, June 8, 2015.
77. John Schmidt, personal interview with the author, June 11, 2015.
78. Rick Dickinson, telephone interview with the author, September 1, 2015.

Chapter Seven: A New Framework for Local Community and Economic Development

1. Mac Holladay, CEO, Market Street Services, personal interview with the author, September 22, 2015.
2. Ibid.
3. M. P. Feldman, "The Character of Innovative Places: Entrepreneurial Strategy, Economic Development and Prosperity," *Small Business Economics* 43 (1) (June 2014): 1–12.
4. Ibid. This definition was developed by Dr. Feldman in the work she did for the U.S. Economic Development Agency.
5. David V. Gibson and John S. Butler, "Sustaining the Technopolis: The Case of Austin, Texas," World Technopolis Association 2 (2013): 64–80
6. Ibid.
7. Julie Huls, personal interview with the author, April 17, 2015.
8. Mayor Roy Buol, personal interview with the author, June 10, 2015.
9. Jose Beceiro, telephone interview with the author, May 6, 2015.
10. Mac Holladay, telephone interview with the author, September 22, 2015,
11. Rick Dickinson, telephone interview with the author, September 1, 2015.
12. Mac Holladay, telephone interview with the author, September 22, 2015.
13. Julie Huls, personal interview with the author, April 17, 2015.
14. Dave Lyons, personal interview with the author, June 8, 2015.
15. Ibid.
16. Mayor Roy Buol, personal interview with the author, June 10, 2015.
17. Ibid.
18. Mike Van Milligen, personal interview with the author, June 10, 2015.

19. In this section, we use the term "customer" to describe the individuals and organizations who are the direct recipients of the services provided by the economic development system. We do this even though businesses, education organizations, and citizens who are impacted by the direct economic development processes are also, in the larger sense, considered to be "partners" in the economic development system.

20. W. Edwards Deming, *Out of the Crisis* (Cambridge, MA: Massachusetts Institute of Technology, 1986).

21. Peter S. Pande, Robert P. Neuman, and Roland R. Cavanagh, *The Six Sigma Way: How GE, Motorola, and Other Top Companies are Honing Their Performance* (New York: McGraw-Hill, 2000).

22. John Kania and Mark Kramer, "Collective Impact," *Stanford Social Innovation Review* 9 (1) (Winter 2011).

23. City of Dubuque, Outcomes, *City Focus: Highlighting Issues Important to Dubuque Residents*, March 24, 2015, www.cityof dubuque.org/cityfocus

24. David Ammons and Jonathan Morgan, "State-of-the-Art Measures in Economic Development," ICMA Publications, *PM Magazine* 93 (5) (June 2011), http://webapps.icma.org/pm/9305/public/cover.cfm?author=David%20Ammons%20and...; IEDC, *Making It Count: Metrics for High-Performing EDOs* (Washington, D.C.: Author). Members of IEDC can download the report at www.iedconline.org

Chapter Eight: A New Framework for State Community and Economic Development

1. Edward E. Gordon, *Future Jobs: Solving the Employment and Skills Crisis* (Santa Barbara, CA: Praeger, 2013).

2. Erin Sparks, *Top Trends in State Economic Development* (Washington, D.C.: National Governors Association, August 2013).

3. Jennifer Bradley, "Michigan Gov. Snyder's Regional Recipe Central to Fix-It Agenda," *The Avenue*, Brookings, Institution, January 31, 2011, http://www.brookings.edu/blogs/the-avenue/posts/2011/01/31-state-restructuring-bradley

4. Ibid.

5. Ibid.

6. Amy Liu and Owen Washburn, "A New Generation of Economic Development," *The Avenue*, Brookings Institution, February 24, 2015, http://www.brookings.edu/blogs/the-avenue/posts/2015/02/24-new-generation-economic-development

7. Pete Carlson, "Expanding Growth and Opportunity: Findings from the Brookings-Rockefeller Project on State and Metropolitan Innovation," Brookings Institution, July 23, 2015, http://www.brookings.edu/research/reports/2015/07/23-expanding-growth-opportunity-ca

8. Ibid.

9. Ibid.

10. Ibid.

11. John Kania and Mark Kramer, "Collective Impact," *Stanford Social Innovation Review* 9 (1) (Winter 2011).

12. Shiloh Turner, Kathy Merchant, John Kania, and Ellen Martin, "Understanding the Value of Backbone Organizations in Collective Impact: Part 1," *Stanford Social Innovation Review*, July 17, 2012, http://ssir.org/articles/entry/understanding_the_value_of_backbone_organizations_in_collective_impact

13. Peter S. Pande, Robert P. Neuman, and Roland R. Cavanagh, *The Six Sigma Way: How GE, Motorola and Other Top Companies Are Honing Their Performance* (New York: McGraw-Hill, 2000).

14. www.michiganbusiness.org/about-medc

Chapter Nine: Enabling the Transformation: What It Will Take

1. Joe Nocera, "The Good Jobs Strategy," *New York Times*, July 7, 2015, http://www.nytimes.com/2015/07/07opinion/joe-nocera-the-good-jobs-strategy.html?rref=collection%2Fcolumn%2Fjoe-nocera&_r=0

2. Zeynep Ton is an adjunct associate professor in the operations management group at MIT's Sloan School of Management. She is the author of *The Good Jobs Strategy: How the Smartest Companies Invest in Employees to Lower Costs and Boost Profits.* She is on Twitter at @zeynepton.

3. Joe Nocera, "The Good Jobs Strategy," *New York Times*, July 7, 2015, http://www.nytimes.com/2015/07/07opinion/joe-nocera-the-good-jobs-strategy.html?rref=collection%2Fcolumn%2Fjoe-nocera&_r=0

4. Charisse Bodisch, CEcD, personal interview with the author, April 20, 2015.

5. Rick Dickinson, personal interview with the author, June 8, 2015.

Selected Bibliography

This bibliography includes a selected list of references that provide additional depth on many of the topics addressed in this book. Some have also been included in the notes. It is not intended as a comprehensive bibliography on the topic of economic development.

Ackoff, Russell L. *Creating the Corporate Future*. New York: John Wiley & Sons, 1981.

Behrman, Greg. *The Most Noble Adventure: The Marshall Plan and How America Helped Rebuild Europe*. New York: Free Press, 2007.

Brynjolfsson, Erik, and Andrew McAfee. *The Second Machine Age: Work, Progress and Prosperity in a Time of Brilliant Technologies*. New York: W.W. Norton & Company, 2014.

Davis, Stan, and Christopher Meyer. *Blur: The Speed of Change in the Connected Economy*. New York: Warner Books, 1998.

Deming, W. Edwards. *Out of the Crisis*. Cambridge, MA: Massachusetts Institute of Technology, Center for Advanced Engineering Study, 1986.

Gibson, David V., and Everett M. Rogers. *R&D Collaboration on Trial*. Boston, MA: Harvard Business School Press, 1994.

Goldsmith, Stephen, and Susan Crawford. *The Responsive City: Engaging Communities through Data-Smart Governance*. San Francisco: Jossey-Bass, 2014.

Gordon, Edward E. *Future Jobs: Solving the Employment and Skills Crisis*. Santa Barbara, CA: Praeger, 2013.

Hall, Brian P. *Values Shift: A Guide to Personal and Organizational Transformation*. Rockport, MA: Twin Lights Publishers, 1995.

Manyika, James, Susan Lund, Byron Auguste, Lenny Mendonca, Tim Welsh, and Sreenivas Ramaswamy. *An Economy That Works: Job Creation and America's Future*. McKinsey Global Institute, June 2011. www.mckinsey.com/mgi/our-research

McDonough, William, and Michael Braungart. *The Upcycle*. New York: North Port Press, 2013.

Moretti, Enrico. *The New Geography of Jobs.* Boston, MA: First Mariner Books, 2013.

Motoyama, Yasuyuki, and Jason Wiens. *Guidelines for Local and State Governments to Promote Entrepreneurship.* Kansas City, MO: Ewing Marion Kauffman Foundation, March 2015.

Pande, Peter S., Robert P. Neuman, and Roland R. Cavanagh. *The Six Sigma Way: How GE, Motorola and Other Top Companies Are Honing Their Performance.* New York: McGraw-Hill, 2000.

Piketty, Thomas. *Capital in the Twenty-First Century.* Cambridge, MA: Belknap Press, 2014.

Rokeach, Milton. *Beliefs, Attitudes and Values.* San Francisco: Jossey-Bass, 1968.

Russo, J. Edward, and Paul J. H. Schoemaker. *Winning Decisions: Getting It Right the First Time.* New York: Doubleday, 2002.

Stiglitz, Joseph E. *The Great Divide: Unequal Societies and What We Can Do about Them.* New York: W.W. Norton and Company, 2015.

Stiglitz, Joseph E., and Bruce C. Greenwald. *Creating a Learning Society: A New Approach to Growth, Development and Social Progress.* New York: Columbia University Press, 2014.

Thompson, Derek. "A World without Work." *The Atlantic,* July/August 2015, 50–61.

Ton, Zeynep. *The Good Jobs Strategy: How the Smartest Companies Invest in Employees to Lower Costs and Boost Profits.* New York: Houghton Mifflin Harcourt Publishing Company, 2014.

Unger, Debi, and Irwin Unger. *George Marshall: A Biography.* New York: HarperCollins, 2014.

Selected Websites for Organizations Involved in Economic Development Research and Education

The Aspen Institute—www.aspeninstitute.org
The Brookings Institution—www.brookings.edu
Ewing Marion Kauffman Foundation—www.kauffman.org
International City/County Management Association—www.icma.org
International Economic Development Council—www.iedconline.org
John S. and James L. Knight Foundation—www.knightfoundation.org
National Governors Association—www.nga.org

Index

About the Author

Thomas C. Tuttle, PhD, is president of Tuttle Group International, a strategic management consulting organization located in Annapolis, Maryland. He is also president of the World Academy of Productivity Science and a vice president of the World Confederation of Productivity Science. He was director of the University of Maryland Center for Quality and Productivity for 26 years, where he chaired the U.S. Senate Quality Award process and the Maryland Quality Award Program. In that role, he worked closely with the Maryland Department of Economic and Employment Development and led contract funded programs to enhance the competitiveness of Maryland manufacturing through productivity assessments and technical assistance to firms to accelerate their path to develop and achieve registration for their quality management systems. Tuttle assisted the Maryland secretary of economic development in establishing the first office of technology development within the department and served as its interim director. As a "boundary spanner," he consulted with the Maryland State Department of Education and six local school districts to develop and implement quality management systems in public education. His writing, research, and consulting have focused on quality and productivity management and measurement, strategic planning, and management and the leadership of organizational system change. In 2011, Tuttle received the C. Jackson Grayson Distinguished Quality Pioneer Medal given by the American Productivity and Quality Center for his work as a "lifetime advocate of quality and productivity through strategic change." He is a fellow of the World Confederation of Productivity Science, a lifetime member of the American Psychological Association, and a member of the Society for Industrial and Organizational Psychology.